Baedeker

Rome

How to use this book

Following the tradition established by Karl Baedeker in 1844, sights of particular interest, outstanding buildings, works of art, etc. as well as good hotels are indicated by one or two stars as follows: especially worth attention ★, outstanding ★★.

To make it easier to locate the various places listed in the "A to Z" section of the Guide, their co-ordinates on the large city map are shown in red at the head of each entry.

Only a selection of hotels, restaurants and shops can be given; no reflection is implied therefore on establishments not included.

In a time of rapid change it is difficult to ensure that all the information given is entirely accurate and up-to-date, and the possibility of error can never be entirely eliminated. Although the publishers can accept no responsibility for inaccuracies and omissions, they are always grateful for corrections and suggestions for improvement.

Preface

This Pocket Guide to Rome is one of the new generation of Baedeker city guides.

Baedeker pocket guides, Illustrated throughout in colour, are designed to meet the needs of the modern traveller. They are quick and easy to consult, with the principal sights described in alphabetical order, and practical details and useful tips shown in the margin. The information is presented in a format that is both attractive and easy to follow.

The guide is in three parts. The first part gives a general account of the city, its history, prominent personalities and so on; in the second part the principal sights are described; and the third part contains a variety of practical information designed to help visitors to find their way about and make the most of their stay.

The new Baedeker guides are noted for their concentration on essentials and their convenience of use. They contain numerous specially drawn plans and colour illustrations, and at the end of the book is a large map making it easy to locate the various places described in the "A to Z" section of the guide with the help of the co-ordinates given at the head of each entry. Users of this guide, therefore, will have no difficulty in finding what they want to see.

A water-spouting lion rests at the foot of the Egyptian obelisk in the Piazza del Popolo

Contents

Baedeker Specials

All roads

What it is to be finally in Rome, the "centre of the world", on the banks of the Tiber! Nihil tibi Roma, nothing can compare with you, cradle of Western civil-isation, heart of the mighty Imperium Romanum, nerve centre of Western Christianity. But before embarking on the obligatory walk to the historic ruins of the Colosseum, Palatine and Forum Romanum, before climbing the Capitol Hill, strolling over to the Castel Sant'Angelo, giving oneself up in admiration of the countless temples to the muses, it an excellent idea to sample a little of Rome's "*dolce vita*". Treat yourself a 'caffè' accompanied by irresistible 'dolci' on the magnificent Piazza Navona, the romantic Campo dei Fiori or the Piazza di Spagna, always teeming with people. Enjoy contemplating the lively hustle and bustle taking place right in front of your eyes and drink in the unforgettable atmosphere of the place. Afterwards, why not walk up to the Pincio Gardens and have your first view across the roofs of the Eternal City? The façades of the houses and occasional grand palazzi shimmer in their warm hues, while among them can be seen graceful bell-towers adding their red brush-strokes to the picture, while dome upon dome rises up out of the sea of stone – the highest one visible in the background being that of St Peter's, the most famous church in Christendom. As for the Vatican City itself, it is best to be generous with one's time: its immense collection of artistic treasures cannot be equalled anywhere in the world; the Raphael Rooms and the Michelangelo frescoes in the Sistine Chapel on their own are worth a journey to Rome.

Pantheon
A unique round building of antiquity

Forum of Caesar
with the Temple of Venus

lead to Rome

"Rome is a world on its own and it would take years to become a true citizen of this city". So wrote the German poet Goethe in 1786 during a tour of Italy and over 00 years later nothing has really changed. Although, just as in Goethe's day, the est way to get to know Roma Aeterna is on foot, it can be justly said that the city's even hills exact their own price in terms of a visitor's weary legs! And if, after a substantial programme of culture, the visitor fancies a simple stroll around, he is robably best advised to make for the magic triangle around the elegant Via ondotti, where all the greatest and most illustrious fashion houses are represented. As for entertainment at the end of the day, on warm summer evenings the

whole of Rome turns into a vast open-air banquet. Pavements and roadsides are covered with white-covered tables, people saunter past or sit down outside one of the countless trattorie or restaurants, for instance in Trastevere, probably the oldest district in the city. Rome is not, however, simply the golden city of our dreams, but also a traffic inferno – the chariot races of Ben Hur seem like harmless jaunts in comparison – a vast sea of noise and movement, a city of inefficient bureaucracy with areas of unprepossessing tenement blocks on its outskirts. But as Italy's old man of the cinema, Federico Fellini, once declared: "Once Rome has you caught in her ancient spell, all critical judgements are forgotten. The only thing which matters is what a great joy it is to be able to live here." So if, like many before you, you succumb to the inimitable charm of the Eternal City, be sure not to forget to toss a coin into the Fontana di Trevi and thus make certain that you will return there one day.

Palatine Hill
The foremost among the seven hills of Rome

Rome Cafés
Tempting but expensive

Castel Sant'Angelo
The most powerful fortification of Rome

**Nature, Culture
History**

Facts and Figures

Coat of Arms of Rome
SPQR
Senatus Populus Que Romanus
Senate and People of Rome

General

Capital of
Italy

Rome is the capital city of the Republic of Italy, the province of Rome and the region of Lazio (Latium). It is the seat of the President (official residence the Quirinal Palace) and of both chambers of the Italian Parliament: the Senate in Palazzo Madama and the Chamber of Deputies in Palazzo Montecitorio. The Constitutional Court and the highest court of justice are also to be found here.

Rome	Area: 1507 sq. km/
Capital of Italy	582 sq. miles
Situation: 41°52′ north	Population 2.8 million
12°30′ east	Language: Italian

Within Rome's boundaries is also to be found the smallest state in the world (0.44 sq.km/110 acres), the Vatican City, ruled by the Pope, who is also the head of the Roman Catholic Church.

◄ *A view from the top of St Peter's over St Peter's Square and the Via della Concillianzone*

The city of Rome is still expanding in all directions and the municipality currently occupies an area of almost 1508sq.km/582 sq. miles. The historic city centre contained within the Aurelian walls occupies an area of 140sq.km/54sq. miles in the middle of the hilly Campagna Romana, and is situated on the River Tiber (Tevere), some 20km/12 miles inland from the Tyrrhenian Sea.

Seven is the magic number which defines the topography of Rome: the Eternal City's seven legendary hills are the Capitol (Campidoglio), Palatine (Palatino), Aventine (Aventino), Quirinal (Quirinale), Viminal (Viminale), Esquiline (Esquilino) and Caelian (Celio). The Janiculum (Gianicolo) and Pincian (Pincio) are often mistakenly included, but in fact only came to form part of the city area in a later period.

Just to add to the confusion, these seven hills are in no way identical to the 'sette colli' on which the Latins originally made their settlements almost 3000 years ago. These comprised Subura (a hilltop forming part of the Caelian), Palatium and Germalus (today together forming the Palatine), Velia, Oppius, Cispius and Fagutal, the last three being hilltops on the Esquiline.

The historic centre is bordered on the west by the Tiber, on the east by the Servian Walls (parts of which are still visible), which were built around the city's summit in 387 B.C. Around this central core there had already grown up in ancient times a series of outlying built-up areas which the Emperor Aurelian surrounded with a protective ring of walls at the end of the 3rd c. A.D. In the course of centuries further districts (rioni) developed, such as the Borgo Pio around the Vatican and Ostiense around the church of San Paolo fuori le Mura; and after Rome became the capital of a united Italy in 1870 new quarters including Prati and Paroli developed.

*The double staircase leading to the Palazzo dei Senatori –
the seat of the Mayor and Municipal Council*

Today the suburbs of Greater Rome extend to the east as far as the Alban Mountains, in the west as far as Ostia on the coast, while north and south they stretch far into the surrounding plain, the Roman Campagna. Nineteen more hills have been annexed, most recently Monteverde, Monte Sacro and Colli Portuensi.

Population and Administration

Population

The Comune di Roma is the capital of the province of the same name which has a population of some 4 million and of the Italian region of Lazio (Latium) with a population of about 5.2 million. The Comune itself occupies a land area of almost 1508sq.km/582 sq. miles and is home to nearly 2.8 million people. If the many inhabitants of the surrounding Campagna Romana, not included in these statistics, are also taken into account, then the total population of the Roman conurbation today almost reaches 6 million.

Population development

The rise of Rome to become the capital of the Roman Empire was accompanied by a steady increase in population, so that by the beginning of the Christian era the city had a population of about a million. After the fall of the Western Empire the population dropped to 25,000, recovered during the golden centuries of the medieval period and then fell even lower, before beginning to increase again slowly after the Pope's return from exile in Avignon (15th c.) In 1870 the city's population was 200,000, in 1921 some 700,000. In the last sixty years the total has risen to about three million as a result of the drift of the rural population from the provinces and immigration from the south of Italy. Since 1981, however, the population has started to decrease again slightly, especially in the inner city area. The ambience which defines present-day Rome is by no means influenced just by the Italians themselves: millions of tourists come every year, as well as priests and nuns from all over the world. In addition, Rome has, during the last ten years, become home for over half a million immigrants from Eastern Europe, Somalia, Ethiopia, North Africa, the Philippines and other third world countries.

Religion

In the capital of Catholicism it can be said that almost 98% of the population are, in the truest sense of the word, "Roman" Catholic. Many other faiths have, however, put down roots here, and churches representing other branches of Christianity are to be found, with several other countries having their own national church here. The Jewish faith is represented by six synagogues and in 1995 a huge mosque, by far the largest Islamic cultural centre in Western Europe, was opened on Monte Antenne.

Administration

The Comune di Roma is governed from the Capitol, which is the seat of the Mayor (Sindaco). The Municipal Council (Giunta Munizipale) has 14 members, while the City Council (Consiglio Comunale) has 80 members. Every five years elections to these councils take place and at the end of 1993 the Green politician, Francesco Rutelli was chosen as the new Mayor of Rome.

Districts

From a social, political and historical point of view, there has always been a strict demarcation line in the minds of the citizens of Rome, between those who live in the 22 rioni, the traditional districts situated within the old Aurelian city walls, and are considered to be the only true Romans, and those who live beyond, in the 18 quartieri, or new districts, or further out in the 11 borgate, or outer suburbs. To make such a distinction is hardly justified as the dividing lines within this urban hierarchy are totally blurred. The province of Rome

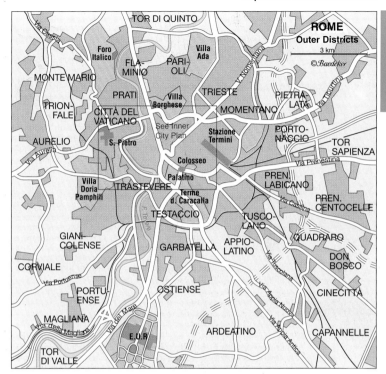

coincides with the area of the old Agro Romano, which stretches out well beyond the outermost suburbs. The Agro Romano provided the capital with fresh meat and vegetables in ancient times, but, after the building of the Aurelian city wall, it in effect became fallow land and over many centuries served as a strategic buffer zone to deter attacks from enemy forces.

In the area surrounding the Roman metropolis several new suburbs or *borgate* have sprung into life since the 1930s. Their population consists primarily of impoverished agricultural workers and the jobless and dispossessed who have come from the Mezzogiorno, or south of the country, hoping to find a better standard of living in the Italian capital. As well as placing strict controls on the movement of immigrants into the capital, the government embarked on a rather half-hearted social construction programme designed to provide new dwellings beyond the city boundaries. The state-run company responsible for social building programmes undertook the planning and construction of the first districts of Gordiani, Pietralata, Prenestino and San Basilio. The results were single-level shacks, constantly overcrowded and lacking basic sanitation, accompanied by a complete absence of public areas and amenities. With the population growth after the Second World War the problem of the homeless continued to be acute. A new generation of *borgate* came into being, the illegal "abusivi", with houses, generally unplastered, such as at Torre Angela, which extended, without formal planning controls,

Borgate

13

into the surrounding Roman Campagna, occupying arbitrarily divided agricultural land and having no proper infrastructure. Everyday life in the borgate is characterized by the high level of unemployment and a spiralling crime rate. The problems of this "vita violenta", as Pier Paolo Pasolini described it so vividly in his novels about the borgate, are also evident, however, in the newer suburbs such as Laurentina, Corviale, Spinaceto and Tor Bella Monaca, which were built legally by the state Communist construction company IACP. Here the barracks of the original workers' settlements have been replaced by inhuman concrete blocks.

Restoration measures in the Eternal City

The enormous increase in vehicular traffic and emissions from oil heaters have over a long period led to a situation where air pollution in Rome represents a major environmental problem. Buildings which have existed for centuries have, in the last few years, become victims of the prevailing smog. Since the 1980s an attempt has been made to arrest this deterioration, with traffic-calmed zones being introduced and comprehensive restoration measures undertaken, of which a large majority were completed before the World Cup Football Championships in 1990. In the long term there is the intention to convert the whole of the inner city area into a traffic-calmed archaeological zone, which will include the closure of the Via dei Fori Imperiali. In the medium term the consequences of very necessary additional restoration work are all too evident to the tourist visiting Rome, with large numbers of buildings shrouded in scaffolding. Costly cleaning processes are being employed and, where appropriate for their conservation, buildings are being given a protective coating.

Economy

International standing

In ancient times Rome was not only the busy capital of the powerful Imperium Romanum, but also the leading economic and commercial centre of the entire Mediterranean region. This supremacy was, however, lost when the glorious period of the Empire came to an end. Neither under the Popes, nor the kings of Italy, nor during the present republic has Rome ever succeeded in regaining a European position of influence, let alone an international one, in economic terms. The industrial revolution which took hold of Western Europe during the second half of the 19th c. had only a marginal impact on Rome. Only in the film and fashion industries has Rome assumed a commercial importance outside Italy during the 20th c. By virtue of its status as a cultural and artistic centre, Rome does however enjoy a world-wide pre-eminence, and this has led to the development of tourism as the city's largest industry and source of wealth.

National standing

For many years Italian industry and commerce has been concentrated in the northern provinces, in Piedmont, Lombardy, Liguria and Veneto. Rome, on the other hand, is the non-industrial capital of a modern industrial state and is first and foremost an administrative centre, accommodating the government and civil service. As to the exact number of the city's inhabitants who are employed in the highly inefficient state bureaucracy, even the government has only the haziest of ideas: it is estimated as being about a quarter of a million. As a large part of the national economy is under state ownership, Rome, as administrative centre of these state industries, occupies a key position in the commerce of the nation. It is also gaining increasing importance as a banking, business and insurance centre.

Industry

It is hard to understand why in a city with such a large concentration of workers and consumers, no commensurate level of efficient indus-

The elegant Via Condotti from the bottom of the Spanish Steps

trial activity has established itself. Even as far back as the closing years of the last century, when the Italian kingdom was founded, and there was an influx of people into the new capital city, no industry of any note took root. Since then there has been a desperate shortage of industrial jobs in the greater Roman area, despite the fact that after the Second World War measures were taken by the Cassa per il Mezzogiorno which have promoted and developed an industrial base in the capital. New industrial areas have been established in the south and south-east of Rome, but the traditional problems of heavy industry, with smoking chimneys and environmental pollution, have at least thereby been avoided. Most of this new industry belongs to the electronic sector and its related fields of telecommunications and information technology. Indeed the highly specialised EDV technology from "Tiburtina Valley" enjoys an international reputation. With a share of over 10% of national production the pharmaceutical industry is also well represented in Rome, while the chemical industry has specialised in high-quality textile fibres. There are also various local food-processing firms which serve the needs of the local population. Closely connected with Rome's role as a capital city and cultural centre is its printing industry with the state printing works at the head.

Agriculture in the Campagna Romana is on quite a large scale with modern efficient farms and around 40,000 people employed in the industry.

Agriculture

The number of firms in Rome belonging to the service sector has risen sharply in the last few years. With around 1.1 million people employed in the service industries it has become Rome's single largest employer.

Service sector

Transport

Tourism

With around 6 million visitors every year it is no surprise that tourism has become the city's largest and most lucrative source of income. Rome has nearly 900 hotels and about 3500 restaurants and total annual receipts from tourism account for more than 7 million lire.

Film and television industries

Rome gained an international standing in cultural and economic terms with the founding of Cinecittà, the Italian Hollywood, in 1935. However, the golden years of the film industry are now past and internationally successful films which have been produced here are now few and far between. In recent times the Roman studios, which have such a long and proud tradition, are now used predominantly for television productions and advertisements, as both the state-run radio and television company RAI and the large private television stations have their headquarters in Rome. The fierce rivalry between RAI and the private television networks is essentially a battle to gain the highest share of advertising revenue, and this in turn has brought a thriving advertising and publicity industry to the city. Silvio Berlusconi, the controversial media tycoon and short-lived leader of the national government, personifies more than anyone the Italian media war. He owns almost all the private broadcasting operators and, though his production base is mainly in Milan, he has a very influential lobby at his disposal in Rome.

Fashion

Romans have an innate feel for style and elegance and the city enjoys a world-wide reputation for fashion. Twice a year large *alta moda* shows are held in which the "haute coutouriers" of Rome put their skills and creativity under the spotlight. For years both Rome and Milan have been vying with Paris for supremacy in the cut-throat world of European fashion and in the Italian economy the fashion industry has always occupied a pre-eminent position. Probably nowhere else are there so many alta moda and prêt-à-porter boutiques as there are in Rome. The most famous couturier in Rome is undoubtedly Valentino, but there are also many other distinguished fashion designers, such as Gucci, Fendi, Battistoni, Trussardi and Pucci, who have established themselves in and around the Via Condotti, the illustrious centre of Roman sartorial chic.

Transport

Harbour

In ancient times seagoing ships could sail right up the 20km/12 miles from the mouth of the Tiber to the city's harbour, but over the centuries the river silted up and is now used only by small craft and houseboats. Ostia, which was one of the largest ports in the Mediterranean in Roman times, is now suitable only for fishing boats and pleasure craft. The Mediterranean port for Rome is now Civitavecchia, 85km/53 miles to the north-west of the city.

Airports

The most important airport is the Aeroporto Leonardo da Vinci at Fiumicino, 25km/15^1/$_2$ miles south-west of the city, with national and international flights. The Aeroporto di Ciampino, situated 14km/ 9 miles south-east from the centre on the Via Appia Nuova, is mainly reserved for charter flights and military use. The Aeroporto di Urbe is reserved for sporting aircraft and flying enthusiasts can book tourist excursion flights from here.

Railway, underground, trams

Rome is an important railway junction for traffic between northern and southern Italy and services to the east of the country, but the railway plays little part in transport within the city. Altogether Rome has only ten railway stations, while even the Vatican has one of its own. The main station is Stazione Termini, at which most long-distance trains arrive, though some use the Tiburtina and Ostiense stations. Most of the city's business and commuter traffic is carried by buses. Rome has two underground railway lines in the Metropolitana system. Line A runs between Anagnina via Cinecittà, Termini and Piazza di Spagna to Via Ottaviano (near St Peter's). Line B runs from Rebibbia via Pietralata and Termini to the south to the E.U.R. district and on to Laurentina. Visitors who are not pressed for time can have a leisurely and inexpensive trip around central Rome on the "Circolare", one of the last surviving tram routes.

Road transport

In ancient Rome nine great consular highways started from the Golden Milestone in the Forum Romanum – the Aurelia, Cassia, Flaminia, Salaria, Tiburtina, Prenestina, Casilina, Tuscolana and Appia. These main highways – now all represented by modern roads following the same routes – were supplemented by new ones, with the result that the province of Rome has an excellent network of roads. Modern traffic is served by an orbital road of motorway standard, the Grande Raccordo Annulare, and a number of motorways (A1 going northwards, A2 going south, A12 going west/north-west with access to the Aeroporto Leonardo da Vinci, A24 going east).

Inner city traffic

For years now administrations have fought shy of taking interventionist measures to alleviate the problems caused by Rome's chaotic inner city traffic, and although today the centro storico is to a large extent only accessible to private motor-cars with special permits, the traffic situation there still remains a problem awaiting a solution. The visitor is best advised to leave his car and use the public transport system or a taxi – if for no other reason than that parking spaces in Rome are at a premium.

Art and Culture

History of Art

The Etruscans

Although Rome's legendary founding by the twin brothers Romulus and Remus on 21 April 753 B.C. belongs to ancient heroic myth, there nevertheless have been archaeological finds which prove, not only that there were even settlements on the site of the present city during the Bronze Age, but also that as early as the 7th c. B.C. it was the location of a major Etruscan centre. Its advantageous situation at the intersection of military and trading routes quickly conferred on the settlement an important commercial and strategic function. Quite early on, the settlement started to develop the permanent features of a town, the forum was paved and a canal and sewage system (Cloaca Maxima) was installed. The period of Etruscan rule of Rome is also reflected in the works of art which have been handed down from this time – mainly burial decorations, sculptures, paintings and artifacts, as well as architectural finds. The highly developed achievements of the Etruscans also received a considerable stimulus from the late-Classical and Hellenistic works of art of Greece, and yet they retained their own characteristic features: a certain stylisation, linear surface modelling, a lack of plasticity and an emphasis on the head and on highly expressive gestures.

Roman art modelled on Greek designs: a frieze of acanthus leaves from the Roman Forum

Capitoline She-Wolf

One of Rome's most famous emblems is the Capitoline She-Wolf (a bronze sculpture from the 5th c. B.C., Palazzo dei Conservatori). A clear, simple physique, modelling without excesses or any plastic details: these are the features of the watchful predator which has become a public symbol for the city.

Ancient world

From the 5th c. B.C. onwards Greek art came more and more to the fore with statues and gold and silver vessels which the Romans brought back from their campaigns in Greece and which aroused an interest in Hellenistic luxury and a considerable acquisitive fever among the cultured and increasingly affluent upper strata of Roman society. Holy images, including those of gods, and even reproductions of such images, were used to decorate buildings and gardens and by the 2nd and 1st c. B.C. a plethora of Greek works of art of different periods and schools could be seen in Rome. As the city began to replace Greece as the pre-eminent centre of artistic activity, some of the outstanding Greek artists and creators were attracted there and a new Roman civic style inspired by these masters came into being. The city itself became important in commissioning new works, for it wished to have essentially Roman concepts represented in historical reliefs, allegorical and mythological pictures, as well as in portraits and architecture, and thereby secure expression for its political and civic ideals.

Many public buildings, thermal baths, amphitheatres, circuses and arenas were erected. Roman civic architecture is most clearly defined by the new style of construction for public squares and spaces and this can be seen at its most manifest in the imperial forums. The axial layout and overall plan are as much a feature of these sites as the way the temple with its peripteros and cella is built into the overall complex. The whole square was enclosed by rows of shops and exchange halls. On the Forum of Trajan (A.D. 97–117) – the last and most impressive of the imperial forums – a basilica with two apses and five aisles was placed between the open square and the temple to serve as a marketplace and court of justice. The ancient buildings were embellished with triangular and segmented gables, brick façades were faced with marble, the larger sections of buildings were frequently given barrel or cross vaulting. In the imperial capital the new type of amphitheatre was developed, whose rising rows of seats were not all at one single gradient, but were arranged in a much less restricted way. The Colosseum, which was opened in A.D. 80, with its oval façade of several storeys, broken up by arched arcades, under which statues were placed, shows this type of architecture carried through to its logical conclusion.

Bathing became a nationally promoted institution during the period of the Empire. As well as the more modest private bathing establishments, magnificent thermal baths were now built: axially arranged series of rooms, sometimes lavishly vaulted, with multicoloured marble facing, columns, pilasters, arcades, stucco and marble decorations. The central building as an influential architectural form in ancient times was first developed within the thermal bath complex, then later on its own as a burial building or temple.

While the Roman upper classes lived in city atrium houses, palaces or in the country in villas, ordinary people had to endure cramped conditions in extremely basic dwelling houses with an appalling level of hygiene and the constant fear of fire or structural collapse.

Many works by masters of antiquity have become lost, or have only survived in fragments or are merely known of through descriptions. Historical paintings like that in the burial building on the Esquiline portray the story of the founding of Rome, while portraits arose both out of a growing need for people to have images of their ancestors and of civic representatives and from a desire for immortality. A well-defined system of decorations was developed for the interiors of palaces, private houses and burial buildings. The walls were divided up by stucco plaster and including the plinth into sections and the way that these were painted was intended to give the illusion of a much larger room. This was achieved first of all through perspective painting, then with architectural features painted on, which offered wide vistas, later enriched by landscape representations. Individual paintings on panels also found their home within this framework. In the Augustan period, large-format mythological figures in painted landscapes were added, conceived specifically for the interior (Villa Farnesina 19 B.C.). This painted architecture started to decline in importance and in the end merely retained the function of dividing up

Architecture

Painting

the surfaces. It made way for a new phase where the entire wall was covered with an ornamental pattern and tiny pictorial motifs. There followed a highly mannered phase where an attempt was made to regain a greater definition of purpose in these wall compositions and a logical construction.

Sculpture

Roman sculpture based itself very much on Greek models: Greek symbols of religion and ritual gave rise to copies and variations which were only slightly altered from the original and in Rome these had no greater significance than as artistic embellishments. The challenge for Roman artists was to attain individuality and an ideal representation of the human form.

Examples of relief sculpture show works exploiting parallel surfaces and depth, without the one having originated in the other. The adventus relief of Domitian (Palazzo della Cancelleria, about A.D. 83–85) displays the figures ranged one behind the other, their movement constrained, while on the reliefs of the Ara Pacis (13–9 B.C.), by means of oblique placing and overlapping, an incredible spatial depth is achieved, which is intensified still further on the Titus Arch (A.D. 81) by the inclusion of light and shade. Scenes of everyday life or mythology can be found on tombstones and sarcophaguses – likewise closely following Greek models.

The Stadium of Domitian on the Palatine

Early Christendom

From very early on, Rome was a main centre of Christianity, its followers facing terrible persecution again and again until the edict of tolerance of Constantine in 313 made Christianity the state religion. Christians buried their dead in catacombs, either in tombs built into the walls or collectively in large burial chambers. These subterranean rooms and passages were decorated with wall and roof paintings using fresco and tempera techniques, either with Christian symbols or with more concrete images: representations of Christ, Mary and child, apostles and martyrs, themes dictated by Christian ideas of redemption. From the 4th c. onwards Christians were allowed to build basilicas (San Giovanni in Laterano, Old St Peter's etc.), the architecture of which inclined towards the basilicas of antiquity, with rows of columns and arcades. Baptisteries were also built with the central font for baptisms being placed in the middle of the building. This central style of building would have been borrowed from the circular rooms to be found in the thermal baths. Today Santa Sabina still gives an impression of what the early Christian basilicas looked like. The mosaics on the walls of the nave in Santa Maria Maggiore recount various scenes from the Old Testament in a vivid and gripping way. Important evidence of early Christian art is furnished above all by lavishly conceived ivory work (diptychs), the impressive wooden doors of Santa Sabina and sarcophaguses (e.g. those to be seen in the Museo Cristiano Pio Lateranense in the Vatican), whose programmes of reliefs represent either scenes from the Old or New Testament or frequently motives of redemption.

In contrast to other cities in Italy there are scarcely any examples of Romanesque architecture to be found in Rome. One reason for this is almost certainly that there was already a large number of church buildings in existence which could be partially extended or altered in the Romanesque style. For instance, at the beginning of the 13th c. Santa Pudenziana was given a campanile (belltower) with sharply protruding ledges and round arch openings on every floor. Between 1204 and 1241 the cloister at San Paolo fuori le Mura was built with its arcade arches supported by pairs of pillars with smooth, fluted or rotated shafts which are decorated with sumptuous mosaics by Pietro Vassaletto. Relatively simple ornaments are assembled in a host of different ways, so that the total effect is highly impressive. Many floors and church fittings were embellished with these stone mosaics, particularly under the direction of the Cosmati family, from whom the term "cosmati work" is derived, used to refer to examples dating from between 1100 and 1300.

The local sculpture tradition had recourse to early Christian models as well as ancient themes and motives. An outstanding example is the 5m/16ft high Easter candlestick (c. 1180) in San Paolo fuori le Mura with scenes from the Passion and the Ascension of Christ, arranged in rows of pictures one above the other. Of key importance in the development of sculpture was Arnolfo di Cambio, a pupil of Nicola Pisano, who, in the ciborium at Santa Cecilia in Trastevere (1293), created a masterly link between architecture and sculpture and between space and physique, with the line becoming an expressive transmitter of dynamics, perspective and space. In his works, which command a wide range of motives, Arnolfo combines Gothic, classical, early Christian and Byzantine influences.

It was not until the late 14th c. that Gothic forms, which previously had been usually introduced as architectural embellishments, began to occur in Roman sculpture. Materials using the mobile figures, reproduced in soft folds, can be seen at the wall altar in Santa Maria in Trastevere or at the relief gable with the coronation of Mary in Santa Maria del Popolo.

Violent feuds among the noble families, or between them and the people or the Pope hindered the development of Gothic architecture. The only large Gothic religious building in Rome is the Dominican church of Santa Maria sopra Minerva (1280 until the end of the 15th c.) Alterations and restoration work have today, however, compromised the observer's impression of a Gothic building.

The flat and schematic forms of frescos and mosaics in the 9th c. (San Clemente, Santa Prassede, San Marco) developed from the 13th c.

Middle Ages

Gothic

onwards into turbulent figures with gentle features, conceptually differentiated physiognomies and undulating folds of clothing. The shape and dimensions of human bodies were fully modelled and underlined by reflections of light and shade. Pietro Cavallini and Giotto, two representatives of this school of painting, which shook off the shackles of the Byzantine tradition, met in Rome.

The changing fortunes of the Castel Sant'Angelo exemplify the dramatic events in the city's history: the building, which was begun by Hadrian as a mausoleum (135), had been used from as early as the second half of the 3rd c. as one of the outlying bastions of the city's fortifications and then subsequently, on account of its advantageous position, was strengthened and made into a bridgehead. The castle's important strategic function – it also served from time to time as a barracks and a prison – is evidenced by its exterior walls crowned with battlements and its four massive corner towers. The imposing round tower with its square-shaped foundations brings to mind the building's original purpose as a mausoleum.

During the Middle Ages the influence of the ancient world on the arts was never completely relinquished, but during the Renaissance it was to enjoy a new golden age. Fresh and influential ideas and stimuli emerged from Tuscany, brought to Rome by newly-arrived architects: Leo Battista Alberti, Rossellino and Giuliano Sangallo. Detailed and exact studies of ancient models by means of drawings and measurements led to the creation of large symmetrical buildings with a use of forms which drew on ancient motifs. The Popes commissioned many new works, bringing distinguished architects and artists to Rome and having their palaces in the city built by them. The Palazzo della Cancelleria (1483–1495) has a façade based on that of the Palazzo Rucellai in Florence and develops it one stage further in terms of splendour and monumental display. In order to avoid the monotony inherent in such a large architectural expanse, the pilasters are grouped in twos or threes. Because of the hierarchical arrangement of the interior rooms, the window openings have more lavish frames on the piano nobile than on the second floor.

The genre of building known as the villa developed in the style of the country houses of antiquity. Peruzzi designed the Villa Farnesina with two storeys, the ground floor having an arcaded loggia, and wings jutting out like towers. Rectangular windows between pilasters, massive ledges and a frieze composed of a garland of fruits divide up the building. At the Tempietto of San Pietro in Montorio (1502), a kind of memorial marking the spot where the apostle Peter was executed, the stylistic development of Bramante can be seen. He did not simply copy details from sources in antiquity, but by close and perceptive observation of forms, was able to create tension through contrasts of depth and surface, and of density and corporeality. The result was a building of wonderful plasticity, its lower storey dominated by its 16 Doric pillars, which support the entablature of the metope and the balustrade. The upper storey is recessed behind the balustrade and is divided up alternately by rectangular and mussel-vaulted niches. The tempietto is crowned by a simple dome.

The range of painting from this period is brilliantly exemplified by the decorations and furnishings of the Vatican. The Chapel of Nicholas V was decorated with paintings by Fra Angelico da Fiesole from 1445–1448 depicting scenes from the lives of St Laurence and St Stephen. These narrative works display monumentality and unity both in their composition and in their figures, while the architecture gains in plasticity, no longer giving the impression of being unreal buildings

Renaissance

Architecture

Painting

◀ *The cylindrical mausoleum built by Emperor Hadrian and named the Castel Sant'Angelo by Pope Gregory the Great*

The "Delphic Sybil" by Michelangelo in the Sistine Chapel

arranged around the figures. Botticelli was employed in the Cappella Sistina (1481–1482) where he painted scenes from the life of Moses in his taut disciplined style of drawing, with mobile folds of clothing, hair and gestures, and figures given linear outlines. Perugino was responsible for the fresco of the handing over of the key to Peter, the scene being enacted on a wide square in front of a central building which has been conceived according to architectural ideals, its proportions exactly fulfilling the laws of perspective, and with an ancient triumphal gate in the background. Michelangelo carried out the ceiling fresco between 1508 and 1512. The voluminous figures from the story of the creation fill the available space and are conceived with a distance viewpoint in mind; they are within a simple frame of simulated architecture. Spiritual expression, richness of movement, the variety of conception of the figures and their physiognomies are even more apparent in his fresco of the Last Judgement on the altar wall (1534–1541). From 1509 Raphael was given the task of furnishing the rooms in the Vatican, where his pictorial inventiveness brings both actions and ideas to life with monumental figures in voluminous garments who are placed in spatial areas which have both depth and perspective.

The fresco decorations at the Villa Farnesina (1508–1511) give us an idea of how the villas of this period were fitted and furnished. Notable painters such as Raphael, Giulio Romano and Peruzzi were given the task of decorating the villa with paintings of mythological scenes. Broad landscape backdrops and simulated architectural details enlarge the spatial area, the painted figures, in some degree recapturing the Greek ideal, move freely and unrestricted, while garlands of fruit adorn some of the compositions. Interior rooms in the Renaissance often had gilded wood-carved coffered ceilings, derived from ancient models, as can be seen in the Salone delle Prospettive.

Besides providing sculptured figures for portals, choir screens, taber- nacles and incidental pieces, the most important duty of a sculptor in the Renaissance was that of providing decorations for tombs. Such sculptors did not normally hail from Rome, but were brought into the Papal city from outside (e.g. from Tuscany), for instance Donatello, Andrea Sansovino, Filarete and the Pollaiuolos. Pope Sixtus IV's tomb in the Vatican (1484–1493) was the work of Antonio Pollaiuolo and marks a definite step in the development from the traditional Gothic memorial slab and the free-standing tomb. The Pope is shown lying down, surrounded by relief slabs which depict virtues and the papal arms. The bronze plinth is also embellished with reliefs, person- ifications of the free arts. The figures are conceived in the definitive Pollaiuolo style with mobile bodies, a vivid fall of the folds and an exactly differentiated surface texture. With the tomb of Innocence VIII (St Peter) Pollaiuolo again shows the Pope lying down, as well as sitting enthroned with his insignia – a novelty which was to point the way for subsequent burial monuments.

In 1505 Julius II commissioned Michelangelo to build his tomb. Originally intended as a free-standing two-storey monument in St Peter's Church above the Confessio Petri, it was installed in San Pietro in Vincoli in 1547 as a wall-mounted tomb with the "Slaves" (now in the Louvre, Paris and the Accademia, Florence), the allegories of active and contemplative life and the figure of Moses. The whole can be interpreted as an allegory of life in bondage, suggested by the slaves or prisoners, and mercy, shown by the seated figures in the upper storey. The prisoners, vividly captured in the block, clearly show Michelangelo's style of working, his figures emerging out of the stone in layers, so that unworked sections are still visible. In 1498– 1500 Michelangelo was occupied with the task of completing the Pietà for San Pietro: the beautiful young Mary seems to accept the death of her son as a necessary sacrifice for the spiritual salvation of mankind. She is wearing a robe, the details of which are painstakingly executed by the artist and show the influence of Donatello. By con- trast, the image of Christ lying lifeless in her lap, comes across as deeply tender. The impression of perfect harmony is strengthened by the way the group is rigidly contained within a triangular area.

The bronze portal by Filarete in St Peter (1433–1445) takes as its theme the stories of the apostles Peter and Paul and portrays both historical and mythological scenes. Closely influenced by the bronze doors of the Baptistery in Florence, the relief sections betray huge inconsistencies both in the way they are proportioned and divided up as well as in their composition. In this respect they act as a pointer to the fact that Rome, even at the beginning of the Quattrocento, was still very much in the second league in terms of sculpture. The exca- vation of important ancient pieces of sculpture (Torso of Belvedere, the Laokoon group etc.) were not without consequence for the devel- opment of sculpture: close study of the ancients' achievements – in respect of movement, expression and proportion – was possible and many copies of these works were made. The damaged sculptures were restored and made good, notably in the Della Porta studio.

On returning to Rome from their French exile in 1417, the Popes devoted themselves to two pressing tasks: the restoration of their residence and the rebuilding of the dilapidated city. From the begin- ning of the 15th c. the most varied assortment of architects and mas- ter builders were involved in the construction of the new cathedral of St Peter, the Papal residence and the public squares around these buildings. Individual phases of construction were completed, but the work did not represent the realization of one overall plan. The choir of St Peter's Church was begun by Rossellini to plans by Leo Battista Alberti, the dome was conceived by Michelangelo, the façade by Maderna, the semi-circular colonnades of the Piazza di San Pietro

St Peter's Church: building started in 1506 and continued under the most famous architects and artists of the day

were the work of Bernini, the gardens with the belvedere were created by Bramante and his followers, while between them Raphael and Michelangelo were responsible for the designs and furnishings of the palace interior. The whole area was intended to provide a visual demonstration of the Pope's supremacy as representative of Christ.

The expansion of the city proceeded on several fronts. First it was necessary to improve communications between the Vatican and the rest of the city over the Ponte Sant'Angelo. With the building of the Ponte Sisto in 1475 a second bridge across the Tiber was provided. Then, in order to improve access to the city from the north for the vast numbers of pilgrims, travellers, couriers and traders, work was begun at the beginning of the 16th c. on redesigning the Piazza del Popolo. Three roads lead in a fan-shape from the square into the city centre.

The hills were intended to become attractive residential areas again, with access to them being facilitated by means of a system of roads with even gradients and the provision of water being guaranteed by new pipes and conduits. Finally, it was a matter of some priority to the Popes to install pilgrimage paths between the seven (later eight) main churches, something which was initiated by Sixtus V and his town planner Domenico Fontana. Apart from the main axes, Sixtus V had another 125 streets paved.

The Popes encouraged the construction of palaces along the more important thoroughfares by awarding special privileges to those who commissioned such buildings. Towards the end of the 16th c. the most important centres in the city had been rebuilt and new quarters such as Borgo and Trastevere had been added. The most important banks had opened up offices on the Strada di Banchi (now the Via Banco Santo Spirito), while the papal mint was set up in the nearby square.

Among further building measures undertaken by the Popes was the construction of monumental public squares, which are distinguished by the wealth of variety which they display; examples include the Piazza Navona, the Piazza di Spagna, the Piazza Barbarini and the Capitol. Often these areas were given a new look by the installation of an ancient monument which had been adapted to acquire a Christian significance in accordance with the Counter-Reformation, through such small changes as the addition of a cross or a sculpture. Church façades were refashioned, particularly during the Baroque period, in the course of alterations to the public squares. Satellite buildings were erected in a symmetrical arrangement, adjoining the church but on a lower level. Their façades provided a complement to the concave or convex shape of the main church (e.g. Sant'Andrea al Quirinale). Fountains, either free-standing or built into the wall, sometimes with a comprehensive array of sculpted figures, acquired extraordinary significance in the public squares and spaces of Rome. The Spanish Steps, which date from the early 17th c., form one of the most impressive examples of this period: the steps lead up from the Piazza di Spagna with the Fontana della Barka, are divided by half-landings into three sections which divide in the middle into two separate flights, and ascend to the Piazza della Trinità dei Monti. The façade of a church and an obelisk standing in front mark the summit of this venerated flight of steps.

Providing a direct link with the Renaissance architectural tradition, the first Baroque building in Rome of seminal significance is Il Gesó, built between 1568 and 1584, first to plans by Vignolas, and then to those of Nicolo della Portas. The façade mirrors the basilica-like arrangement of the interior, its structural division by means of arrangements of pilasters, ledges, window openings and niches giving a plastic character to the wall, which, through its lavishly fashioned central portal, its window in the upper storey and its triangular gable with the side volutes has a strong pull towards the centre. Inside, the short spacious crossing seems to be totally subordinate to the central dome. The side rooms are connected to the main hall in such a way that they do not detract from its unity and stylistic homogeneity – a notable and momentous achievement of early Baroque. The principle of a church with a large main hall and a domed crossing was adopted for many other churches; however, the proportions were enlarged and the wall was made less severe and given more emphasis by sculpted features such as completely round pillars, arches and sculptures. What had been uniform and evenly distributed structural elements were now split up and regrouped, with effects of light and shade being consciously added. In Sant'Andrea al Quirinale (1658–1670), Giovanni Bernini created a façade executed in travertine with a portal framed by an aedicule which is crowned by the coat of arms of the church's founder in front of the large semicircular window, with the result that the entrance area shows a pronounced emphasis on sculpture. Large isolated forms are brought into a supposedly hierarchic harmony. Through the use of an oval for the building's ground-plan, extended by eight chapels, Bernini created an important type of Baroque church, which can transmit a feeling of calm to the observer by means of the clarity of its composition and tectonic structure. Beside the extensions to St Peter's Church, the main construction project in Rome during the Baroque period was the laying of the square in front of the church.

The vast oval square was designed by Gian Lorenzo Bernini between 1656 and 1671. It is formed by two vaulted colonnade arms, each with three aisles, and its transverse axis consists of the obelisk, the two fountains and the colonnade projections. The columns support the entablature and the balustrade on which the statues of saints are positioned. The columns, which are arranged in four rows and

Baroque

Architecture

enclose the open area of the square, give the whole a solidity, while at the same time affording a sense of unfettered space. The proportions have been chosen in such a way that the columns seem colossal to the observer, yet are nevertheless almost dwarfed by the façade of St Peter's Church which by comparison appears even higher and more imposing.

With the façade of the Palazzo della Propaganda Fide (1662) – a late work of Borromini – the pilasters opposite the back wall and the entablature show great gains in originality. The windows also form an extra feature with their unconventionally formed gables. Roman Baroque architecture no longer had anything schematic about it; instead Maderna, Bernini, Borromini, Cortona and others incorporated their personal ideas directly into their buildings.

Painting

The hallmarks of the work of the Bolognese Annibale Carracci were emphatic gestures, large forms evoking deep pathos and relaxed postures and settings. These contrasted with the realistic painting methods of Caravaggio, whose overall sombre coloration contrasts with sections which are effectively lit, the juxtaposition strengthening the dramatic qualities of his artistic scenes. These two artists formed opposing poles of artistic activity in Rome at the start of the Baroque period. In 1595 Carracci moved his studio to Rome with the aim of reviving the artistic school of Raphael. He was followed by other artists from Bologna. The frescos which Carracci created for the galleria of the Palazzo Farnese (1597–1604) were of great importance for the development of monumental painting. The scenes of the barrel divided into three are all subordinated to the central idea of the elevation and metamorphosis of the human soul through divine love. The figures are portrayed as being totally free of all constraint, almost lost to the world, surrounded by an atmosphere of joyousness, their movements being especially expressive by means of rotations and foreshortenings. The complicated quadruple-layered compositions are given clarity through the cleverly thought-out use of colours. These frescos provided an important stimulus to increases in light effects in painting and in dynamics without compositions losing their strength. Domenichino's fresco in the church of Sant'Andrea della Valle (1623–1626) portrays the life of the apostles in dramatic terms by means of just a few figures, while never forsaking moderation and order. These paintings, in the way they are adapted to structural conditions (e.g. in the apse calotte), are a masterly example of the architectural painting in Rome in the 17th c. Caravaggio, on the other hand, was no frescoist and began in Rome with smaller works, mainly pictures of people conceived as half-figures. It was only very gradually that large commissions started coming his way (the Contarelli chapel in San Luigi degli Francesi, the Cerasi chapel, Santa Maria del Popolo) and gave an indication of his importance as a painter. Monumental groups of figures are clearly and powerfully composed, individual people are given weight and are finished off in a sculpturally effective way, rotations intensify the expression. Chiaroscuro effects and the considered application of colouring direct the observer's attention to the essence of the work, with landscape and space often only being hinted at.

Pietro Corina is considered to be the most important representative of the High Baroque in Rome. He painted vast ceiling areas in churches and palaces and also carried out private commissions for churches, creating altar-leaves or paintings with mythological contents. The frescos of Santa Maria in Vallicella (1647–1665) show the true range of his colour, his ability to create spatial illusions and blend his compositions in with the surrounding architecture.

Giovanni Lorenzo Bernini is by common consent the central figure of the Baroque period in Rome and, like many of his colleagues, he went far beyond the limitations of the genres in which he was expected to work. Early works such as the Amalthea goat (Villa Borghese) bear testimony to his extraordinary skill. In the statues at the Villa Borghese it is already possible to observe the individual characterization of details and the powerful structural control of the sculpture; yet the group of Apollo and Daphne (1622–1625, Museo Borghese) shows that Bernini was able to free his sculptures from distracting details and to give a greater strength and precision to the expressive and corporeal aspects of his work. What is extraordinary about this group of figures is the multiplicity of angles from which it can be advantageously viewed. Bernini captures the moment in which Apollo, passionately in love, seeks to reach the fleeing Daphne, who is saved by being turned into a tree, which is hinted at by the leaves on her arms and legs. The artist here narrates a story in a most concentrated way and implies the passage of time merely by his depiction of the two figures. What is so gripping is the state of the two people's feelings – the passion of the god and the fear of the girl being pursued, which is not only perceptible in the bearing and gestures of each, but is even visible in the way the sculptor has fashioned the ends of their hair. In accordance with this aim Bernini had created the busts of his two subjects in quite different ways, using distinct methods of expression and structure. Bozzetti's models in wax and terracotta inspired him to test the effects of light and shape in his works in cast bronze. With his monument to Pope Urban VIII (1628–1647, St Peter) Bernini followed the conventions of that time with a sarcophagus, a statue of the dead man in a sitting position, and the allegorical marble figures, while at the same time taking a course of his own by his personification of death, which writes the name of the Pope while contemplating the theme of dying. The ciborium above Peter's tomb (1633, St Peter) was created jointly by Bernini working with Borromini and Maderno. The ornamental bronze spiral columns were intended to call to mind the ciborium of the Constantine church of St Peter, just as the surmounting was fashioned with it in mind, but here artistic considerations triumphed with the result that the four columns are combined to form one monument by means of four large volutes. These are surmounted by the terrestrial globe, on which the cross stands.

Bernini's Baroque sculpture "The Rape of Proserpina"

If Bernini's works were all created very much with the Pope in mind – he was forbidden to work for any other client without the agreement of the latter – other young artists such as Alessandro Algardi and François Duquesnoy were very dependent on private patrons for their livelihood. Although they maintained their own studios, they were never able to demonstrate the same success as Bernini.

The church and the nobility had lost their dominant role in the classical period and in terms of commissioning works of art they very much retreated into the background, artistic production becoming the province of the new merchant class, the petty nobility and the elevated bourgeoisie. Genre pictures, vedute and portraits were new artistic forms which became very popular. The great demand for graphic works was certainly closely connected with these trends. During his second stay in Rome Giovanni Battista Piranesi set himself the task of

Classicism

recording the city and its antiquities in the form of engravings. This new-found consciousness of the architectural heritage of the ancient world was a distinguishing feature of this epoch and also found its expression in Johann Joachim Winckelmann's exhaustive studies of antiquity which he undertook during long stays in Italy and finally during his period of office as president of antiquities at the Vatican library.

From a formal point of view this new trend also made itself felt in the architecture of the period. Alessandro Galilei successfully won the commission to build the façade of San Giovanni in Laterano (1733–1736). This show wall, with its large, uncluttered proportions and austere layout, is one of the earliest examples of classical architecture in Rome. It unites both floors of the building in a vast overall design which contrasts with the deeply recessed windows of the two storeys. A broad entablature, triangular gables, a balustrade with sculpted figures complete the front of the building. Piranesi's façade for Santa Maria del Priorato (1764–1766) succeeds in giving a strictly classical impression by virtue of the clear demarcation of its forms, the use of antique elements and ornamental motives.

Anton Raphael Mengs developed his academic brand of classicism during his extended stays in Rome. The ceiling painting in the Villa Albani is conceived like a panel picture: a firm, self-contained symmetrical composition with statuesque figures which have little connection with the side ovals. Canova was responsible for important works of sculpture of the period. In his tomb for Pope Clement XIV the pathos of the figure of the Pope – a gesture from the former Baroque period – contrasts with the classical severity of the sarcophagus and the representations of the virtues "Moderation" and "Gentleness", each a unity in itself, motionless within an unbroken outline.

19th c.

During the 19th c. Rome attracted many artists from the north. The Nazarenes moved back to Rome to the convent of Sant'Isidoro in 1810 in order to fulfil their ideal of a strictly secluded, religious way of life (Brothers of Luke). Overbeck and Pforr were the initiators and they were joined by Cornelius, Schadow, Schnorr von Carolsfeld and others. They championed a Christian art drawing on old German painting, as opposed to the 'unfeeling academicism' which they saw around them. The early Raphael and Perugino were other models for them. By working communally they wanted to fill vast rooms with monumental wall paintings as the old masters had done. In 1817 they were commissioned to decorate the villa of the Palazzo Zuccaro with frescos depicting the story of Joseph (now in Berlin). They were also asked to decorate the garden house of the Marchese Carlo Massimo in Laterano with themes from Dante, Tasso and Ariosto – a project which was left unfinished.

After the unification of Italy and the elevation of Rome to the status of capital city in 1870 there were important new building projects. Eclectic building styles were chosen for the government ministries and these were intended to reflect the various historical epochs. Two Renaissance palaces on the Piazza Venezia were pulled down to make way for the national monument to Victor Emmanuel II, a vast structure of white marble conceived in classical forms by Giuseppe Sacconi (1885–1911). Over the tomb of the unknown soldier stands the "Altar of the Fatherland". The monument is dominated by the austere columned portico with its broad entablature and bronze four-horsed chariots which emphasize the two sides of the portico.

20th c.

It is only possible to touch on a few aspects of the varied manifestations of fine arts and architecture in the 20th c., developments of which have not generally been affected by any one particular location, mainly because of the international nature of cultural interaction and mobility. Virgilio Guidi was instrumental in defining the Roman

National Monument to Victor Emanuel II on the south side of the Piazza Venezia

milieu at the start of the 20th c.; he was very attached to the secessionist movement, but also took part in exhibitions of valori plastici, which established a rigid mysterious world by excessive definition in the modelling of objects and from 1920 encouraged a trend towards Quattrocento models. The journal "Valori Plastici", which was published in Rome from 1918, with which de Chirico and Carrà were closely connected, became an important organ for the movement. After 1923 the term "Stile Novecento" was used to refer to works by these artists, who set so much store by the clarity and transparency of their compositions and the serviceability of their architecture. The chief representatives of the "Roman school" were Mario Maffai and Scipione. They turned against the rhetorical monumentalism of the rationalists and in the 1930s strove towards a more enigmatic Baroque-influenced style of painting. Just before the Second World War warning signals can be detected in their pictures. Developments after the war were rich in new stimuli, many artists being influenced by the more informal trends coming from America. In 1947 the first Gruppo Forma met in Rome to defend abstract art, followed in 1950 by the Gruppo Realista. At the beginning of the 1960s there were concerted efforts to reduce artistic features to a minimum, "arte povera" as it was called. Followers of this trend set store by a conscious simplicity of expression and poverty of form and made use of plain and trivial materials which they formed only sparingly. The 'transvan-guardia' which followed this returned to classical media, painting and drawing, and revived forms from the past.

Architects in Rome at the beginning of the 20th c. remained commit-ted to historicism, as Cesare Bazzani's Museo d'Arte Moderna, built in 1911, demonstrates. In 1928, behind the scenes of the exhibition 'Esposizione dell'architettura razionale', a struggle raged between the rationalists and the academics to gain the favour of the young Fascist regime, repressive measures not being taken against the former until 1937. A number of rationalist buildings were created by Mario Ridolfi: the post office building in the Quartiere Nomentano (1932) and a house on the Via Valentino. In the 1950s he designed, with other architects, the district of Tiburtino, which was destined to become a symbol of Italian neorealism by virtue of its irregular structure and traditionalistic houses. Between 1950 and 1954 the standardized mu-nicipal houses known as 'case a torre' were built on the Viale Etiopia. In 1926 Marcello Piacentini built the Hotel Ambasciatori in an eclectic style, i.e. using elements from different styles. With the seizure of power by the Fascists he quickly became one of the leading repre-sentatives of the new regime's architecture, which made use of neoclassical and historicist elements. One of the many commissions which Piacentini was given was that of designing the Via Concil-iazione: a monumental thoroughfare which cuts off the Borgo and leads directly onto St Peter's Square. He also worked on the great E.U.R. project (Esposizione Universale Roma), the buildings for the world exhibition planned for 1942 – today a district of the city with administrative and commercial offices. Futuristic skyscrapers stand isolated because of rigorous building regulations, while spaciously laid-out streets and enormous squares give the area the distinctive character of a satellite town. Evidence of modern architectural trends is provided by Rome's main railway station, built between 1938 and 1950 by Calini, Castellazzi, Fadigati and others. The main admin-istrative building is divided up by horizontal rows of windows which contrast with the curved roof shape of the entrance hall. Light construction materials, travertine cladding, glass and marble give the building its transparent airy appearance.

Education and Science

General

The Eternal City has only been the capital of the whole of Italy since 1870. Its traditions and status in this role are therefore rather modest in comparison with more centrally organized countries in Europe, even though for centuries Rome was the centre of the Papal States. Its dominant role as political capital and Vatican City does naturally have a relevance in cultural and scientific areas. With its many universities, academies, institutes, libraries and archives, Rome does retain an abundance of cultural assets which are not just connected with the city's glorious past. There are a total of two state and 15 papal universities and higher education establishments with some 300,000 students. The National Library alone has a stock of about 4 million books, while the Vatican Library possesses over 1 million volumes. It would be difficult to put a figure on the number of locally based foreign research and educational establishments. Countless young foreigners come to Italian language courses in Rome, while just within the city itself there are 1900 state schools.

Universities

The state university 'Università degli Studi di Roma' ('Sapienza') was founded between 1932 and 1935. Before that the only higher educa-

View of the centre of Rome – political capital and Vatican City

tion establishments in the city were the Papal colleges and institutes belonging to religious orders. Today 'Sapienza' boasts over 170,000 students in 14 faculties. There is also the state recognised Catholic university for medicine ('Università Cattolica del Sacro Cuore'). Other centres of higher education include the private 'Università Internazionale degli Studi Sociali' whose curriculum areas range over law, politics and economic science, as well as a two-year training in journalism. The Papal 'Università Gregoriana' is purely a Jesuit college and offers training for the priesthood to students from all over the world. Citizens from countries of the European Union as well as those from other foreign countries are all basically eligible to study at Rome's universities.

Besides the above mentioned National Library and the Vatican Library there are a large number of state, papal and private libraries which provide not only the most up-to-date literature but also books, incunabula and old manuscripts for all kinds of studies. Of special note are the 'Biblioteca Italiana per Ciechi', a library for the blind, and the 'Biblioteca Teatrale del Burcardo', which specializes in theatrical literature. | Libraries

With its historical monuments, churches and museums Rome offers a unique range of opportunities for artistic, historical, archaeological, religious and theological studies. Numerous state and papal academies and institutes are devoted to research into Rome's past and the furtherance of science and culture, e.g. the 'Accademia Nazionale dei Lincei', founded in 1603, and the 'Accademia Nazionale San Luca' (with gallery). In addition many foreign countries maintain important academies, libraries and cultural and scientific institutes in Rome. | Academies and Institutes

Cultural Scene

Music

As far as large-scale musical events are concerned, Rome cannot really escape the taint of provincialism; whether in terms of classical music or rock music, the Italian capital has very little to offer. The musical centres of excellence are all situated in the north of the country, in Milan or Turin, where the international stars are more frequent guests. The reason for this is not just the general organizational complacency of Rome but above all the lack of suitable venues: apart from the 'Pala EUR' the city possesses no large public hall. The events which take place every summer either in the open air or in marquees (the Estate Romana) offer only limited compensation for this state of affairs. However, when local rock stars and songsters perform in the parks and public square, the demands of the younger generation of Romans are at least satisfied to some extent. Tourists who take an evening stroll through Trastevere at any time of year will come across numerous bars and restaurants with live music, the Roman jazz scene being particularly active. For lovers of classical music it is worth their while to check up on events which may be happening during their stay, as the orchestra of the 'Accademia di Santa Cecilia', the Opera, the RAI (state-run television and radio corporation), not to mention the city's chamber orchestras, guarantee a high level of music making. Because of the lack of modern and well-equipped concert halls, concerts tend to take place in the venerable surroundings of historic palaces and churches. Opera performances, which until 1994 took place in July and August in the Caracalla Baths and now are held at the Villa Borghese, also enjoy an outstanding reputation.

Theatre

In terms of quantity alone, Rome is the largest theatrical centre in Italy, with more than 40 theatres fulfilling the demand for drama and entertainment and new companies continually being formed. The Teatro Argentina is a municipal theatre with a long tradition – it staged the first performance of Rossini's "Barber of Seville". The great contemporary stage directors, such as Giorgio Strehler and Dario Fo, possibly the most famous of the Italian theatrical avant-garde, no longer choose to stage their productions in Rome, however, instead preferring Milan. The less popular Carmelo Bene does, however, work in Rome. It is, though, first and foremost the many small experimental companies to which Rome owes its reputation as a theatrical city. In spite of the large number of permanent ensembles a large proportion of classical theatre performances are by guest companies. Particularly popular with Roman audiences are the plays of Pirandello and the, for their time, highly innovative comedies of Goldoni. Foreign dramatists, such as Shakespeare, Brecht and Strindberg are, however, also frequently performed. The theatre season runs from October to June, although many theatres also put on summer performances.

Cinema

In the days when Cinecittà, the Italian Hollywood, was enjoying its heyday, Rome was an exciting centre for film-making. It was above all in the 1950s that international screen stars came here to disport themselves and perform what came to be known as 'dolce vita' and Rome certainly owes its present vibrant film tradition to this golden period of forty years ago. The city still has a total of some 170 active cinemas whose contribution is supplemented in the summer months by a large number of film showings which form part of the 'Estate Romana' cultural festival. The film scene has a diversity of both programmes and entry prices. In the top 'prima visione' (first performance) category can be found showings of the latest international films, while the 'seconda visione' category is devoted to second showings. The film clubs which form part of the 'Cinema d'Essai' show old films and films of artistic merit. Children's films are generally shown in the church community cinemas.

The inexorable progress of private broadcasting started relatively early in Italy and since 1976 the three channels of the state broadcasting corporation RAI have enjoyed fierce competition. At first this competition consisted of just a few local and regional operators, but recently a stage has been reached where a small number of companies have over a number of years enjoyed a complete monopoly. Three large private networks dominate Italian television and can boast higher viewing figures than the state-run 'Mamma RAI'. The owner of these three private channels (Canale 5, Rete 4 and Italia 1) is the media tycoon, Silvio Berlusconi, who, during his short period as prime minister of Italy, tried to reform the RAI for his own personal benefit.

TV and Radio

The whole of Italy has access to television entertainment and newscasting, the provinces as well as the main cities. The inhabitants of Rome can tune in to RAI 1, 2 and 3, as well as some 30 broadcasting stations. Any tourist in Rome who investigates the channels available on the television set in his hotel room will soon realize that the games shows and entertainment programmes are that much more frenetic, the advertising breaks that much more intrusive, than he is likely to be used to in his own country.

The number of private radio stations in Rome runs into hundreds, all competing with one another for the limited range of frequencies. There is a preponderance of stations broadcasting continuous light music at a high volume, often only occasionally interrupted by commercials. More challenging material is offered by the small politically-run stations which are the product of the so-called alternative culture of the 1970s. Some, such as 'Radio Radicale', are on the far left of the political spectrum.

There is probably no other city which can offer as many museums and art galleries as Rome. There is probably no finer museum, however, than the city itself. The impact of this 'museum city' with its countless architectural monuments and over 70 museums and galleries is overwhelming. Leaving aside the Vatican Museum, which has over 1.5 million visitors every year, Rome's most frequented museum is the 'Museo Nazionale Etrusco' in the Villa Giulia, with around 100,000 visitors annually, followed by the recently extended 'Museo Nazionale Romano', while the other museums and galleries are much less visited. Rome would not be Rome, however, if there were not an appropriately 'Roman' explanation for the relatively low numbers of visitors at these smaller establishments: poor attendance can be laid at the door of essential restoration work, which can often drag on for years and means that only a small part of the museum's collection can be put on display.

Museums and Galleries

Cinecittà – the Hollywood of Rome

Italy's film pioneer, the Italian counterpart to the Lumière brothers in France or Edison in America, was the inventor, producer and director, Filoteo Alberini. At the beginning of 1895 he gained a patent for his film camera, in 1901 he opened the Cinema Moderno in Rome, in 1905 he founded the Cines company, built the first film studio and made "La Presa di Roma" ("The Capture of Rome"), a film spectacular which told the story of Victor Emmanuel II's entry into Rome in 1870.

How it all began

But Rome was not at this time the only centre of the Italian film industry; there was competition from both Milan and Turin. And from Turin came the most costly and important films of those days, the effects of which can still be detected in Italy's film industry to this day, notwithstanding the fact that it has now been centred in Rome for many years. "Cabiria" is the name of the monumental historical film made by Giovanni Pastrone in 1914, which is set in the 3rd c. B.C. and depicts Etna erupting, slaves revolting, the maiden Cabiria falling into pirates' hands, a hero called Maciste distinguishing himself and even Hannibal crossing the Alps, the latter a sequence for which, so the story goes, all the available elephants in Italy were pressed into service.

Historical blockbusters and diva wars

The film "Cabiria", which made consistent use of such cinematic innovations as tracking shots and artificial lighting, and numbered the American director D. W. Griffith among its admirers, was actually only one of a whole series of historical films which, in an Italy intent on expansion and national aggrandisement, probably performed a propagandist function. "The associations with the glory of the Roman empire and the power of the Caesars were welcomed with open arms", wrote the cinema historian Jerzy Toeplitz of the relationship obtaining at that time between the cinema and politics.

Italian cinema in those days, heavily influenced by the cult figure, Gabriele d'Annunzio, a writer of excesses, who was also involved in the gestation of "Cabiria", did, it is true, forge a reputation for itself in other types of film. The popular comedy was one of these, but scarcely a place could be found for more realistic pieces, or those which might have drawn on the works of the great writer, Giovanni Verga. Of greater impact was the invention of the 'film diva' – a typically Italian phenomenon – and the resulting stir caused by the 'war' between stars such as Lydia Borelli and Pina Menichelli, which often produced bigger headlines in the newspapers than the real war which was taking place at the time. "The cult of the diva", wrote Ulrich Gregor, "led Italian cinema further and further into a romantic and escapist fantasy world". Not only that – it led Italian cinema, which in the 1920s found itself exposed to American competition, into complete ruin.

Talkies

Italian cinema did not recover from this disastrous state of affairs until the advent of talkies towards the end of the 1920s. Production was now concentrated in Rome, where it had been transferred by the entrepreneur and monopolist, Stefano Pittaluga. In 1930 nine or ten of the new talkies, which initially served mainly as a vehicle for tourism and hits such as "O sole mio", were shot in the recently constructed Cines studios in Rome. Soon, however, directors directed their cameras towards Italian everyday life, a trend viewed by the Fascist government with great suspicion. Up until this point Mussolini had not taken a great interest in the film industry, now however he prescribed aesthetic guidelines for it, demanding that the actors should retain a typically Italian appearance, should speak 'pure' Italian, and that foreign films should be dubbed. In 1935 he finally founded a film school and studio in Rome, the latter opening in 1937 under the name Cinecittà.

Neorealism

The new film school numbered people such as Rossellini, Antonioni and Visconti among its students and, given that the Fascist regime in Italy was less rigorous in its political control of culture and arts than the equivalent regime in Germany, the journal 'Cinema' was able to publish a kind of manifesto for neorealism in 1943. This led to the paradoxical state of affairs by which in the early 1940s Rome and Cinecittà were not only producing propaganda films as well as escapist melodramas and light entertainment films which were lumped together under the sardonic and dismissive label 'white telephone cinema', but were also leading the way in the new neorealism, thereby ensuring that Italy would always occupy a leading place in

A scene from Fellini's film "La dolce vita" with Marcello Mastroianni and Anita Ekberg

the history of the cinema. Italian cinema, as the writer Carlo Lizzani has said, has always been characterized by the conflict between the pomp and pathos of 'annunzionism' and the love of the spontaneous and unscripted which defines the verismo movement. In such masterpieces as Rossellini's "Rome – open city" (1945), which deals with the anti-Fascist resistance, Visconti's "La terra trema" (1948), whose theme is the struggle of fishermen against exploitation, and de Sica's "Bicycle Thieves", an appeal for social justice, realistic cinema gains the upper hand in the history of film for one glorious, if brief, moment. These are films which often employ non-professional actors, in which dialect is spoken and original settings are used. Even by the 1950s, genuine neorealistic cinema was played out, the victim, among other things, of political manouevring by a Christian democratic government which did not want to see an impoverished country depicted on cinema screens.

The age of comedy returned, along with the media-conducted battles of jealous divas such as Gina Lollobrigida and Sophia Loren, and even the historical film – albeit shorn of the propagandist tendencies which it had displayed heretofore – made a reappearance on the cinema screen, enjoying a renaissance with unpretentiously colourful adventures involving such musclemen as Hercules or Maciste (famous from "Cabiria"), who bravely blast their way through the world of antiquity. "Cinecittà films have always been spectaculars, decked out by people who were incapable of simulating the real world, and in any case never had any desire to, preferring to create a dream world." So wrote Georg Seesslen, and he went on: "This is how Cinecittà films shine – in a way that the real world never can. The falseness of this brilliance is completely calculated – ephemerality is everything. Cinecittà dreams of wealth, as only the poor can dream of

The colourful world of Cinecittà

37

wealth. Every scene is packed with more objects of breathtaking and ostentatious glamour than could in reality ever be contained in a single room, or temple, or indeed in the whole world."

In whatever genre it chose to involve itself, Cinecittà tended to produce its own cheaper and often very idiosyncratic version of Hollywood. With the often politically contentious 'Italo-western', which came to the fore at the end of the 1960s and the beginning of the 1970s, Cinecittà came up with a true hybrid, which sometimes went one better than its American original and in its aesthetics was heavily indebted to its parent. Actors such as Clint Eastwood have used Italy as a stepping-stone to stardom, along with many others from all over the world, and in addition Cinecittà makes itself available for international co-productions, so that it is not at all unusual to see Americans at work on productions in Rome.

Of course Italian cinema does not just consist of the colourful world of Cinecittà. Indeed its reputation does not come from actors in Adriano Celentano fashions showing their paces in the soft sex films of Tinto Brass, but from directors such as Michelangelo Antonioni, who films understated yet fascinating studies of bourgeois life such as "La notte" (1960); Luchino Visconti and his elegiac films about the decline of the nobility and the bourgeoisie ("The Leopard", 1962, "Death in Venice", 1970); Francesco Rosi and his analytical thrillers about power and morality ("Who shot Salvatore G.?", 1962; "Lucky Luciano", 1972); the Taviani brothers, who in their best works found a perfect blend of realism and poetry ("Padre Padrone", 1977; "The Night of San Lorenzo", 1982); and finally in the works of Bernardo Bertolucci, who combined politics, sociology and psychology in equal measure as well as the traditions of melodrama ("1900", 1974–1976, "La luna", 1979).

The end of
Cinecittà?

There is in fact no rigid dividing line between the commercial world of Cinecittà and the work of genuinely artistic film-makers. Sergio Leone ("Play me the Song of Death", 1968; "Once upon a time in America", 1984) began his career in the genre of spectaculars set in ancient times, often referred to as 'sandal films' ("The Colossus of Rhodes", 1960), while the genre encompassing mafia films and political thrillers has also had its share of masterpieces. A director such as Federico Fellini, who in "La strada" (1954) had insisted on using authentic locations, was content to have a replica of the Via Veneto constructed for some of the scenes in "La dolce vita" (1959) and subsequently shot his films almost exclusively at Cinecittà.

Cinecittà's golden age is now, however, very much in the past, just as the era of the great Italian film directors is at an end, with those who have not died, such as Bertolucci, now a long way from the zenith of their powers. The crisis caused by the slump in Italian films – at the beginning of the 1990s the Italian industry's share of the domestic market had plummeted to just 10% – seems to have been surmounted and the share has now climbed back to about 25%, with Carmine Cianfarani, president of the association of Italian film-makers, now able to approach the future with some degree of optimism. The comedian Roberto Benigni has even managed to beat off all American opposition with his film "The Monster" (1995) and taken first place at the box-office. Particularly exciting in recent years has been the work of Nanni Moretti with his playful examinations of the Italian scene ("Dear Diary", 1993) and Gianni Arnelio, who in his large-scale and deeply human films such as "Stolen Children" (1992) and "Lamerica" (1994) renews contact with the neorealism tradition and is able to make it relevant for the jaded palates of today's cinema-goers. The Italian film industry can probably not entirely overcome its structural problems; it has to struggle against the overwhelming competition of Hollywood and with the other media, as is the case with all the national cinema industries in Europe. Most of Cinecittà's activities now fall within the fields of television and advertising. Fellini once even went to court over the constant interruptions for commercials that his films were subjected to when shown on television. And in his film "Intervista" (1987), actually set in Cinecittà, the image of the enemy is provided by a weird forest of television aerials – even though "Intervista" was originally filmed in order to be shown on television. Incidentally, the commercials which have been produced at Cinecittà include the highly successful Campari advertisements, attractive, light-weight and highly intelligent – but then they were after all made by Fellini.

Prominent Figures in Roman History

Pope Alexander VI
(c. 1431–1503)

Posterity has branded Pope Alexander VI (1492–1503) as a nepotist and libertine. Though he brought no credit to the Church, his reign is commemorated by a small coat of arms on the walls of the Vatican Palace (at the end of the right-hand colonnade, near the post office). His main object was the aggrandisement of the Borgia family to which he belonged; using the Papacy as an instrument, he sought to establish himself as the ruler of a hereditary monarchy and for this purpose to secularise the States of the Church.

A cardinal at the age of 26, he learned in the world of the Italian Renaissance to forget all scruples. Although a man of driving energy and a great patron of the arts, he dishonoured his position as the "vicar of Christ" and successor to St Peter by his addiction to sexual pleasures. Savonarola, falling foul of the Borgias, died at the stake; the Papacy survived.

Augustus
(63 B.C.–A.D. 14)

Augustus, originally Gaius Octavianus, Caesar's grand-nephew and adoptive son, became the first Emperor (Imperator) of the Roman Empire. In 43 B.C. he allied himself with Mark Antony and Lepidus as a member of the Triumvirate established to conduct the war against Caesar's murderers. The three triumvirs divided the territories held by Rome between them, Augustus taking the west, Mark Antony the east, Lepidus Africa. After defeating Antony and Cleopatra at Actium in 31 B.C., Augustus became sole ruler. In the Augustan age which followed he pacified the Empire, strengthened its frontier defences and was a generous patron of art and learning. The poets of the period included Virgil, Horace and Ovid. His most notable monuments in Rome are his Mausoleum, with the Ara Pacis (Altar of Peace), and his house on the Palatine. A bust and a marble statue in the Vatican Museums depict him in a magnificent – if idealised – aspect.

Gian Lorenzo
Bernini
(1598–1680)

Baroque Rome would be unthinkable without Gian Lorenzo Bernini, son of the sculptor Pietro Bernini, who left his mark on the city, both as architect and as sculptor. Popes and cardinals commissioned countless buildings and works of sculpture from him, and his patrons can often be identified by the heraldic devices which he incorporated into the decoration of a building. Under the 17th c. Popes, Urban VIII (1623–44: the three bees of the Barberini family), Innocent X Pamphili (1644–55: a dove holding a branch surmounted by lilies) and Alexander VII Chigi (1655-67: a tree and a star over a hill), Bernini created a whole series of masterpieces, spurred on by his bitter rivalry with his great contemporary Borromini: the bronze baldacchino and the tomb of Urban VIII in St Peter's, the figure of St Theresa in ecstasy in Santa Maria della Vittoria, the Fountain of the Four Rivers in the Piazza Navona, St Peter's Square with its colonnades, the Church of Sant'Andrea al Quirinale, the Scala Regia in the Vatican and the statues now to be seen in the Villa Borghese Museum, to name only a few.

Julius Caesar
(100–44 B.C.)

Gaius Julius Caesar, a talented general, ambitious politician, generous victor and historian, who prided himself on his literary skill, was the outstanding figure of the closing years of the republican period, of such commanding historical stature that his name was given to the holder of supreme political power, the Caesar (which later gave the German "Kaiser").

Originally destined for the priesthood, he began his military career in 81 B.C., studied in Rhodes from 76 to 73 and was elected to the post of

Julius Caesar

Bernini

Emperor Hadrian

Pontifex Maximus in 63. He allied himself with Pompey and later with Crassus, and thereafter, as a member of the first Triumvirate, was able to put his political and social ideas into effect against the will of the Senate. From 58 to 51 he was engaged in the Gallic War, first dealing with the Helvetii and then subduing Gaul (53 B.C.); in 55 he crossed the Rhine into Germany, and in that and the following year launched two brief invasions of Britain. In 49 he crossed the River Rubicon in northern Italy, thus bringing his army, without permission, into territory under the authority of the Senate. After fighting in Spain and Greece, spending half a year in the Egyptian city of Alexandria (where the Egyptian queen Cleopatra bore him a son) and waging further wars in Africa and Spain, he was appointed Dictator in 48 B.C. and confirmed in that office with a ten-year tenure in 46. As Dictator he ruled like an absolute monarch, lived in regal state and claimed quasi-divine veneration (in the Forum of Caesar which he built below the Capitol). All this increased the number of his enemies, and on the Ides of March he was murdered by a group of conspirators, including his "son" Brutus.

Giorgio de Chirico was born in 1888 in Volos, capital of Thessaly, Greece, of Italian parents. He studied at the Academy of Art in Munich from 1906 to 1909, where he was introduced to the paintings of Arnold Böcklin and Max Klinger, and to the writings of Schopenhauer and Nietzsche. The artist moved constantly, but after the Second World War he settled in Rome, where he died in 1978.

Giorgio de Chirico
(1888–1978)

De Chirico, with Carlo Carrà, is considered to be the founder of the "Pittura Metafisica" movement of modern Italian painting. His pictures, harsh and three-dimensional, portray mundane objects and townscapes, which are made to appear alien and mysterious through the unusual combination with other objects, particularly mannequins. There is an emptiness in the restrained use of colour which is infused with a sense of metaphysical dread. From 1919/20 onwards de Chirico abandoned the Pittura Metafisica. Of his earlier works, forerunners of Surrealism, the most important are: "The Soothsayer's Reward" (1913), "Secret and Melancholy of a Street" (1914), "The Great Metaphysician" (1917) and "Large Metaphysical Interior" (1917).

Constantine (Flavius Valerius Constantinus) lived as a young man at Diocletian's court, and thus gained at an early age some understanding of the conduct of public business, as well as witnessing the Diocletianic persecution of Christians. In 306 he became joint Caesar with Maxentius, whom he defeated at the Milvian Bridge (still standing) in 312. In 324 he defeated his other rival Lucinius. With the Edict of Milan (313), which allowed Christians freedom of worship, he prepared the way for

Constantine I, the Great
(c. 285–337)

41

Prominent Figures in Roman History

Christianity to become the state religion. In 330 he transferred the imperial capital from Rome to the newly founded city of Constantinople (later Byzantium, and still later Istanbul). He was baptised shortly before his death in 337, and is venerated as a saint by the Greek, Armenian and Russian churches.

Remains in Rome dating from his reign include the Basilica of Maxentius in the Forum (which he completed), Santa Costanza (built to house the tomb of his daughter), parts of a colossal statue of the Emperor in the Palazzo dei Conservatori on the Capitol and the early Christian basilicas which were begun while he was in power.

Enrico Fermi
(1901–1954)

The physicist Enrico Fermi was born in Rome; he was chiefly concerned with the theories of quantum mechanics (of Werner Heisenberg, 1925, and others). His research led to the discovery of the production of new artificial radioactive elements, and he was awarded the Nobel Prize for Physics in 1938.

In 1942 Fermi succeeeded in producing the first controlled nuclear reaction at the University of Chicago, in a purpose-built uranium reactor which he had developed. The first commercial breeder reactor (Detroit, USA) was named after him, as was the US Atomic Energy Commission's Enrico Fermi Prize, awarded annually since 1954. Fermi died in Chicago.

Pope Gregory I,
the Great
(c. 540–604)

Gregory was a scion of the Roman senatorial aristocracy. The judgements of his contemporaries and of ecclesiastical historians range from admiration to condemnation, for he was a man of contrasts, with good qualities and bad. He is perhaps best known nowadays for sending the first missionaries to England. Extremely wealthy, he himself founded the monasteries in which he lived as a Benedictine monk. He had voluntarily chosen a lowly manner of life, but there was no true humility in this, for he strove too hard and too blatantly to gain the favour of the Romans. In the style "servant of the servants of God", which he assumed for himself and his successors, there is an element of the false modesty which counts itself as a merit. Gregory was a monk, a vocation which in him seemed to carry with it a certain narrowness and pettiness, but this nevertheless had the result of enhancing the religious dimension of the Papacy. When old and ailing, tortured by gout, he wrote edifying literature, including a "Pastoral Rule", which was diligently studied by the churchmen of the Middle Ages.

Pope Gregory VII
(c. 1019/1030–
1085)

Gregory VII (Pope 1073–85), "a monk from his mother's womb" – fanatically devoted to the spiritual life and despising all things terrestrial, uncompromising to the point of self-forgetfulness – restored the standing of the Papacy after centuries of decadence. The "monk Hildebrand", feared and cursed by emperors and kings but canonised by the Church, sought to bring the Church back to purity. Small in stature and physically unimpressive but filled with inflexible determination, with a manner that was seldom winning and usually harsh and challenging, he had only one objective – to raise the status of the Papacy and renew the spirit of the Church – and he was strengthened in his endeavours by the assurance of his transcendental mission. He employed a variety of means to help towards achieving his aims – the prohibition of simony (the sale of ecclesiastical offices) and the marriage of priests, the excommunication of King Henry IV of Germany, crusades against the infidel. He did not scruple to enforce the Church's claims by the sword. Nor did he conceal his urge to dominate and command; he demanded only one thing – obedience. Showing little love for any man and inspiring little love in return, a bitter hater and bitterly hated, he drove the course of history on, and the German king was compelled to do penance at Canossa. Gregory had no sense of moderation, but had he not set himself such far-reaching goals, the Papacy would have sunk into mediocrity.

Hadrian (Publius Aelius Hadrianus), Trajan's successor and, like him, born in Spain, was Emperor from 117 to 138. One of the first concerns of his long reign was to strengthen the defences of the Empire, and he was responsible for the construction of two fortified frontier lines, Hadrian's Wall in England and the Limes in Germany, of which substantial remains survive. He liked to travel widely and is said to have visited every province in the Empire; as far away as Luxor in Egypt there is an inscription in his name on the Colossi of Memnon. This emperor, with the beard of a philosopher, whose favourite city was Athens, was a great admirer of Greek culture and promoted the diffusion of Hellenistic thought in the Roman world. He was a great builder, and there is much evidence of this still to be seen in Rome – the Mausoleum of Hadrian (Castel Sant'Angelo), the Pantheon and Hadrian's villa at nearby Tivoli.

Hadrian
(76–138)

The desperate rising of the Jews under Bar Kochba in Judaea (132–135) took place during Hadrian's reign.

A member of the Lombard nobility who became Pope at the age of 37, Innocent III was a man of commanding personality. Imperious and a born ruler, he nevertheless sought conciliation. There were many sides to his nature; he could be haughty and commanding or mild and sympathetic, winning and humorous or majestic and unapproachable. He saw the kingdoms and peoples of the world as fit subjects for his rule. Innocent was a shrewd politician, but not wise enough to leave politics alone on occasion, and too much of a politician to be always wise. He was the most fully rounded man to occupy the Papal throne, and during his reign the Papacy was seen in its most powerful form.

Pope Innocent III
(c. 1160/1–1216)

Two Popes are generally granted the style of "the Great", Leo I and Gregory I. Leo (Pope 440–461), a Tuscan, was determined to assert his rule and extend the powers of the Papacy and use them to the full. He was the first Pope to realise clearly the potentialities of his office, and the pride of the aristocrat whose secular power had been destroyed by the fall of the Western Empire was now projected into the spiritual field. The primacy of the Church in Rome was established and consolidated through Leo's skill in formulating its doctrine and its bold conception of the role of the Pope; it was reflected in the practical administration of the Church and given expression in the orthodox creed. Leo's courage was demonstrated during the troubled period of the great migrations. Raphael did him honour in the Stanze in the Vatican, Leo XII in a marble relief in St Peter's (far end of the left-hand aisle).

Pope Leo I, the Great
(d. 461)

Marcus Aurelius Antoninus was Emperor from 161 to 180. Born in 121 he attracted the interest of Hadrian at an early age and by his desire was adopted by Hadrian's successor Antoninus Pius and initiated into the business of government. Marcus Aurelius was faced throughout his reign with ever increasing external dangers – the Chatti in Germany, the Caledonians in Britain – while in Syria the Parthians shook off the Roman yoke. The security of the Empire was threatened by risings of the Quadi, the Marcomanni, the Jazyges, a people of herdsmen in the Nile delta, and the Moors in Spain. Marcus Aurelius died in Vindobona (Vienna) in 180. In spite of his numerous wars he is thought of as the philosopher on the Roman Imperial throne.

Marcus Aurelius
(121–180)

Michelangelo Buonarotti, a Renaissance genius who was sculptor, painter, architect and poet, and perhaps the greatest artist of all time, was born in Caprese (Casentino, Tuscany) and spent his youth and period of apprenticeship in Florence, to which he constantly returned after a year spent working in Bologna (1494–5) and several long stays in Rome. Florence was then ruled by the Medici, those great patrons of the arts, for whom Michelangelo produced numerous works.

Michelangelo
(1475–1564)

Prominent Figures in Roman History

Marcus Aurelius

Michelangelo

Raffael

His first stay in Rome, during which he created the "Pietà" in St Peter's, began in 1496. In 1505 Pope Julius II della Rovere summoned him back to the Vatican and invited him to design his tomb. (This commission was a burden to Michelangelo for most of his life; even after the Pope's death there were still disputes with his heirs.) Between 1508 and 1512 Michelangelo laboured on the frescoes of the Creation on the ceiling of the Sistine Chapel; in 1513–14 he carved two figures of slaves (now in the Louvre) for Julius' monument, and thereafter until 1516 worked on his famous figure of Moses, now in San Pietro in Vincoli in Rome. The completion of the Pope's tomb continued to be delayed, with repeated alterations in the design.

In Florence (1520–34) Michelangelo was responsible for the building of the Medici chapel of San Lorenzo and the sculpture for the Medici tombs.

Between 1536 and 1541 he created the famous fresco of the Last Judgment on the altar wall of the Sistine Chapel, perhaps the most magnificent painting in the world. In 1545 Julius II's tomb was finally set up in San Pietro in Vincoli. Michelangelo now increasingly occupied himself with architecture, working on the Palazzo Farnese, the Piazza del Campidoglio and St Peter's, whose gigantic dome is his greatest architectural achievement.

After a richly creative life, during which he had known difficulties but could look back on tremendous achievements, Michelangelo died in Rome in 1564. His tomb is in the Church of Santa Croce in Florence.

Alberto Moravia (1907–90)

Alberto Moravia was born A. Pincherle in Rome, the son of Moravian immigrants. He is considered one of the leading exponents of psychological realism in Italy. He was president of the International PEN Club from 1959 to 1962. The author deals mainly with the inter-relationship between the sexes and family psychology. As a keen, though ironic and distanced observer, he relates episodes from the lives of the middle classes and from the prostitute's environment. Moravia mercilessly criticises the middle classes and their moral indifference; alienation and boredom are constant themes in all his works. As well as many novels and short stories, Alberto Moravia has written plays, essays and travel guides.

Nero (A.D. 37–68)

Claudius Drusus Germanicus Nero, who liked to see himself as a poet, musician and painter rather than as a ruler required to take political decisions, was Emperor from A.D. 58 to 68. Coming to power as a mere youth, he was only 31 when he died. In his early years of rule he behaved with moderation, but later instituted a reign of terror, in the course of which he murdered both his mother (A.D. 59) and his wife

Octavia (A.D. 62). He was believed to have been responsible for the burning of Rome in 64, though he himself attributed the blame to the Christians, whom he accordingly persecuted. In the year 68 there was unrest in many provinces of the Empire, and Nero, outlawed by the Senate, committed suicide.

The name of the Colosseum comes from the colossal statue of Nero which stood there. His "Golden House", a gigantic palace on the Mons Oppidus, provided a stimulus for Renaissance painters and sculptors.

This Pope of the Baroque period can fairly be mentioned in the same breath as the great figures of antiquity; indeed he himself invited the comparison by setting up a statue of himself on the façade of St Peter's, with the inscription "Paulus Burghesius Romanus" and a crowned eagle in his coat of arms. During his reign he incurred the charge of nepotism, though in other respects his life style was modest.

Pope Paul V
(1552–1621)

It was long since the world had revolved round Rome (indeed it was now known to revolve round the sun; Galileo's first trial was held in Paul's reign), and the States of the Church were now only of marginal importance in European affairs. Although this was apparent to others, Paul – a cultivated but stubbornly contentious lawyer – did not fully appreciate it and overestimated his influence on the great powers. All the efforts of his diplomats could not prevent the outbreak of the Thirty Years' War, in which the whole of Europe was soon embroiled.

Luigi Pirandello, born in Sicily, studied philology in Palermo, Rome and Bonn. In 1925 he founded the "Teatro d'Arte" and received the Nobel Prize for Literature in 1934.

Luigi Pirandello
(1867–1936)

The author, one of the most important dramatists and novelists of this century, first wrote realistic novels and stories set in his native Sicily. He turned to stage plays when he was over 50 years old and liberated the Italian theatre from its mainly provincial traditions. Pirandello's principal theme is the constant reversal of appearance and reality; man can never be fixed as a natural or social being and is never sure of his own reality. Psychologically Pirandello anticipates existentialist thought which emerged after the Second World War, particularly in French literature. His plays, such as "The Fool's Cap" (1917) and "Henry IV" (1922) are more like sketches than complete stage plays. In "Six Characters in Search of an Author" (1921) Pirandello created an effective vehicle to portray the interaction of appearance and reality, when six people enter a play rehearsal, looking for an author to write the drama of their own lives.

Raphael – Raffaello Santi or Sanzio – was born in 1483 in Urbino (Marche region) and died in Rome in 1520. Like Michelangelo he was a painter, sculptor and architect, but it is mainly his paintings that have earned him his world renown. He began his career as assistant to his father, Giovanni Santi, who was also a painter, and thereafter he became a pupil of Perugino. In 1504 he went to Florence and in 1508 to Rome, where seven years later, at the age of 32, he was put in charge of the building of St Peter's and made conservator of ancient monuments. The young painter gained the favour of Roman society and was given many commissions, while he appealed to ordinary people with the fervent piety of his Madonnas, works of incomparable beauty. His greatest achievement is to be seen in the Stanze di Raffaello in the Vatican – the magnificent frescoes which represent the high point of Renaissance painting.

Raphael
(1483–1520)

Whether Romulus and Remus ever existed may be questioned, but at any rate legend ascribes the foundation of Rome to Romulus, who is said to have established the first settlement on the Palatine, to have laid down military and civil regulations for the new town and to have

Romulus and
Remus

formed the Romans on the Palatine and the Sabines on the Quirinal into a single community. His origins were also shrouded in legend. Romulus and Remus were said to have been the twin sons of the god Mars and Rhea Silvia, daughter of King Numitor of Alba Longa. Amulius, Numidor's brother, had driven him from the throne and made Rhea Silvia a vestal virgin (and accordingly subject to a vow of chastity), thus securing undisputed power for himself. He caused the twins, Romulus and Remus to be exposed soon after their birth, but they were suckled by a she-wolf (which became the heraldic animal of Rome) and later found by a shepherd named Faustulus. They then killed their uncle, founded Rome and carried out the rape of the Sabine women to provide wives for the men of Rome. During the battle with the Sabines Romulus killed his brother Remus.

The death of Romulus was also the subject of numerous legends. he was said to have been murdered, to have disappeared into the earth, together with his horse, on the site of the Forum and to have ascended to join the gods. However this may be, he was worshipped in Rome as a god.

Trajan
(A.D. 53–117)

Trajan (Marcus Ulpius Traianus) was the first native of Spain to become Emperor. Having been adopted by the Emperor Nerva by virtue of his outstanding military and political capacity, he came to the imperial throne in 98 and reigned until 117.

During Trajan's reign the Roman Empire reached its greatest extent. In the two Dacian wars he subdued Dacia, a country rich in gold (cf. the scenes on Trajan's Column), and in the Parthian war he advanced into Mesopotamia and Assyria. In 117, however, the oppressed Parthians and Jews rose against Roman rule. Trajan's frequent campaigns earned him the name of the "soldier Emperor". He died in the town of Selinus in Asia Minor on his way back from the Persian Gulf.

He left his monument in the form of the Forum of Trajan, with the famous column, originally crowned by a statue of the Emperor.

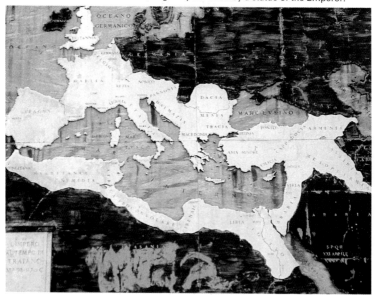

The Roman Empire reaches its greatest extent under Trajan

History of Rome

Many explanations have been advanced as to how and why the cradle of European civilization should have developed out of Etruscan, Latin and Sabine hill settlements at the narrowest place along the lower valley of the Tiber. For Rome, the "eternal city", has a unique role not just in European but in world history – the "urbs" of the powerful Imperium Romanum, the "head of the world", the centre of Western Christianity and the Catholic Church. And yet it is one of the secrets of history exactly how the great empires of political power and civilization come into being, and so Rome's meteoric rise to glory in the final analysis must remain one of the mysteries of the past.

Caput Mundi – Head of the World

From its earliest origins to its position as dominant Mediterranean power

The year 753 B.C. (1 ab urbe condita) was used by the Romans as the basis for their calendar, thereby confirming the mythological date of the founding of their urbs quadrata by the demigods Romulus and Remus, the legend of whom was passed down by the 1st c. historian Livius. According to him everything began with King Numitor, the ruler of the old Latin capital of Alba Longa, the legendary settlement which was the precursor of Rome itself. The daughter of King Numitor, Rhea Silva, who was condemned to remain unmarried and childless, was given the twin princes Romulus and Remus by the god of war, Mars. Amulius, the wicked uncle of Rhea Silvia, who had usurped the crown, thereupon threw his niece into prison and turned the twin boys out into the marshy area at the foot of the Palatine. There they were suckled by a she-wolf (Lupa Capitolina) and later found by a shepherd. As young heroes they killed the tyrant Amulius and on 21 April 753 B.C. founded Rome – Romulus on the Palatine and Remus on the Aventine. In a subsequent dispute over the setting of the town boundaries Remus was killed by his brother. The legend says that Romulus was the first King of 'Roma' – until the gods summoned him to heaven where he was revered as the god Quirinus.

Origins shrouded in legend

Historical sources verify that the early history of Roman begins in the 10th c. B.C. with the founding of a settlement on the Palatine. By the 9th c. B.C. all seven of Rome's hills – the Palatine, Aventine, Capitol, Caelian, Quirinal, Esquiline, and Viminal – were thinly settled by Latino-Sabine tribes of farmers and shepherds. The area of their settlement was situated exactly between the territories of two rival civilizations. From the 8th c. B.C., to the north of Rome extended the kingdom of the emergent Etruscans. At the same time the colonizing ambitions of ancient Greece were being constantly reinforced in the south of Italy (Magna Graecia). While the Greeks sought to establish peaceful trading relations with the newly-established Rome, the expansionist ambitions of the Etruscans led them to use a surprise attack to subjugate the local population. It was probably the Tarquin branch of the Etruscans who in 616 B.C. captured the not insignificant settlement of Rome, urbanized it and made it the location of one of their royal residences. The impact of the already highly civilized Etruscans on the simple farmers and shepherds who had settled at the ford on the Tiber must have been tremendous. The cultural achievements and civilized life-style of the Etruscans left their mark on the Romans in many different ways. Many things which we think of as typically Roman, such as irrigation techniques, temple building, gladiatorial contests and the toga, were in fact part of Etruscan culture.

Early history and Etruscan period

Under the Etruscan kings Rome was systematically developed during the 6th c. B.C. into a fully-fledged town following the model of the great Etruscan towns such as Arezzo and Volterra. The marshy areas at the foot of the town's hills were extensively drained (Cloaca Maxima) and with the Forum Romanum Rome was given its first central public square with its first large buildings. It is likely that Etruscan Rome was divided into three districts (tribus), which, while obliged to pay tributes to the king, were granted a considerable degree of independence in order that a thriving public life would develop. The power of the king was upheld by privileged Etruscan noble families who quickly mixed with the influential indigenous Latin families.

The military strength of Rome enabled the town to enlarge the area of its influence and before long the territory over which it ruled extended over the greater part of present-day Latium (Lazio). As the outermost boundaries of the loosely knit Etruscan kingdom started to be violated, Rome took advantage of a favourable moment, rebelled and put an end to Etruscan external rule. Tarquinius Superbus, the last of the Etruscan kings of Rome, was driven out in 509 B.C..

The first republic
5th and 4th c. B.C.

In shaking off Etruscan domination Rome also got rid of the kingdom which had been imposed on it and turned itself into a republic (res publica) with senate and consuls. The new form of government was exclusively based on the power of the patrician nobility, however, and had hardly any similarities with a republic as we know it today. It was not long, though, before the common people, the plebeians, demanded a voice in the political process, but the patricians yielded to the will of the people (populus) only after tough discussions and the threat of secession from the city state (secessio). A sense of communal identity started to grow among the Romans, the new rights of the plebeians were codified and in 450 B.C. recorded in the Twelve Tables, set out for everyone to see in the Forum Romanum. At the end of the class wars a new leading class established itself, the nobility, as it was called, a patrician-plebeian city class which occupied all political offices and controlled the hierarchically organized executive state. Consuls, praetors, quaestors, censors and aediles ruled the aspiring city state and organized every facet of public life. With the temple to Saturn, the Concordia temple, the Servian Walls and the municipal aqueduct Rome gained its first monumental buildings. At this time the city's wealth was derived predominantly from agriculture, as trade and commerce still played a subordinate role.

In parallel with this internal consolidation and cultural development Rome was continually enlarging its territory and strengthening its external political position. The Etruscans were still the ruling force in the central area of northern Italy, which led Rome to adopt a tactical policy of links with the peoples in the areas surrounding the Etruscans. At the beginning of the 4th c. B.C. Rome violated the borders with Etruria for the first time and conquered Veii (396 B.C.) and the Etruscan towns of Nepi and Sutri. However the sudden invasion of the Celtic Gauls (387 B.C.) put an abrupt halt to Rome's expansionist ambitions. Only the Capitol hill was saved from the ravages wrought by the Gauls and the work of rebuilding and fortification lasted for decades. It was not until the Appian Way (Via Appia, 312 B.C.) was built, under the censor Claudius Caecus, that Rome was able to make a decisive resumption to its expansion both to the north and south. After the overthrow of the neighbouring Etruscans, the Samnites and the Senones, only the Greek Tarentines offered any resistance. But in the end even Pyrrhus, the King of Epirus, who was hastily called on to offer aid to the besieged Tarentines, proved powerless against the military might of the Romans, who adopted the powerful infantry formation of the phalanx on the battlefield. In 272 B.C., with the fall of Tarentum, Rome disposed of the last resistance to its advance across southern Italy. Now the hitherto fledgling republic felt strong enough to take up the struggle for domination of the whole of the Mediterranean.

The expansion of the Empire
3rd and 4th c. B.C.

In the early years of the 3rd c. B.C. Rome initiated its tenacious policy of overseas conquest with the support of its allies in the rest of Italy. Its expansion into Gaul and Spain soon led to conflict with the powerful

Carthaginians in North Africa. The first two Punic Wars (264–241 and 214–201 B.C.) brought Rome close to downfall. It took the Third Punic War (149–146 B.C.) to result in the merciless sacking of Carthage and the colonization of the Roman province of Africa. Yet of far greater significance was the conquest of the decaying Hellenic empire in the eastern Mediterranean. The victorious Illyrian Wars (229–219 B.C.) brought Rome in touch with the material and cultural riches of Greek civilization. The expansion eastwards had an enormous effect on the development of Rome and led to a complete hellenization of the Roman city state which had hitherto still remained in essentials wedded to its agrarian heritage. The abundance of war booty kindled a vigorous expansion of economic activity. Rome's harbour, Ostia, and the road network were constructed, markets were established and overseas trade flourished. The conquest of the east brought Rome not only great wealth and rudimentary capitalist structures but also fundamentally changed the Romans' way of life. Art, religion and literature, indeed public life as a whole, now became heavily influenced by Greek culture. In 166 B.C. Rome celebrated its first theatrical performance with the play "Andria" by Terence. In spite of these far-reaching changes within society, the old aristocratic-plebeian nobility succeeding in holding on to their political power base within the Senate.

However the structural problems created by the over-expansion of the empire were soon to bring massive internal tensions in their train. The *populares*, or party of the people, demanded reforms but ran into resistance from the Senate, whereupon the people's tribunate tried to implement these reforms (land reform etc.) without higher authority. The Senate responded by declaring a state of emergency. Riots and unrest inflamed the revolutionary atmosphere and the consequence was a series of civil wars – under the Gracchus brothers (133–121 B.C.) and under Marius and Sulla (88–82 B.C.) – and an uprising of slaves under Spartacus (73–71 B.C.) which ended with the crucifixion of more than 6000 people along the Appian Way. The army emerged out of the unrest as the strongest political force. Under the conservative general Sulla a brutal dictatorship was established, which was sanctioned by the Senate.

Civil wars
100 B.C.

Sulla's death was followed by the arrival in 70 B.C. of three characters on the political stage, Gnaeus Pompeius, Gaius Julius Caesar and Marcus Licinius Crassus, who blocked all attempts by the Senate to reassert its powers and at the same time strengthened the capital's grip over the provinces.

First triumvirate
60 B.C.

After the dissolution of the first Roman triumvirate, Caesar stepped into the role of absolute dictator. This brilliant commander and *pontifex maximus* took just a few years to romanize virtually the whole of the Mediterranean area, flaunted hitherto unknown heights of splendour and demanded total submission from all around him. His rule was totally autocratic, the Senate and people's tribunate retaining only the external trappings of power. In Rome new temples and public buildings were built, including the Pompeius theatre, the first theatre to be built of stone, while the Forum Romanum was restored on a lavish scale. Yet as Caesar heavy-handedly sought the elusive aura of a monarch, senatorial opposition rose up one last time. On the Ides of March (the 15th) in 44 B.C. the charismatic dictator was murdered by Brutus in the name of republican ideals.

Gaius Julius Caesar

A year after Caesar's murder Gaius Octavian, Marcus Antonius and the lesser known Lepidus together formed the second triumvirate. They divided the empire between them and effectively annulled the republican constitution. However, Octavian, the great-nephew and testimentary heir of Caesar, acted decisively to break the grip on power of this unstable triumvirate and in so doing sounded the beginning of the great period of the Roman Empire.

Second triumvirate
43 B.C.

Roman Empire

Augustan age
(27 B.C.–A.D.14)

On 23 January 27 B.C. Octavian was confirmed as *princeps* by the Senate and, with the honorary appellation of Augustus Caesar, assumed control of the Roman Empire. As 'first citizen' of Rome he claimed the full powers of dictatorship, retaining, however, the old republican institutions. Augustus's reign heralded a period of peace and of economic and cultural prosperity. The army was drastically slimmed down and massive building projects were to alter the Roman cityscape. The 41 years of his reign were glorified as a golden age and era of peace. The Pantheon was erected, the Forum Augustus built, arts and sciences were promoted and flourished. The population of Rome passed the million mark for the first time. A public welfare system guaranteed the provision of food for all the citizens. The all-powerful Augustus, who refused to tolerate any kind of open religious worship, left behind him a flourishing 'marble' city which had advanced to be politically, culturally and economically the head of the European world – *caput mundi*. The influence of the Augustan period of empire, or principate, lasted until well into late antiquity.

The Julian-
Claudian
Emperors and
the Flavian
dynasty
(14–96)

The Roman Senate entrusted the principate to Augustus's adopted stepson Tiberius (14–37), from the Claudian family, for the duration of his life. Although Tiberius continued the policies of Augustus, the seeds of the Roman Empire's proverbial decadence and corruption were sown during his reign. He pursued relentlessly the slightest imagined personal attack and had large numbers of his republican opponents executed. His successors (Caligula, Claudius, Nero, Titus and Domitian) were, like him, shameless squanderers and power-drunk autocrats. Ill-defined arrangements for the succession led to continual intrigues and incest was the order of the day. Caligula even had himself worshipped as a god. Yet, in spite of the decadence and political ineptitude, the Roman metropolis grew and flourished. Building programmes were pursued on a vast scale. Nero even ordered the destruction by fire of the city's slums in order to be able use the resulting open spaces for magnificent new buildings, including his Domus Aurea ('Golden House'). The zenith of building activity in the 1st c. A.D. was reached, though, with the completion of the Colosseum. This monumental arena symbolizes the life-style and aspirations of the average Roman citizen. But the bloodthirsty arena spectacles and the free rations of bread – *panem et circenses* – only served as a smoke-screen to hide the real underlying social tensions which existed in the capital of the Empire.

Adoptive
emperors
(96–193)

Under the five so-called 'adoptive emperors' (Nerva, Trajan, Hadrian, Antonius and Marcus Aurelius) Rome remained a place of relative peace and prosperity. The 2nd c. was, seen as a whole, a period of 'humanitarian and enlightened' imperialism in which the rulers wielded power predominantly with the people's goodwill and in harmony with the Senate. Under the emperor Trajan, the most charismatic personality since Augustus, the empire reached its greatest extent: from Scotland to Mesopotamia, from the Danube to Morocco – the relief band on the Trajan column depicts the progress of this policy of conquest.

Soldier emperors
(3rd c.)

Increasing unrest on the borders of the empire gave an early warning of a period of population upheaval and migration. Moreover the emperors were becoming less and less successful in holding their vast army in check. With Septimus Severus (193–211) began the period of the so-called 'soldier emperors'. Suddenly the internal politics of the empire started to be determined by the army and military commanders were arbitrarily appointed emperor. Scarcely any of them reigned for longer than two years, hardly any of them died a natural death, many of them never setting foot in Rome during their brief reigns. The century when all these soldier emperors were in power (over 30 between 235 and 284) was also a period of systematic persecution of Christians. The Bishop of Rome for the first time claimed the highest authority for himself. The need to fortify Rome with the powerful Aurelian Wall (270–282) was a clear sign of the external and internal dangers which the empire faced. Only the reform of the empire under Diocletian (284–305) brought a period of relaxation and the division of the empire into a western and eastern half granted ancient Rome its last golden age. In the 3rd c. the construction of the monumental profane and military architecture which had symbolized the empire came to a halt and the Romans confined themselves to conserving what had already been created.

Late Antiquity

Under Emperor Constantine I (306–337) Rome's internal power structure yielded to pressure and began to undergo decisive changes. The edict of tolerance enacted by Emperior Galerius in 311, which gave religions parity of treatment, put an end to the persecution of Christians and enabled Christians to erect public places of worship. The victory of Constantine in 312 over the official joint emperor Maxentius (who wanted to establish the cult of Hercules as a state religion) at the Pons Milvius, one of the Roman bridges crossing the Tiber, opened the way for Christianity to become the dominant religion. For strategic reasons Constantine moved the capital of the Roman empire to Byzantium and gave it the name Constantinople (present-day Istanbul). Rome, however, continued to dominate the 'spiritual empire'. The large buildings which were erected during the new Christian era were places of worship; from modest beginnings developed sacred buildings of formal beauty, as the great basilicas of the 4th and 5th c. testify. As successor to St Peter, the Bishop of Rome assumed a position of pre-eminence in the Western Roman Empire or Occident. However the western empire was becoming increasingly troubled along its borders with Germany and the turmoil caused by population movements destroyed this first bloom of Christian civilization. Rome was captured and sacked in 410 by the Western Goths under Alaric and in 455 by the Vandals under Gaiseric (although without the notoriously barbaric destructiveness which is associated with the word 'vandal'). With the overthrow of the last emperor Romulus Augustulus in 476 at the hands of Odoacer the Western Roman Empire officially came to an end. Theoderic, Odoacer's successor, established a period of Gothic rule in Italy which lasted until about 535. Rome enjoyed an era of peace and prosperity with extensive restoration work to the fabric of the city.

From Constantine to Theoderic (4th–6th c,)

Christianity becomes a state religion

From 535 the Eastern Roman Empire set about the task of crushing the Gothic kingdom. One of the key battle areas was Christian Rome which eventually came under Byzantine rule. Large parts of the city were destroyed or severely damaged in the Gothic Wars (535–553). The population dropped to less than 50,000. The surrounding farmland was devastated and most of the patrician families were systematically exterminated. When the leader of the Eastern Goths, Totila, reduced the city to rubble in 546, Rome is said to have gone for 40 days without any form of human life. With the invasion of the Langobards in 568 Rome faced a new threat. In spite of the Germano-Byzantine power struggle for the legacy of Rome, which continued for several centuries, it was in fact Christianity which enabled Rome to regain the world role which it had once possessed.

The fall of Rome

Middle Ages

Evolution into a Church State (8th–13th c.)

When Pope Stephen II called on Pippin, the King of the Franks, to his aid against the Langobards, Rome's fortunes began to improve. Pope Stephen went specially to Paris and gave Pippin the honorary title of 'patricius' of Rome. Two years later the Frankish king defeated the Langobards and gave the Pope the liberated regions of Emilia-Romagna and Latium. This gift from King Pippin became the kernel of a sovereign state ruled over by the papacy. Pippin himself became the first 'King by the mercy of God'. Furthermore the newly created church state secured its gift by an alliance with the German kings. Charlemagne extended the territory of the church by donating it Tuscany and northern Campania. With the crowning of Charles as Emperor on Christmas Day 800 in St Peter's Church by Pope Leo III, the imperial sovereignty over Rome alongside that of the papacy was strengthened. Around 1000 new churches were built in Rome, intended to reinforce the status and importance of the Popes. The investiture dispute stirred up by the reformist Pope Gregory VII between the Church and the kingdom of Germany culminated in 1077 in the legendary walk to Canossa, where the excommunicated Emperor Henry IV subjugated Pope Gregory VII. In 1084 Rome had to endure merciless plundering at the hands of the Normans and this devastation marked the final eclipse of the ancient city. The incensed citizens of Rome expelled Pope Gregory. A century later Innocence III (1198–1216), probably the most powerful of the Popes, gained the upper hand over the Holy Roman Empire of the German Nation. However, from the time of the resistance of Arnold of Brescia (1144–1155) to the power of the papacy, Rome remained a bone of contention between pope, nobility and bourgeoisie and as a result never achieved the importance of the other emergent Italian city republics in the late Middle Ages.

Exodus of the Popes to Avignon (1309–1377)

The Eternal City faced a new threat when the Popes were forced by the French kings to go into exile to Avignon in France. This 'Babylonian captivity' caused a hiatus in the Church's temporal power and a drying-up of the Popes' incomes. Bitter struggles broke out in Rome itself between various factions and culminated in 1347 in the short-lived people's rule under the last 'people's tribune', Cola di Rienzo. The population of the city fell to just 20,000 and many churches, palaces, roads and squares were left deserted. The return of Pope Gregory XI to Rome took place at the initiative of a woman: St Catherine of Siena. As, however, a pope continued to reside in Avignon, a situation developed which came to be known as the Great Western Schism, in which there could at times be as many as three popes all in competition with one another. In 1417 the schism was ended and the Vatican finally became the only papal residence.

Renaissance and Baroque

15th c.

In the 15th c. there were many intelligent and politically adroit popes and noble families who, inspired by humanism and the burgeoning Renaissance, knew how to capitalize on Rome's inheritance and gradually give back to the city its world importance. The rebuilding of the city at first however proceeded only in fits and starts. In 1455 the first great renaissance palace, the Palazzo Venezia, was built. Slowly but surely the Eternal City became a worthy setting for the might and splendour of the papacy and one of the world's most beautiful cities came into being, a magic garden of churches, squares, fountains and avenues, which embodied all the ideals of the Renaissance to overwhelming effect. The sheer exuberance of the architecture recalled the epoch of the earlier emperors. The Popes were active and enthusiastic in fostering the arts and commissioned the most gifted artists and craftsmen of the Renaissance to work for them. The Popes all wanted to leave something behind with which their name was directly connected and which also reinforced the authority of the Church. In 1506 work was begun on St Peter's Church, one of the most magnificent buildings of all.

While the papal patrons were pursuing their ambitious self-interests by assisting in the flowering of Renaissance art in Rome, they left no stone unturned in their efforts to safeguard their hold on power in political and military terms. When Clement VII sought, however, to counteract imperial supremacy in Italy through a pact with the French, Rome was seized by the German and Spanish troops of Charles V. The 'sacco di Roma', as it came to be called, put a sudden halt to the new construction activity and resulted moreover in wild plundering. The plague broke out in the devastated city, which was also gripped by famine. The population plummeted to 50,000 and the church was compelled to make reparations on a horrendous scale. The terror and humiliation left behind by Charles V created an almost apocalyptic atmosphere in Rome. Never again would the Popes be in a position to interfere openly in world politics.

Sacco di Roma (1527–1528)

After the shock of the *sacco di Roma* and the ensuing political neutrality imposed on the Papal States, the nobility in Rome occupied the most important offices in church government. Although now politically subject to the Spanish, the Popes were able to assert themselves in the Counter-reformation struggle and to keep the essentials of the traditional Roman Catholic faith separate from the reformatory tendencies. In the late 16th and 17th c. the long-established noble families provided the prelates, cardinals and popes and endowed Rome

Popes and noble families in the 16th–18th c.

Life on the Piazza Navona in the 18th century (etching by Giovanni Battista Piranesi, 1756/1762)

with magnificent palaces and churches in the late Renaissance and Baroque styles of architecture. Centre-stage were such famous Roman names as Colonna, Orsini, Farnese, Borghese and Chigi. The city's building programme was now on a scale hitherto unknown. Sixtus V sought to publicise himself as the reviver of Rome's past glories and Urban VIII, assisted by the architects Bernini and Borromini, made good his claim to be the Pope of the Baroque. Rome glowed in its new-found splendour. In many instances the ruins of antiquity were used as building materials. In the second half of the 17th c. the golden age of the papacy slowly drew to a close, the church's financial means dried up and the building of St Peter's Square was the last major city building project. During the 18th c. Rome's political role was more or less negligible.

19th century

Napoleon

The French Revolution and the whirlwind which accompanied Napoleon's dismantling of the European political order, even affected the relatively peaceful, uneventful and apolitical world which Rome had become. In 1798 Rome was made capital of a Roman Republic based on the French model, whilst between 1809 and 1811 it became the second capital of the French empire and seat of the 'King of Rome', Napoleon's only son. The Congress of Vienna in 1815 restored the Papal States and the Pope returned to Rome as sovereign.

Risorgimento

In the European Year of Revolution of 1848 a wave of unrest swept down through the Italian peninsula. Il Risorgimento, as the liberation movement which sought the unification of Italy was known, came into being. Giuseppe Mazzini and Giuseppe Garibaldi were the central figures of the Risorgimento movement. On 9 February 1849 a Republican triumvirate assumed power in Rome which was joined by Mazzini. Pope Pius IX fled and asked the French to intervene. Garibaldi meanwhile was instrumental in organizing the defence of Rome. In 1950, however, the Pope returned to Rome with the help of French troops and had over 20,000 supporters of the Risorgimento movement driven out of the city.

Capital of
Italy

The national Risorgimento movement proclaimed the kingdom of Italy in 1860 under the leadership of the Piedmontese king Victor Emmanuel II. However the Papal States successfully refused to join the new nation state until 1870. Only when the French protection forces were removed in order to fight in the Franco-German War did Pius IX concede to the inevitable and hand the city over to the king and withdraw to the Vatican. In 1871 Rome became capital of the unified kingdom of Italy and the Quirinal became the royal residence. The city's reconstruction programme was soon resumed as the new country desired to have a government worthy of it. Rome became a city of civil servants and government offices. The requisite administrative buildings were erected all over the city and blended in with the architectural styles of past epochs. In spite of the improved infrastructure large sections of the population continued to suffer destitution. The Vatican was marginalized and the Pope felt himself to be a prisoner.

20th century

Mussolini
1922

After the march on Rome Benito Mussolini assumed power in Italy in 1922. Under the *duce* building activity in Rome was revived and the city expanded to become the most populous in the Mediterranean, although with enormous housing and supply problems.

With the Lateran Treaties of 1929 Mussolini succeeded in establishing peace between the Papacy and the Italian government. The popes were granted the tiny Vatican state along with a number of extraterritorial enclaves which together constituted a sovereign territory. As compensation for its territorial losses the Vatican was given the then enormous sum of 2,000 million lire. With this concordat the Church became an important ally of fascism in the struggle against liberal and socialist movements.

Lateran Treaties 1929

In 1940 Italy entered the war on the German side. In 1943 the Italians arose against the dictator Mussolini. In July 1943 Mussolini was arrested, in September of that year Italy capitulated, Rome was occupied by German troops and experienced the Gestapo terror. When the allied forces moved to take Rome, the German army withdrew on June 4 and declared Rome an "open city".

Second World War

Roma Città aperta

On 2 June 1946 after a referendum Italy was declared a republic and Victor Emanuel III abdicated. In the first national elections the Christian Democrats emerged as victors, followed by the socialists and communists. Rome became the capital of the republic of Italy. In line with the economic recovery the city expanded and new suburbs (borgate) were built on the edges of the city. Unfortunately this sensibly conceived municipal policy had no overall plan for the effective use of available land and thus came to grief with hideous overdevelopment of the surrounding area and over 600,000 illegally erected dwellings.
   The city's population rose to an estimated 3 million.

Italian Republic

In stark contrast to Rome's local politicians Pope John XXIII was very popular among the poor. He smoothed the way for long overdue church reforms which were negotiated from 1962–1965 at the Second Vatican Council.

Second Vatican Council 1962–1965

After massive political protests and demonstrations in the early 1970s the Romans elected a communist administration for the first time in 1976. Despite its optimistic plans it came to grief when confronted with the chaotic reality of the city and its way of life.

1976

John Paul II was the first foreigner for 453 years to be chosen to be Pope. In the same year the abduction and murder of the popular Christian Democrat prime minister, Aldo Moro, took place in Rome.

1978

A new concordat was passed to regulate relations between church and state – the Roman Catholic faith ceased to be the state religion of Italy.

1984

As a result of the football World Cup (Mondiale 1990) being held in Italy many buildings in Rome were restored and new renovation and building projects were carried through.

1990

At the beginning of December the Romans elected the Green politician Francesco Rutelli to be the new Mayor of Rome.

1993

In June the largest mosque in western Europe was opened on the Monte Antenne.

1995

As the Catholic Church is celebrating the year 2000 as a 'holy year', it is intended that Rome should appear to the world in fresh splendour. Many monuments are being restored, museums modernised and works of art being made more easily accessible. It is hoped to have improved public transport services in time for the millennium.

1996–2000

Quotations

Ammianus
Marcellinus
(b. about A.D. 330)

(The Emperor Constantine visits Rome in the 4th c.)
"As the Emperor reviewed the vast city and its environs, spreading along the slopes, in the valleys and between the summits of the Seven Hills, he declared that the spectacle which first met his eyes surpassed everything he had yet beheld. Now his gaze rested on the Temple of Tarpeian Jupiter, now on baths so magnificent as to resemble entire provinces, now on the massive pile of the amphitheatre, massively compact, or Tivoli stone, the summit of which seems scarcely accessible to the human eye; now on the Pantheon, rising like a fairy dome, and its sublime columns, with their gently inclined staircases, adorned with statues of departed emperors; not to enumerate the Temple of the City, the Forum of Peace, the Theatre of Pompey, the Odeum, the Stadium and all the other architectural wonders of eternal Rome. When, however, he came to the Forum of Trajan, a structure unequalled by any other of its kind throughout the world, so exquisite, indeed, that the gods themselves would find it hard to refuse their admiration, he stood as if in a trance, surveying with a dazed air the stupendous fabric which neither words can picture nor mortal ever again attempt to rear."

François-René de
Chateaubriand
(1768–1848)

"Whoever has nothing else left in life should come to live in Rome; there he will find a land which will nourish his reflections, walks which will always tell him something new. The stone which crumbles under his feet will speak to him, and even the dust which the wind raises under his footsteps will seem to bear with it something of human grandeur."

Charles Dickens
(1812–1870)

"We entered on the Campagna Romana; an undulating flat . . . where few people can live; and where for miles and miles there is nothing to relieve the terrible monotony and gloom . . . We had to traverse thirty miles of this Campagna, and for two-and-twenty we went on and on, seeing nothing but now and then a lonely house, or a villainous-looking shepherd . . . tending his sheep. At the end of that distance, we stopped to refresh the horses, and to get some lunch, in a common malaria-shaken despondent little public-house . . . When we were fairly going off again, we began, in a perfect fever, to strain our eyes for Rome; and when, after another mile or two, the Eternal City appeared, at length, in the distance, it looked like – I am half afraid to write the word – like LONDON!!! There it lay, under a thick cloud, with innumerable towers, and steeples, and roofs of houses, rising up into the sky, and high above them all, one Dome. I swear, that keenly as I felt the seeming absurdity of the comparison, it was so like London, at that distance, that if you could have shown it me in a glass, I should have taken it for nothing else."

Edward Gibbon
(1737–94)

"It was at Rome on the 15th of October, 1764, as I sat musing amidst the ruins of the Capitol, while the barefooted friars were singing vespers in the Temple of Jupiter, that the idea of writing the decline and fall of the city first started to my mind."

Johann Wolfgang
von Goethe
(1749–1832)

"I have now been here for seven days, and am gradually getting some general idea of the city. We walk about Rome most diligently, and I familiarise myself with the layout of the ancient and the modern city, look at the ruins and the buildings, and visit this villa or that. I take the principal sights very slowly, look at them attentively, go away and come back again; for only in Rome can one prepare oneself for Rome.

I must confess, however, that it is a bitter and sorry business disentangling the old Rome from the new; but one has to do it, and must hope that one's efforts will be rewarded. One encounters traces of inconceivable magnificence and inconceivable destruction: what the barbarians left standing the builders of modern Rome have devastated."

"Rome will give you so many pretty girls that you will say,'This city has everything that the world can offer.' As many fields of corn as has Gargara, as many grapes Methymna, as many fish the sea, as many birds the trees, as many stars the sky, so many girls has this Rome of yours."

Ovid
(43 B.C.–A.D. 17)

I found that (Rome) flourisheth beyond all expectation, this new even emulous to exceed the old, the remnants of the old adding to the splendour of the new . . . A man may spend many months at Rome and yet have something of note to see every day."
("Il Mercurio Italico; an Itinerary contayning a Voyage made through Italy in the yeare 1646 & 1647", 1648)

John Raymond
(17th c.)

"The society of Rome is excellent; and the circumstance of every man, whether foreigner or native, being permitted to live as he pleases, without exciting wonder, contributes essentially to general comfort. At Rome, too, every person may find amusement: for whether it be our wish to dive deep into classical knowledge, whether arts and sciences be our pursuit, or whether we merely seek for new ideas and new objects, the end cannot fail to be obtained in this most interesting of Cities, where every stone is an historian."
("Traveller's Guide", 8th edition, 1832)

Mariana Starke

"The head and crown of all churches is without any doubt St Peter's; and if the ancients held it a misfortune not to have seen the Temple of Olympian Jupiter, this could be said even more aptly of St Peter's. For this building is larger than the temples of the Greeks and Romans and surpasses them all in architectural quality and magnificence. I never go there without praising God for granting me the happiness of seeing this wonder, of seeing it and learning to know it over many years."

Johann Joachim
Winkelmann
(1717–68)

"All roads lead to Rome."

Proverb

**Rome from
A to Z**

Sightseeing tours

The recommendations which follow are intended for the tourist who is in Rome for the first time and only has a limited amount of time at his disposal; if followed they should ensure that his stay is as memorable as possible. Names of places and monuments which appear in the walks in bold print can be looked up in the "A to Z" where a more detailed reference or description will be found.

Flying visit

For anyone who is only visiting Rome for a few hours and yet still wants to see the most important sights, an organized sightseeing tour is recommended (see Practical Information, Sightseeing Tours) or alternatively a short work through the historic centre. From the Termini railway station it is best to take the underground to ★Colosseo, to walk from there across the ★★Foro Romano to the ★★Campidoglio/Capitolino, and then into the middle of the historic centre to the ★★Pantheon. After that a good idea might be a stop for refreshment at one of the cafés in the lively ★★Piazza Navona, and then finally to continue to the ★★Piazza di Spagna in order to finish this short visit in the elegant shopping district around the Via Condotti.

Circular walks

refer to City Plan pp. 62/63

Walk no. 1

In order to gain an overview of the historical and cultural influences which have shaped Rome, a walk is recommended through the city from the ancient centre to that of the present day. The starting-point is the mighty ★★Colosseo, from where it is just a short walk to the ★★Foro Romano and ★★Palatino, both with impressive ruins which repay a short walk round. Once back on the Via dei Fori Imperiali go past the ★Fori Imperiali of Augustus and Trajan and climb the ★★Campidoglio or Capitol, for centuries the political heart of the city. On the northern side is the vast towering ★Monumento Nazionale a Vittorio Emanuele II, which overlooks the ★Piazza Venezia, teeming with traffic – crossing it can be quite an adventure! The tour goes past the famous art collection of the ★★Galleria Colonna on to Rome's most magnificent fountain, the ★★Fontana di Trevi. It is said that throwing a coin into the fountain ensures that the visitor will return to the Eternal City some day. Only a few steps away is the ★Museo delle Paste Alimentari where the story of Italy's most popular dish – pasta – is told. The busy Via del Corso leads up to the ★Piazza del Popolo where a stop for coffee can be made. Anyone wanting to get a view across the roofs of the city for the first time should not fight shy of climbing the ★Pincio. Afterwards the walk proceeds to the delightful ★★Piazza di Spagna and the ★★Via Condotti, Rome's most exclusive shopping area.

Walk no. 2

The second circular walk begins at the ★★Vatican/Città del Vaticano and an adequate amount of time should be allowed for a visit here. Not only is there the famous St Peter's Church, but also the Vatican museums which have no equals anywhere else in the world. After such an extensive cultural programme it would make sense to have a breath of fresh air by walking across the ★Gianicolo and enjoying the beautiful view over Rome. At the bottom of the hill lies the ★★Villa Farnesina, a truly luxurious renaissance palace with an enchanting

◀ The Roman Forum – a mecca for all visitors to Rome

garden. The walk then continues across the Tiber and through the bustling old centre of the city to the ★★**Piazza Navona**, a favourite spot for street musicians and pavement artists. A short distance away stands the best preserved building from Roman antiquity, the ★★**Pantheon**. The route then goes to the south, passing the church of ★**Santa Maria sopra Minerva** with its Egyptian elephant obelisk, and then reaches the busy ★**Piazza Venezia** and the mighty ★**Monumento di Vittorio Emmanuele II**. The Via dei ★**Fori Imperiali** then leads to the imperial fora and, as a fitting climax to the whole walk, to the ancient ruins of the ★★**Foro Romano**, ★★**Palatino** and ★★**Colosseo**.

After a time-consuming day spent trailing round the obligatory ancient monuments, such as the ★★**Colosseo**, ★★**Palatino**, ★★**Foro Romano**, ★**Fori Imperiali**, ★**Terme di Caracalla** ★★**Terme di Diocleziano**, the next day ought to be devoted to the *centro storico* and the Vatican City. The starting-point is the lively ★★**Piazza di Spagna** at the foot of the Spanish Steps. From here the walk goes through the very elegant ★★**Via Condotti**, centre of Rome's most illustrious fashion houses, and on to the busy Via del Corso. The visitor comes into contact with Rome's more recent history and, indeed, the present day with the parliament building (Camera dei Diputati) on the Piazza di Montecitorio. To the south a stop must be made at the Piazza della Rotonda to view the magnificent domed building, the ★★**Pantheon**. From here the walk goes through narrow winding streets, across the spacious ★★**Piazza Navona** with its splendid fountain, past the venerable ★**Chiesa Nuova** to the Tiber, crossing at the ★**Ponte Sant'Angelo** to the ★**Castel Sant'Angelo**. Turning to the left the visitor will get a fine view across to the ★★**Vatican/Città del Vaticano**. The wide sweeping Via della Concilazione leads directly to the church of ★★San Pietro in Vaticano and to the open square of the ★★**Piazza San Pietro**. After viewing this, the remainder of the afternoon can be kept free for seeing the marvellous artistic treasures of the ★★**Musei Vaticani**.

An atmospheric finish to the day would surely be a stroll through the lively district of ★**Trastevere**, which – at least according to its inhabitants – is the oldest area of Rome. In the little streets and alleys around the church of ★**Santa Maria in Trastevere** there are many 'trattorie' providing ample opportunity to sample the highly-praised cuisine of Rome.

Walk no. 3

Evening walk

Recommendations for a longer stay

Apart from enabling the visitor to get to know the most important sights of the city, to visit many of the different museums and thereby derive slightly more lasting impressions of Rome, the advantage of a longer stay is that it is possible to make excursions into the surrounding area. Places worth visiting, both from an archaeological and scenic point of view, are the ★**Via Appia Antica**, where a short section of the old Roman road and graves of Roman families can be seen, as well as the ★**Catacombe di San Callisto**, one of the largest complexes of catacombs. An excursion should also be made to ★★**Tivoli** with the wonderful park of the Villa d'Este dating from the 16th c. and the Villa Adriana dating from the period of the Empire. Also recommended is a visit to ★★**Ostia Antica**, the port of ancient Rome, and the attractive mountain and lake scenery of the ★**Colli Albani**.

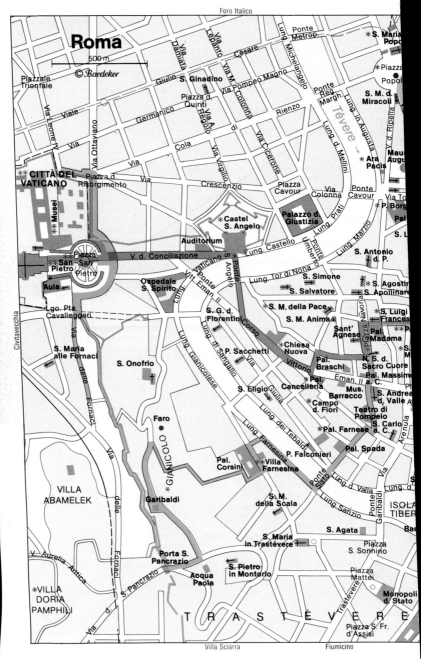

Roma

500 m

© Baedeker

Foro Italico

Piazzale Trionfale

Piazzale Trionfale

S. Ginadino

Piazza d. Quiriti

Piazza d. Risorgimento

** CITTÀ DEL VATICANO

** Musei **

Via Leone IV

Via Ottaviano

Viale

Via

Via

Via Damiata

Via Lepanto

Giulio Cesare

Via M. Pompeo Magno

Via M. Colonna

Via A. Regolo

Germanico

Cola

Via Virginio

Via Cicerone

Rienzo

di

Crescenzio

Piazza Cavour

Via Colonna

* S. Maria d. Popolo

* Piazza

Popol

S. M. d. Miracoli

Lung. in Augusta

V. d. Ripetta

Tèvere

Lung. d. Mellini

Maus Augu

* Ara Pacis

Ponte Cavour

Via To

* P. Borg

Pal

S. L

Lung. d. Marzio

** Piazza San San Pietro Pietro

Aula

Lgo. Pta. Cavalleggeri

Civitavecchia

Via delle Fornaci

S. Maria alle Fornaci

S. Onofrio

Faro

VILLA ABAMELEK

GIANICOLO

Garibaldi

* VILLA DORIA PAMPHILI

V. Aurelia Antica

S. Pancrazio

Porta S. Pancrazio

Acqua Paola

* Castel S. Angelo

Auditorium

V. d. Conciliazione

Ospedale S. Spirito

S. G. d. Fiorentini

Lung. di Sangallo

P. Sacchetti

S. Eligio

Giulia

Pal. Corsini

Lung. Castello

Vaticano Ponte Vitt. Eman. II

Ponte S. Angelo

Lung. Tor di Nona

Corso

* S. M. della Pace

Vittorio

* Chiesa Nuova

Pal. Braschi

Eman. II a. C.

* Pal. Cancelleria

Mus. Barracco

* Campo d. Fiori

Lung. dei Tebaldi

* Pal. Farnese

P. Falconieri

** Villa Farnesina

GIANICOLO

S. M. della Scala

S. Maria in Trastevere

* S. Pietro in Montorio

Palazzo d. Giustizia

Lung. Prati

Ponte Umberto I

S. Antonio d. P.

S. Simone

S. Salvatore

S. M. Anima

Sant' Agnese

N. S. d. Sacro Cuore

Pal. Massimo

S. Andrea d. Valle A

Teatro di Pompeio

S. Carlo a. C.

Pal. Spada

Arenula

Ponte Sisto

Lung. d. Valla

Lung. d.

Ponte Garibaldi

Lung. Sanzio

S. Agata

Piazza S. Sonnino

ISOLA TIBER

Ba

S. Agostin

S. Apollinar

* S. Luigi Frances

* Pa

Pal. Madama

* S. M

Trastevere

TRASTEVERE

Villa Sciarra

Fiumicino

Piazza Mattei

Monopoli d. Stato

Piazza S. Fr. d'Assisi

E

Via Isonzo

* VILLA BORGHESE

Galoppatoio

Porta
Pinciana

Ch. Luterana

d'Italia

Villa
Medici

PINCIO

Via Boncompagni

Inner City plan
with Circular Walks

Walk 1
Walk 2
Walk 3

Depretis

** Piazza
di Spagna

Trinità
dei Monti

S. Isidoro

S. Maria
Concezione

** S. M. d.
Vittoria

Min.
delle
Finanze

Piazza d.
Indipendenza

S. Andrea Macelli

Via Ludovisi

Via Mercede

P. S. Silvestro

Piazza
Barberini

Via Barberini

** Pal.
Barberini

** Terme di
Diocleziano

S. Maria
d. Angeli

Piazza d.
Repubblica

Via Marsala

** Fontana
di Trevi

QUIRINALE

* Museo
d. Paste

Min. di
Difesa

S. Carlo
4 Font.

Piazza d.
Cinquecento

Stazione
Termini

Piazza
olonna

S. Croce

Piazza
d. Quirinale

S. Andrea
Quirin.
San Vitale

Teatro
d. Opera

** Pal.
Massimo

Pal. Sciarra

Univ.
Gregoriana

Pal.
Espos.

Via Giolitti

S. Ignazio

Pal.
Rospigliosi

Min. d'
Interno

Piazza d.
Esquilino

** S. Maria
Maggiore

ollegio
Rom.

** SS. Apostoli

Banca
d'Italia

S. Lorenzo

Piazza S.
M. Maggiore

Pal.
Colonna

Pal.
Doria P.

S. S.
Nome
d'Maria

** Foro
Traiano

SS. Dam.
e Sisto

S. Agata

* S. Prassede

Piazza
Venezia

Mon.
Vitt. Eman.

* S. M.
Aracoeli

* Foro
Augusto

* Museo N.
d'Arte
Orientale

* Mus.
Capitol.

Campidoglio

V dei Fori Imperiali

ESQUILINO

P. Senat.

Conserv.

Arc.
Sett. Sev.

SS. Cosma e
Damiano

* S. Pietro
in Vincoli

OPPIO

Domus Aurea

Teatro
arcello

CAPITOLINO

** Foro Romano

S. Francesca

S. Omolono

** Colosseo

* S. G. i
Velabro

** PALATINO

* Arco di
Constantino

Piazza d.
Colosseo

Via San Giovanni in Laterano

Tempio
di Vesta

* S. M.
Cosmedin

S. Anastasia

Tempio
di Claudio

Circo

SS. Giov.
e Paolo

V. S. Stefano Rotondo

Massimo

S. Gregorio
Magno

Tivoli, Colli Albani
San Giovanni
in Laterano

Rome from A to Z

★Ara Pacis Augustae   D 5

Location
Via di Ripetta/
Piazza Augusto
Imperatore

Buses
70, 81, 90, 119
913, 926

Opening times
Tue.–Sun.
9am–1.30pm,
Tue.,Thu., Sat.
also 4–7pm

Between the Mausoleo di Augusto (see entry) and the Tiber stands Augustus' Altar of Peace. Nowadays protected against the elements by an unlovely concrete shelter, it was first dedicated in 9 B.C..

After the troubles of the civil wars, social unrest such as the Spartacus uprising and victories in Gaul and Spain, Emperor Augustus finally secured peace for the Roman Empire – the Golden Age of Augustus had arrived. Accordingly, as recorded in Res Gestae, "the Senate resolved to erect the Altar of the Augustan Peace as a votive offering on the Field of Mars". Although re-discovered in the 16th c., reconstruction of the altar only became possible in the early 20th c.

This masterpiece of the Roman sculptor's art wholly immortalises the Imperium Romanum with its religious roots and ceremonies, its all-conquering claim to power, its Imperial house and the institutions on which it was based. The lower part of the screen around the altar, of Carrara marble, is richly decorated with reliefs of foliage – acanthus, ivy, laurel, vines – interspersed with birds and reptiles. The upper part is taken up by a sculptured frieze, running round all four sides. On the ends the allegorical figures and mythological scenes include the four elements, Aneas' sacrifice and, near the entrance, the cave where the she-wolf is supposed to have suckled Romulus and Remus. The reliefs along the sides tell of historic events, with the frieze facing the Via Ripetta showing illustrious members of the Imperial family, among them Augustus, Agrippa, the Empress Livia and Gaius Julius Caesar. A flight of ten steps leads up to the platform (11.62 ×10.60m/38×35ft), in the centre of which stands the altar, guarded by lions, with about a third of its reliefs of sacrificial rites still intact.

★Arco di Constantino   E 7

Location
Piazza del
Colosseo/Via di
San Gregorio

**Underground
station**
Colosseo (line B)

Buses
11, 27, 81, 87,
186, 673

Trams
13, 30

The massive Arch of Constantine in the shadow of the Colosseum (see Colosseo) was probably begun by the Emperor Hadrian (117–138) rather than Constantine (306–337). This was the conclusion arrived at in the early Nineties during the restoration of the great monument when the marble and its background was subjected to precise analysis. Hitherto the assumption had been that the triumphal arch was erected by the Senate after Constantine's victory over Maxentius at the Ponte Milvio (see entry) in 312 in honour of the "liberator of the city and bringer of peace", but presumably the bottom part of the arch dates from Hadrian's time while the upper part was added in later centuries. This is the largest (21m/69ft high, 25.7m/84ft wide, 7.4m/24ft deep) and best preserved of the Roman triumphal arches, although it, like the Colosseum, was incorporated in the castle of the Frangipane family and was not disengaged until, the 16th c. (partly) and the 19th c. (completely). Since the arch, in three sections, is mainly decorated with reliefs taken from earlier structures, the scenes depicted have little to do with Constantine and his military achievements. The north side, facing the Colosseum, has reliefs of a boar and lion hunt, a sacrifice to Hercules and Apollo from a hunting monument of Hadrian's day, river gods and victories, etc. Reliefs on the south side include a bear hunt, more river deities and battle scenes from the reign of Constantine (conquest of Susa and battle of the Milvian Bridge) and Marcus Aurelius, as well as sacrificial celebra-

Arch of Constantine – the largest of the Roman Triumphal Arches

tions for Diana and Sylvanus. The east side shows Constantine's Triumph while the victory of Crispus is on the west side . The attica on the Colosseum side bears the Latin inscription "To the Emperor Caesar Flavius Constantinus Maximus, pious, fortunate, august, the Senate and the people of Rome dedicate this arch in honour of his triumphs because, inspired by Divinity and greatness of spirit, he freed the Republic by just wars from tyranny and from factions".

Basilica di Porta Maggiore   H 6/7

This underground shrine (probably 1st c. A.D.), although well preserved, is still something of a puzzle to archaeologists. Discovered 13m/40ft below ground level in 1917, it has the form of a basilica measuring 19×12m/62×39ft, with a porch and a semicircular apse. With its mosaic pavement, stucco decoration on the ceiling and cycles of mythological scenes, it seems to have been the shrine of some mystical cult (perhaps the Neo-Pythagoreans). It was probably this type of building, which was widespread throughout the Empire, that also influenced the development of the Christian basilica.

Location
Via Prenestina 17

Trams
13, 14, 19, 19b,
516, 517

Borsa   D 6

The Roman Exchange, occupies part of the site of a large ancient temple, eleven Corinthian columns from which are preserved along one side. Long thought to have been a temple of Neptune, this has now been identified as the Hadrianeum, a temple erected in honour of the deified Hadrian. The floor of the temple now lies below street

Location
Piazza di Pietra

Buses
26, 87, 94

level. In 1691–1700 the temple was absorbed into the new customs house, now the Exchange, built by Carlo and Francesco Fontana under Pope Innocent II.

Camera dei Deputati (Palazzo Montecitorio)   D/E 6

Location
Palazzo
Montecitorio,
Piazza di
Montecitorio

Buses
52, 53, 56, 58,
58b, 60, 61, 62,
71, 81, 85, 88, 90,
90b, 95, 115

The Palazzo Montecitorio, begun by Bernini in 1650 for Pope Innocent X Pamphili and completed in 1694 by Carlo Fontana, has been occupied since 1871 by the Chamber of Deputies, the lower house of the Italian Parliament. At the beginning of this century the palace was enlarged to meet the Parliament's needs.

The Piazza di Montecitorio holds an ancient Egyptian obelisk (594–589 B.C.). Here German archaeologists uncovered what is claimed to be the largest sundial in the world. It dates from the 2nd c. A.D. and the obelisk was the gnomon. The great bronze face of the sundial, 60m/200ft in diameter, is behind the Chamber of Deputies at a depth of 6.5m/20ft below the present street level. Below it is the still more famous sundial of Augustus.

★★Campidoglio · Capitolino   D/E 6

**Underground
station**
Colosseo (line B)

Buses
46, 57, 90, 181,
186, 710, 718, 719

The Capitol, the smallest of Rome's seven hills, was the political and religious centre of the ancient city. On its two summits stood the city's two most important temples, dedicated to Jupiter Optimus Maximus Capitolinus and Juno Moneta, on the sites now occupied by the Palazzo dei Conservatori and the church of Santa Maria in Aracoeli (see entry). The lower area between them is now occupied by Capitol Square, the Piazza del Campidoglio.

The square, flanked by palaces and approached by a ceremonial ramp and staircase, still conveys a feeling of the grandeur and dignity which the city has preserved down the centuries. Here victorious Roman generals came to celebrate their triumphs, making their way to the Capitol along the Sacred Way (Via Sacra); here in the Middle Ages poets were crowned and tribunes of the people were acclaimed; here in 1955 the Treaty of Rome was signed, establishing EURATOM and the European Economic Community; and here, in the Palazzo dei Senatori, the Mayor of Rome has his residence and receives distinguished visitors to the city. Since time immemorial this has been the political centre of Rome and counterpart to the spiritual and religious centre of the city in the Vatican (see entry).

★Piazza del Campidoglio

The Piazza del Campidoglio is reached from Via del Teatro di Marcello by way of the ceremonial ramp and staircase designed by Michelangelo, passing a monument (on the left) to the tribune Cola di Rienzo, and statues of the Dioscuri (Castor and Pollux), the Emperor Constantine and his son Constantine II.

The square, also designed by Michelangelo, is bounded by the façades of three palaces, the Palazzo dei Senatori (to the rear), the Palazzo dei Conservatori (on the right) and the Palazzo Nuovo (on the left). It is not, however, totally enclosed, since there are openings between the buildings which allow passage to streets leading down to the Forum (see entry). The palaces are not set at right angles to one another but form a trapezoid, within which Michelangelo laid out an oval (marked by steps) and a star formation (marked by lighter-coloured paving). This gives emphasis to the centre of the square

Statues of the Dioscori flank the ceremonial ramp (by Michelangelo)

which at one time held an equestrian statue of Marcus Aurelius (161–180 A.D.). The bronze statue, which was originally gilded, had previously stood in front of the church of St John Lateran (see San Giovanni in Laterano). It was thought to represent the Emperor Constantine, who favoured Christianity, and was accordingly preserved from destruction despite its heathen origins. Its true identity was recognized in the 15th c. by Platina, the librarian to the Vatican, from comparison of the likenesses of the two emperors on their coins, and in 1538 Pope Paul III had it transferred to the Piazza del Campidoglio. The statue was taken as a model for the greatest equestrian statues of the Gothic, Renaissance and Baroque periods, including Donatello's Gattamelata in Padua and Verocchio's Colleoni monument in Venice. The statue, which had been badly damaged by air pollution, was restored in 1990 and can now be seen in the Museo Capitolino.

The Palazzo dei Senatori was built in the 16th c. on the remains of the Tabularium the record office of ancient Rome, and now houses the Mayor and the City Council. The double staircase leading up to the entrance was designed (1541–1544) by Michelangelo, who also installed here ancient statues of the river gods of the Nile (sphinx) and Tiber (she-wolf). In the centre is a fountain with an ancient porphyry statue of Minerva, then revered as the patron deity of Rome. The façade, completed in 1605, is the work of Giacomo della Porta and Girolamo Rainaldi; the handsome bell-tower, modelled on a medieval campanile, was added by Martino Longhi between 1578 and 1582.
Palazzo dei Senatori

The Palazzo dei Conservatori, built by Giacomo della Porta in 1564–75 to the design of Michelangelo, contains function rooms used by the City of Rome for official receptions, and also houses some of the collections of the Capitoline Museum. Items on show here include
★Palazzo dei Conservatori

67

**★★Capitoline
She-Wolf**

**★Pinacoteca
Capitolina**

**★Museo
Capitolino**
(Palazzo Nuovo)

fragments of a colossal statue of the Emperor Constantine, 12m/40ft high, from the Constantine Basilica, and two statues of captive Barbarian princes (in the courtyard). One particular highlight is that symbol of Rome and papal jurisdiction, the Capitoline She-Wolf, a bronze by the Etruscan Vulca di Veio from the 6th c. B.C. (its hind-quarters were struck by lightning in 65 B.C.) – the figures of Romulus and Remus were added during the Renaissance. Other interesting exhibits include parts of the Fasti consulares et triumphales, a list of consuls and their victories, and the "Boy with a Thorn" (Spinario), a Hellenistic copy in bronze of a 3rd or 5th c. original. One room in the palace, the Sala delle Oche, is named after the geese whose cackling was said to have saved Rome from capture by the Gauls in 385 B.C..

The palace also contains the Capitoline Picture Gallery (Pinacoteca Capitolina), eight rooms with paintings by Titian ("Baptism of Christ"), Tintoretto (Passion series), Caravaggio ("John the Baptist"), Rubens ("Romulus and Remus"), Veronese ("Rape of Europa"), Lorenzo Lotto ("Portrait of a Bowman") and Velázquez ("Portrait of a Man"), etc. (open Tue.–Sat. 9am–2pm, Tue., Thu. also 5–8pm, Sat. also 8.30–11pm; Sun. 9am–1pm).

The Capitoline Museum, founded by Pope Sixtus IV in 1471, is the oldest public art collection in Europe and has a rich store of classical sculpture. The collection is on show in the Palazzo Nuovo, built about 1650 and modelled on the Palazzo dei Conservatori opposite. Highlights among the sculpture include the "Dying Gaul", a Roman copy of the figure of a dying warrior from the victory monument erected by King Attalus of Pergamon in the 3rd c. B.C. after victory over the Galatians; the "Wounded Amazon", a copy of a work by Cresilas (5th c. B.C.; the "Capitoline Venus", a Roman copy of the Cnidian Aphrodite of Praxiteles; two Hellenistic works, "Amor and Psyche" and the

The classical sculpture collection in the Palazzo Nuovo

"Drunken Old Woman"; collections of 64 portrait heads of Roman Emperors and members of their families, and 79 busts of Greek and Roman philosophers and scholars. Since 1990 the equestrian statue of Marcus Aurelius has stood, behind glass, in the museum courtyard. This work, one of the greatest achievements of antique sculpture, radiates quiet strength, and the Emperor's right hand is raised in a gesture of peace. Originally there was the figure of a defeated king under the horse's raised right front hoof (open Tue.–Sat. 9am–1.30pm, Tue. and Sat. also 5–8pm, in summer 8–11pm; Sun. 9am–1pm).

★★Equestrian statue of Marcus Aurelius

Campo Verano   H/J 5/6

In line with ancient Roman tradition, the Campo Verano, the city's biggest cemetery, is located outside the city walls, on the Via Tiburtina, the road to Tivoli (see entry). The cemetery mirrors the class structure of the city, with the grand family tombs and mausoleums in the park-like sections and poorer folk having to make do with low-cost "loculi", tall structures of marble and travertine with numerous compartments to take the many sarcophagi. The Campo Verano is particularly busy on All Saints Day (November 1st) when the Romans come here every year to visit their dead and decorate their graves.

Location
Via Tiburtina

Buses
11, 63, 65, 71, 109, 111, 163, 309, 311, 411, 415, 490, 492, 495

Trams
19, 19b, 30, 30b

Capitolino

See Campidoglio

★Castel Sant'Angelo   C 5

The Castel Sant'Angelo is one of the most imposing buildings to survive from antiquity. It was originally a mausoleum, begun by Hadrian (A.D.117–138) in the closing years of his reign to provide a last resting place for himself and his successors, and completed by Septimus Severus (A.D.193). When Rome was endangered by Germanic raiders from the north and was surrounded by Aurelius with a new circuit of walls (see Mura Aureliane) the mausoleum, strategically situated, was incorporated in the defences and became the strongest fortress in Rome. The original name of the structure (Hadrianeum) was changed to Castel Sant'Angelo after a vision vouchsafed to Pope Gregory the Great in 590, when he saw an angel hovering over the mauseoleum and sheathing his sword, heralding the end of the plague which was then raging in Rome. Hence the figure of an angel which now crowns the castle (by Piet van Verschaffelt, 1753).

In 1277 Pope Nicholas III linked the castle with the palaces of the Vatican (see entry) by building a wall known as a "passetto" since it contained a covered passage. Pope Alexander VI, the Borgia Pope whose adventurous policy of conquest made adequate protection against attack very necessary, fortified this passage and strengthened the castle by building four corner bastions. In times of danger the Popes were able to take refuge in the Castel Sant'Angelo, as did Gregory VII (1084) when threatened by the German king Henry IV, Clement VII during the attack on Rome by the Emperor Charles V (1527, sack of Rome) and Pius VII when in danger of capture by Napoleon's forces. Celebrated prisoners were confined in the castle, and executions took place on its walls. For a time it housed the Papal treasury and secret archives.

The Mausoleum of Hadrian consisted of a circular structure 64m/ 210ft in diameter and 20m/65ft high standing on a square base (84m/

Location
Lungotevere Vaticano/ Lungotevere Castello

Buses
41, 46, 46b, 62, 64, 280, 808

Opening times
Daily 9am–2pm (closed 2nd and 4th Tue. every month)

Castel Sant'Angelo

Castel Sant'Angelo

275ft each way, 15m/50ft high). Around the top of the walls, built of dressed travertine and tufa, were set a series of statues, and on the highest point was a bronze quadriga (four-horse chariot). This cylindrical structure with its simple geometrical forms and massive walls, within which were the tomb chambers of the Imperial family, formed the core of the Papal stronghold. In the course of 1500 years the building was altered by successive Popes according to their particular needs (whether for defence against attack or for purposes of display, with sumptuous decoration). From 1870 until 1901 the Castel Sant'Angelo served as both barracks and prison, then it was renovated and furnished as a museum.

Its 58 rooms, some decorated with fine murals, hold an interesting collection of weaponry, models of the history of the building of the fortress, several chapels and a treasury. From the upper platform there is a magnificent view over the city.

Ponte Sant'Angelo

The finest of the ancient Roman bridges, the Ponte Sant'Angelo was built by Hadrian in A.D.136 to give access to his Mausoleum over the Tiber and was known as the Pons Aelius, using one of the Emperor's forenames. The three central piers are original. The entrance to the footbridge is guarded by statues of Peter, by Lorenzetto (1530), and Paul, by Paolo Romano (1463), erected in the mid 16th c. under Clement VII. Clement IX commissioned the ten figures of angels which line the bridge from Bernini (see Famous People) who was 70 at the time. The figures, carrying the instruments of Christ's passion, were carved to Bernini's specifications between 1660 and 1668 by his pupils, among them Antonio Raggi, Antonio Giorgetti and Ercole Ferrata.

Statues of angels by Bernini line the Ponte Sant'Angelo

Catacombs

The catacombs were originally the legally recognised burial places of Christians (and also heathens) who called them by the Greek name of Coemetaria (resting places). Until the beginning of the 9th c. the coemetaria with their martyrs' graves enjoyed general veneration, and many remains were transferred as relics to other churches. Then the burial places fell into decay and even the old name was forgotten. The name catacomb comes from Catacumbas, one of these burial places which was situated in the area of the basilica of St Sebastian. Scientific investigation began at the end of the 16th c. and was considered a matter of honour by the Church. As more recent research has revealed, catacombs served merely as burial places and as places where masses for the dead were said and not as refuges for the Christians or where regular services were held.

The layout is very simple; narrow passages, in the walls of which several long niches were formed for the reception of the corpses. For non-Christians these niches were used for urns containing ashes. The niches were sealed by marble or terracotta tablets. Decoration with painting but little sculpture follows the style of the pagan art of the time; symbolic representations predominate, depending on the contents – the sacrificial lamb, the fish, representing the Greek word "ichthys", the Greek initials of "Jesus Christ, Son of God and Saviour", the Greek initials of "Jesus Christ, Son of God and Saviour". There are also impressive early representations of the Last Supper and the Virgin Mary. The older inscriptions only give the name of the dead person.

★Catacombe di Domitilla   F 10

Location
Via delle Sette
Chiese 283

Buses
93, 671, or 118
and change to
94, 218

Opening times
Mon., Wed.–Sun.
8.30–12 and
2.30–5pm (5.30
in summer)

The Catacombs of Domitilla are among the most impressive of Rome's catacombs. They were not used solely by Christians but most wealthy and prominent Romans preferred to be buried in one of the cemeteries beside the great roads leading out of the city. Domitilla was a descendant of Vespasian who, after her conversion to Christianity, allowed Christians to be buried in the family tomb. Christians met to celebrate the commemorative day of notable members of their community at their tomb.

The Catacombs of Domitilla hold the basilica of SS Nereus and Achilleus, a very striking underground church with its columns and marble fragments. From the basilica visitors enter the catacomb corridors, with their tomb chambers and wall recesses, where there are still well-preserved frescoes on such Christian themes as the Good Shepherd, Daniel in the Lions' Den, and Christ and His Disciples.

Fosse Ardeatine

The Fosse Ardeatine, about 300m/330yds from the catacombs, has a memorial to the 335 Italian hostages who were shot here by the Germans in March 1944 in reprisal for a bomb attack.

★Catacombe di Priscilla   G 2

Location
Via Salaria Nuova
430

Buses
135, 235, 319

Opening times
Tue.–Sun.
8.30–12 and
2.30–5pm
(in summer
5.30pm)

Rome's oldest catacombs are thought to be named after Priscilla, from the house of Acilia, who became a Christian and was killed on the orders of Domitian. They contain a number of wall paintings of saints and early Christian symbols.

The tomb of Velatio has frescoes of Abraham's Sacrifice and the Hebrews in the Fiery Furnace. Particularly notable is a Greek chapel, a square chamber with an arch which contains 2nd c. frescoes of Old and New Testament scenes. Above the apse is a Last Supper. Nearby the painting from the early 3rd c. of the Virgin and Child with the Prophet Balaam is the oldest depiction of Mary other than the theme of the Virgin and the Magi. The one here dates from the late 2nd c.

Other Catacombs:
Catacombe di San Callisto: see Via Appia Antica
Catacombe di San Ciriaca: see San Lorenzo fuori le Mura
Catacombe di San Sebastiano: see San Sebastiano
Catacombe di Sant'Agnese: see Sant'Agnese fuori le Mura

★Cerveteri   (Excursion)

Location
51km/32 miles
NW, just off the
Via Aurelia

Opening times
Tue.–Sun.
9am–4pm
(5pm in summer)

Cerveteri, a corruption of Caere Vetus, occupies the site of Caere, a city that from the 8th to the 4th c. B.C. served as an important trading and power base for the Etruscans. Their necropolis at Banditaccia, north of present-day Cerveteri, provides an insight, thanks to the wealth of burial gifts found in the tombs there, into the life and the funerary cult of these mysterious people, who occupied all of central Italy before the Romans and developed a high degree of artistic achievement in architecture, painting, sculpture and metalwork. The Etruscan gold and bronze pieces, vases, funerary urns and paintings found here can nowadays been seen in museums throughout the world, including Paris, London and Rome.

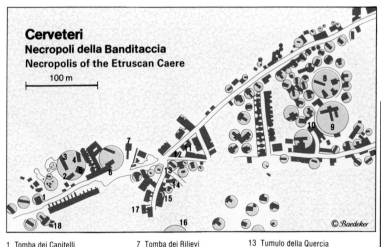

Cerveteri
Necropoli della Banditaccia
Necropolis of the Etruscan Caere

100 m

© Baedeker

1 Tomba dei Capitelli	7 Tomba dei Rilievi	13 Tumulo della Quercia
2 Tomba dei Letti e Sarcofagi	8 Tumulo del Colonello	14 Tumulo dei 2 Ingressi
3 Tomba della Capanna	9 Tumulo Mengarelli	15 Tumulo della Cornice
4 Tomba dei Dolii	10 Tumulo Maroi	16 Grande Tumulo della Tegola Dipinta
5 Tomba dei Vasi Greci	11 Tomba di Marce Ursus	17 Tomba dei 6 Loculi
6 Tomba dei 13 Cadaveri	12 Tomba della Casetta	18 Tombe della Spianata

★Chiesa Nuova (Santa Maria in Vallicella)   C 6

The church of Santa Maria in Vallicella was begun in 1575 for St Philip Neri, founder of the Congregation of the Oratory. It was built on the site of an earlier (12th c.) church dedicated to St John, and is still popularly known as the "New Church". The exterior of the relatively recently restored church is imposing with its massive façade (by Fausto Rughesi) and central dome rising high above the close-packed houses in the older part of the city. Notable features in the sumptuously gilded interior of this high cruciform basilica with a nave and two aisles are the mid-16th c. frescoes by Pietro da Cortona (God the Father and Christ in the dome, and the Assumption in the apse) and early works by Rubens on the high altar (the Virgin with Angels and other images of saints). Left of the choir is the sumptuous chapel of St Philip Neri with his tomb of marble inlaid with mother-of-pearl.

Location
Piazza della
Chiesa Nuova
(Corso Vittorio
Emanuele II)

Buses
46, 62, 64

Immediately to the left of the Chiesa Nuova is the Oratory of the Filippini, the community which St Philip founded. It was built for the priests of the Oratorio – who were very popular with the Romans – by Borromini (1637–50) as a place where they could live, work and pray together. A notable feature of the building is the finely articulated façade, which contrasts with the adjoining church in height, form and colouring. The Sala del Borromini, in the former Oratory, is now used as a concert hall. The Oratory also contains the Biblioteca Vallicelliana, Rome's oldest library open to the public.

Oratorio
dei Filippini

73

The "New Church" founded by St Philip Neri in the 16th century

Circo Massimo   D/E 7

Location
Via dei Circo
Massimo

**Underground
station**
Circo Massimo

According to legend, the Circus Maximus, lying to the south of the Palatine (see entry), was constructed by Tarquinius Priscus on the site of the rape of the Sabine women. The Circus was, in fact, established in 329 B.C. for chariot racing. It could hold around 150,000 spectators (see Baedeker Special, "Bread and Circuses") and the track itself was 500m/547yd long and 80m/87yd wide. The remains of the buildings date from the time of Nero and Trajan. The obelisk erected at the Circus during the reign of Augustus now stands on Piazza del Popolo (see entry).

Obelisco
di Axum

The 24m/79ft high Axum Obelisk which stands at the south-east end of the Circus Maximus on the Piazza di Porta Capena was brought to Rome from Ethiopia's holy city of Axum following the Italian invasion of Abyssinia in 1937.

Città Universitaria   G/H 5/6

Location
Viale delle Scienze

Buses
11, 71, 109, 111,
309, 310, 311,
411, 415, 492

When the Papal University, the Sapienza on the Corso del Rinascimento, became too small, plans were being drawn up from 1870 onwards for replacing it with new university buildings. This large new complex was built by Mussolini in 1932–35, but it has long since become too small to cope with contemporary student numbers. The University City also has several small museums.

★Colli Albani (Excursion)

In the past many patrician Roman families and Popes built castles in these hills, which is why the region is also known as Castelli Romani (Roman Castles). Today many Roman citizens have their retreats here, drawn by the purer air and quieter surroundings of an area which lies considerably higher than Rome. These volcanic hills rise to a height of 949m/3114ft in Monte Cavo. The craters of the volcanoes have formed two lakes, the Lago Di Albano (Alban Lake) and the Lago di Nemi (Lake Nemi). An excellent wine known as Castelli Romani is produced from grapes grown on the slopes of the hills. Around the old castles a series of little towns have grown up, including Frascati, known for its healthy climate and dry white wine, Grottaferrata (see below), Marino, picturesquely located on a ridge, Castel Gandolfo (see below), Albano, Ariccia, Genzano, Nemi, with its small ship museum, and Rocca di Papa, surrounded by beautiful woodland on the rim of a large old volcanic crater, the Campo di Annibale.

Location
20–30km/12–18 miles SE

Rail
Ferrovia Roma-Albano

No tour of the Castelli Romani would be complete without a visit to the old abbey of the Basilians (an order of the Greek Catholic Church) at Grottaferrata (altitude: 329m/1080ft; population 52,000). The abbey church was described by Pope Leo XIII at the end of the 19th c. as "a jewel of the Orient in the Papal diadem". The abbey, which has almost entirely rebuilt in 1754, is not only an imposing Renaissance fortress but also a venerable cloister with some notable works of art, including frescoes by Domenichino (1609/1610) in the chapel of St Nilius.

★Grottaferrata

Location
21 km/13 miles
SE of Rome

Lake Albano is quite a large lake, about 3.5km/2 miles long, 2km/1 mile wide and up to 170m/558ft deep (altitude 293m/962ft), set in a delightful landscape. At one time it was overlooked by the Etruscan city of Alba Longa (now Castel Gandolfo), until its destruction by Rome. The level of water in the lake is kept constant by a 2.5km/1$^1/_2$ mile long underground canal (Emissarium), with the excess fed into the Tiber. The first version of this was built by Roman engineers as early as 397 B.C. due to a prophecy that otherwise the Romans would not conquer the Etruscan city of Veji.

★Lago di Albano

Wonderfully located above Lake Albano, Castel Gandolfo (altitude 426m/1398ft; population 52,000) is famous as the site of the Pope's summer palace. This was begun in 1624 by Carlo Maderna under Urban VIII and together with the nearby Villa Barberini has extraterritorial status as part of Vatican City. From the little town, which is said to have been founded by Ascanius, son of Aeneas, and, as the Etruscans' Alba Longa, was later destroyed by Rome, there are sweeping views down to the lake below and over the Roman Campagna as far as the dome of St Peter's. The mid-17th c. church of San Tommaso di Villanova in the main square, opposite the Papal palace, is by Bernini.

★Castel Gandolfo

Location
25km/15 miles
south-east of
Rome

★★Colosseo E 7

The monumental Colosseum, the mighty Flavian amphitheatre, is the largest closed structure left by Roman antiquity, and has provided the model for sports arenas right down to modern times; the way we view sporting contests today is no different from the way devised by the architects working for the Flavian Caesars, Vespasian and Titus. With the Colosseum these emperors were trying to satisfy the Romans' appetite for "circenses" (games), circuses and entertain-

Location
Piazza del
Colosseo

ment, even though the bloodthirsty gladiatorial contests and animal-baiting were not to everyone's taste.

A bronze cross in the arena commemorates the blood of Christian martyrs shed in the Colosseum under the Caesars, although historians have cast doubt on whether in fact very many Christians were put to death here.

The structure of the Colosseum is so well preserved that it gives a very good idea of what it was like originally, but it has also been so badly damaged that all its scars are there to see as well – from such ravages of time as fire, earthquake, neglect and dilapidation when the games were abandoned under the Christian Empire, conversion into a fortress for the Frangipani, cannibalizing of its ornamentation, marble, travertine and brick for Rome's palaces (Palazzo Venezia, Palazzo della Cancelleria, Palazzo Farnese), and, last but not least, the pollution created by the constant traffic.

The building of the Colosseum was begun by Vespasian in A.D.72 on the site of a colossal statue of Nero (hence the name Colosseo) which stood within the precincts of Nero's Domus Aurea (see entry). Vespasian's son Titus enlarged it by adding the fourth storey, and it was inaugurated in the year 80 with a series of splendid games. The Colosseum was oval in form (though it appears to be almost circular), 186m/610ft long by 156m/510ft across, with an arena of 78×46m/ 260×150ft which could be used for theatrical performances, festivals, circus shows or games. It stood 57m/190ft high and could hold some 50,000 spectators – the Imperial court and high officials on the lowest level, the aristocratic families of Rome on the second level, the common people on the third and fourth.

Underground station
Colosseo (line B)

Buses
11, 27, 81, 85, 87, 186

Trams
13, 30

Opening times
Mon., Tue.,
Thu.–Sat.
9am–3pm
(7pm in summer),
Sun., Wed.
9am–1pm

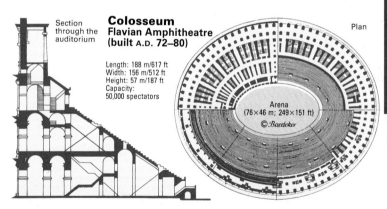

Section through the auditorium

Colosseum
Flavian Amphitheatre
(built A.D. 72–80)

Length: 188 m/617 ft
Width: 156 m/512 ft
Height: 57 m/187 ft
Capacity: 50,000 spectators

Arena
(76×46 m; 249×151 ft)
© Baedeker

Plan

Around the exterior, built of travertine, are pilasters – of the Doric order on the ground floor, Ionic on the next tier and Corinthian on the third. The interior structure was contrived with immense skill, the rows of seating and the internal passages and staircases being arranged so as to allow the 50,000 spectators to get to their places or leave the theatre within a few minutes. On the top storey there were originally 240 masts set round the walls to support an awning over the audience. Unfortunately the sumptuous decoration of the interior

◀ *The remains of the mighty Flavian amphitheatre – the Colosseum*

Bread and Circuses

"**E**verywhere sports grounds, fountains, marble halls, temples, workshops, schools . . . delightful plays of every kind and festive contests without number", thus Aelius Aristides described Rome in his panaegyric in A.D.156. The writer Juvenal, on the other hand, a few decades earlier had gained quite a different impression of the centre of the Roman Empire: "Even in the most pitiful hovel you live better than here in the mad hurly burly of the capital with its thousand dangers, collapsing houses and fires . . . The shabby lodging is expensive, the meagre meals are expensive and feeding the slaves is expensive . . . Because sleep is impossible Rome is full of sick people, and the sickness comes from the . . . heavy stomach-churning food. All night long wagons roll through narrow alleys, corners where flocks get stuck and bring down the drovers' curses . . ." Since during the day the footways were impassible and constant building caused traffic jams, the vast amounts of comestibles for the daily provisioning of Rome's population of 1.5 million usually had to be transported into the city by night, to the sound of the clattering of the wagon wheels on the paving of the main roads and the cries of the suppliers and dealers. The wares found their buyers in two central markets, 190 corn-halls, over 250 mills and countless warehouses, shops, stalls, taverns and bars. For the water supply there were eleven large aqueducts, some of them delivering 2200 litres a second – by the end of the 1st c. Rome's water consumption was 700,000 cubic metres a day. In addition the city still had around 1150 wells where most people came to fetch their water by the bucketful, or had it brought by water carriers, since only the homes of the rich were on the drinking water supply. Although there was a system of canals for carrying away sewage only a few private citizens benefitted from it, such as the owners of the 1800 or so villas and of course the public institutions. The poorer people, who lived packed together in the 50,000 or so tenements, some of them six floors high, had to carry their pails of sewage and dirty water down to a cesspit in the cellar or to the nearest sewage trench, accompanied by the inevitable stench. The dark cramped tenements were sparsely lit by sooty lamps, heated by portable metal coal stoves and cooking was done on open fires. The staple diet was a broth of grain and vegetables, bread, olive oil and salted fish. About a quarter of Rome's population were also entitled to free public grain rations. In the 1st c. the city had to import 5.50 million cwt. of wheat from Africa, 2.75 million cwt. from Egypt and 0.5 million cwt. from Sicily. The Emperor and other leading figures made themselves popular with ordinary folk by distributing free food, drink and sweetmeats in the concourse on the approach to events in the circus or amphitheatre, where the plebians were allowed free places in the top tiers. Over time the free distribution of food and a regular entertainment programme, known as Bread and Circuses, became the means used by the political rulers to prevent social unrest, increase their popularity and their fame and, finally, also by their "offerings" to get the Gods to look

Roman mosaic pavement from the 2nd c. A.D. showing gladiators fighting

favourably upon them. The Romans certainly had more than enough free time for all kinds of amusement. The plebians, mostly impoverished landless peasants and destitute war veterans, lived on the streets from hand to mouth and were grateful for any distraction from their miserable existence. The rich had others to do the work for them and could thus indulge their idleness. Only the artisans and slaves had to work really hard from the crack of dawn, but the normal working day usually ended around noon, and every few days there was some kind of festival going on in the city. In the Colosseum, as the Flavian amphitheatre was called, built to hold 50,000 spectators, the bloodthirsty games began in the morning with the March of the Gladiators – their name came from "gladius", Latin for short sword. Magnificently robed, they completed a lap of honour then saluted the Emperor, with "Hail Caesar, we who are about to die salute you!", whereupon they withdrew, giving ▶

way to all kinds of entertainers, dwarves and other comical characters. Fanfares then announced the entry of the gladiators, who armed either with shield, sword or lance, armour-plating round their arms and legs, or with a shoulder guard, net and spear, would proceed to fight to the death. A badly wounded gladiator could beg for mercy from his opponent who was free to deal the death blow or let him live. The crowd might well have something to say about this, and when the Emperor was present the decision was his – thumbs up for mercy, thumbs down for death. The victors were hailed as the people's heroes and might well be chosen by rich patrician ladies as lovers overnight. The gladiatorial contests originated in the Etruscan funeral ceremonies to honour the deeds of the dead. Over time they became bloodier and more professional and from the beginning of the 1st c. B.C. were staged in public until banned by Emperor Honorius early in the 5th c. The fighters were recruited from slaves captured in battle, convicted criminals and a few volunteers who had to undergo a long and arduous training before they were allowed to appear in the arena. The enthusiasm of the Romans for this bloody spectacle is hard to understand today, but evidently was based on widely respected Roman ideas of discipline, endurance, courage in the face of death and self-sacrifice. Seneca the Younger (d. A.D.65), however, was highly critical of this doubtful pleasure: "I chanced to come upon a show at lunchtime; I expected diversion, joking and some relaxation, people resting their eyes with the blood of their fellow men; the opposite is the case . . . In the morning people are thrown to lions and bears, in the afternoon they are thrown to the spectators. The spectators demand that the victorious killers have new people thrown to them again for them to kill, and then keep the victors back to kill again".

The amphitheatre was also the scene of wild animal shows, with the arena transformed into animal preserves where hundreds of lions, tigers, ostriches, crocodiles, deer, etc. were baited and killed by professional hunters. Even sea battles were staged in the arena which could be filled with water. Just as the victorious gladiators were feted, so was the best charioteer at the circus. This circus was the Circus Maximus, Rome's oldest stadium – first mentioned in 329 B.C. – where in the Caesars' time 150,000 spectators would watch the two or four-horse chariots (quadriga)

has been totally destroyed by fire, earthquake and quarrying. In fact part of St Peter's is built from travertine blocks from the Colosseum and was not until the early 19th c. that Pius VII awarded the unique ruins protected status. Underneath the arena were changing cubicles and training rooms for the gladiators, cages for the wild beasts, and store-rooms, the walls of which are now visible since the collapse of the arena floor.

Ludus Magnus school for gladiators

On the Via Labicana, not far from the Coliseum, excavations have uncovered the remains of the Ludus Magnus, Rome's greatest gladiatorial school, with its practice arena and barracks for the gladiators. This is where for many years slaves, prisoners of war and a few volunteers underwent their training.

thundering round the track in great clouds of dust. Up to twelve chariots running simultaneously had usually to complete seven circuits of the 550×80m/600×88yds track. With whip in hand, reins wound around their body, feet strapped to the floor of the chariot and a dagger bound to their upper arm to cut themselves free if they fell, each charioteer tried to get ahead of the rest.

The theatres could seldom match the great spectacles which drew crowds of spectators to the amphitheatre and the circus. The theatre of Pompeius held about 27,000, that of Marcellus around 10,000 and of Balbus some 8000. They put on plays and comedies but these eventually degenerated into shallow, showy entertainments, with many special effects and stylised mime and dance pieces in garish costumes and masks, with the Chorus speaking the words.

Another generally popular pastime was to visit the baths in order to relax – men and women separately – in steam, hot and cold baths, enjoy a massage or a beauty treatment, exercise in the adjoining gymnasium, read in the reading room or simply chat and exchange the latest gossip. The way through the city passed by the showcases of the jewellers, cloth merchants, and vendors of art and furniture. Nowhere else in the ancient world had as much luxury on offer for every aspect of living as Rome. When the baths closed at sunset the citizens would go gambling, often for high stakes, or pay a visit to one of the officially regulated brothels.

The better circles would meanwhile be filling their evening with a lavish meal of seven courses to a background provided by musicians, dancers and acrobats. Delicacies from various regions of the Empire would be served, accompanied by plenty of wine, often mixed with water: hazelnuts in honey, plums from Syria, pomegranates and sausages to start; steamed giblets, figs, goose, lobsters, barbel and honeycakes as a first course; stuffed poultry, roast hare and boar, mushrooms, quail and dates as second and third courses; a roast pig stuffed with sausages as next course; veal, fruit, stuffed goose-eggs as the fifth course and, for dessert, apples from Crete, oysters, snails, mussels and puddings. Eventually, sated with pleasure, you would have your slaves carry you home in a litter, content in the knowledge that you lived in Rome, a city without equal and the centre of the world.

Domus Aurea   E 6/7

The burning of Rome in A.D. 64 proved very convenient for the Emperor Nero (see Famous People). In the huge area thus cleared of buildings he built a huge and sumptuously appointed new palace, Domus Aurea, the Golden Palace. Although the whole vast project, covering an area greater than that of the present-day Vatican City, was never completed and the magnificent Golden Palace was destroyed by a great fire in 104, the site was used by Nero's successors for other buildings. These included the Colosseum (see entry), which more or less took the place of Nero's artificial lake. Excavations which began in the Renaissance in the area between the Forum (see Foro Romano)

Viale Monte Oppio

Underground station
Colosseo (line B)

Buses
81, 85, 87

and the Esquiline Hill brought to light a whole host of works of art, frescoes and marble statues, including the famous Laocoön group, now in the Vatican Museum (open Tue.–Sun. 9am–1pm).

★E.U.R. – Esposizione Universale di Roma   H–K 10–12

Underground stations
EUR Marconi,
EUR Fermi
(line B)

Mussolini planned an enormous international exhibition that was to take place in Rome in 1942. Work was begun in 1938 headed by Marcello Piacentini and, despite being interrupted during the war years, was completed in 1951. Mussolini's plan for his "Espozione Universale di Roma" envisaged a satellite city between ancient Rome and the sea that with its modern accomplishments would outshine the old palaces of Papal Rome. Its broad streets, residential quarters, public buildings and squares covering 420ha/1038 acres in the monumental style of the Fascist era were intended as architectural pointers that would set the modernist tone. Today E.U.R with its wide green spaces ranks generally as a pleasant residential area.

Palazzo della Civiltà del Lavoro

One of the most imposing buildings of the Mussolini era is the neo-Classical Palace of Labour on the Quadrato della Concordia, a six-storey rectangular building 68m/223ft high, with 216 round-arched arcades reminiscent of the Coliseum. Its architects were La Padula, Guerrini and Romano. The double-domed Palazzo dei Congressi on Piazza John F. Kennedy is from the same period and was designed by Adalberto Libera in 1938; the atrium has frescoes of the history of Rome by Gino Severini and Achille Funi.

Palazzo dei Congressi

Evidence of the Fascist era: the monumental Palace of Labour

★ Museo della Civiltà Romana

The Museum of Roman Culture (Piazza Giiovanni Agnelli 10), opened in 1937 and housed in a building presented to the city of Rome by the Fiat company, seeks to illustrate the history of Rome using models and reconstructions. It offers an excellent overview of the development of the Roman world and of the changing architecture of Rome under the Republic and the Empire. A very special feature is the scale model (1:250) of ancient Rome at the time of Constantine the Great which was begun in 1937 by Italo Gismoni and completed in 1970. Also worth seeing are the plaster casts of Trajan's Column, made for Napoleon III in 1861.

Opening times
Tue.–Sat.
9am–1.30pm,
Thu. also 4–7pm,
Sun. 9am–1pm

★★Model of
ancient Rome

Piazza Giovanni Agnelli

1 Vestibule	23 Central administration	39 Tombs
2 Atrium	24 The Imperial court	40 Houses
3 Hall of Honour	25 The Roman triumph	41 Museum administration
4 Map of Roman Empire	26 Provinces of the Roman	and records
5 Roman legends; the	Empire	42 Family life
earliest Roman culture	27 Regions of Italy	43 Religion
6 Beginnings of the city	28 Building, tunnelling, mining	44 Portraits
7 Conquest of the	29 Baths, aqueducts,	45 Hoards of silver
Mediterranean area	fountains, cisterns	46 Roman law
8 Caesar	30 Theatres, amphitheatres,	47 Libraries
9 Augustus	arenas, sports grounds	48 Musical instruments
10 Family of Augustus; the	31 Fora, temples, basilicas	49 Literature and science
Julio-Claudian Emperors	32 Arches and gates	50 Medicine and pharmacy
11 The Flavians	33 Roads, bridges,	51 Casts of the reliefs on
12 Trajan and Hadrian	milestones, vehicles	Trajan's Column
13 Roman Emperors Antoninus	34 Gates from Aphrodisias	52 Industry and crafts
Pius to the Severans	(Asia Minor) and Leptis	53 Agriculture, stock-farming,
14 Roman Emperors from	Magna (Libya)	land surveying
Macrinus to Justinian	35 Social relations	54 Hunting, fishing, food
15 Christianity	36 Schools	55 Commerce
16–19 The Roman army	37 Model of Rome in the time	56–58 Roman art (outstanding
20–21 The Roman navy	of Constantine the Great	examples)
22 Ports	38 Plans of Roman towns	59 Column of Marcus Aurelius

Fontana dell'Acqua Felice   E 5

Location
Via Orlando
(cnr Piazza San
Bernardo)

Buses
16, 37, 60, 61, 63

The fountain, which has a figure of Moses as its central feature and is also known as the Fountain of Moses, was commissioned by Pope Sixtus V in 1585. The Pope, Felice Peretti (hence the name of the "fortunate" fountain), to whom Rome owes so many magnificent buildings, was less fortunate in his choice of a sculptor for Moses. Prospero Antiche, from Brescia, who carved the statue, is said to have died of grief, or even committed suicide, when he compared his work with Michelangelo's Moses in San Pietro in Vincoli (see entry).

★Fontana delle Tartarughe   D 6

Location
Piazza Mattei

Buses
26, 44, 58, 60, 65,
75, 170, 710, 718

The charming Fountain of the Tortoises was created by the Florentine sculptor Taddeo Landini in 1581–84 to the design of Giacomo della Porta. From the marble basin rises a base decorated with four shells, and four slender youths with outstretched arms support the upper basin. The tortoises sitting on the rim of the basin were added in the 17th c.

★★Fontana di Trevi   D 5/6

Location
Piazza di Trevi

**Underground
station**
Barberini (line A)

Buses
52, 53, 56, 58,
58b, 60, 61, 62,
71, 81, 85, 95,
116, 119, 160,
204, 492

Rome's greatest fountain, the Fontana di Trevi, stands in a small square narrowly hemmed in by buildings and was painstakingly restored in 1988-1991. It is supplied by an aqueduct originally constructed by Agrippa, the great art patron of the 1st c. B.C., to bring water to his baths, and later restored by the Popes. The fountain was created for Pope Clement XII between 1732 and 1751 by Nicolò Salvi, and is accounted his masterpiece. The fountain, 20m/65ft wide and 26m/85ft high, is built against the rear wall of the palace of the Dukes of Poli, and depicts the "kingdom of the Ocean": the sea god Oceanus (Neptune), with horses (one wild, the other docile), surrounded by Tritons and shells. The water swirls round the figures and the artificial rocks and collects in an enormous basin. The basin is full of the coins thrown into it by visitors on the basis of the old tradition that this will ensure they return to the Eternal City some day.

★Fontana del Tritone   E 5

Location
Piazza Barberini

**Underground
station**
Barberini (line A)

Buses
52, 53, 56, 58, 60,
61, 62, 71, 80, 415

The Fountain of the Triton, a masterpiece created by Bernini in 1632–37 for Pope Urban VIII, a member of the Barberini family, stands in the middle of the Piazza Barberini. Four dolphins support the Barberini coat of arms with its three bees, and on a large scallop shell sits a Triton blowing a conch shell. Opposite, at the end of the Via Veneto (see entry), is the Bee Fountain (1644), also created by Bernini for Urban VIII.

The "Kingdom of the Ocean" depicted on the fountain of Trevi ▶

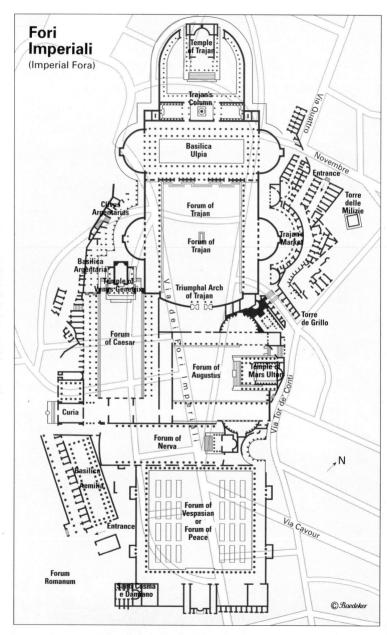

Fori Imperiali
(Imperial Fora)

Temple of Trajan

Trajan's Column

Basilica Ulpia

Forum of Trajan

Forum of Trajan

Clivus Argentarius

Basilica Argentaria

Temple of Venus Genetrix

Triumphal Arch of Trajan

Trajan's Market

Torre delle Milizie

Entrance

Via Quattro

Novembre

Torre de Grillo

Forum of Caesar

Forum of Augustus

Temple of Mars Ultor

Via dei Fori Imperiali

Via Tor de' Conti

Curia

Forum of Nerva

N

Basilica Aemilia

Entrance

Forum of Vespasian or Forum of Peace

Via Cavour

Forum Romanum

Santi Cosma e Damiano

© Baedeker

★Fori Imperiali   E 6

Large parts of the Fori Imperiali – imperial fora – are covered over by the 6-lane highway of the same name which runs alongside the Foro Romano linking the Campidoglio with the Colosseo (see entries). Discussions have been under way since 1980 about taking up the road – put in under Mussolini in 1932 – and thus giving archaeology priority over the car. The 64,000sq.m/690,000sq.ft of asphalt have been laid over ruins from the great days of the Imperium Romanum which undoubtedly would repay excavation. On the other hand, the Via dei Fori Imperiali is also one of Rome's main traffic arteries.

Via dei Fori Imperiali

Buses
11, 27, 81, 85, 87, 186

Underground station
Colosseo (line B)

★★Foro di Traiano

The Forum of the Emperor Trajan (A.D. 98–117; see Famous People), the last, largest and best preserved of the Imperial fora, comprised a considerable complex of buildings, including a temple and basilica as well as three monuments erected in honour of the Emperor himself – a trumphal arch, an equestrian statue and a victory column. Trajan's adjoining markets extended north-east up to the Quirinal Hill.

Opening times
Tue.–Sat. 9am–1.30pm (in summer Tue., Thu., Sat. also 4–7pm), Sun. 9am–1pm

The forum, designed by Apollodorus of Damascus, was begun in A.D. 107 and completed in 143. During the Middle Ages new buildings were erected in the area of the forum by the Colonna and Caetani families, among them the Torre delle Milizie (see entry) still to be seen in Via Quattro Novembre, and later the twin churches of Santa Maria di Loreto (see entry) and Santissimo Nome di Maria. Lastly, in the early 20th c., came the roads cutting through the site, the wide Via dei Fori Imperiali and a number of smaller streets.

Excavations carried out since 1928 have revealed the layout of the forum. A triumphal arch erected in A.D. 116 gave access to an open rectangular area, in the centre of which stood an equestrian statue of the Emperor. At the far end was the Basilica Ulpia, a hall measuring 130×125m/430×410ft and bearing Trajan's family name, from which justice was administered. In the present state of the site it is difficult to imagine a building of these dimensions, and indeed it was no easy matter at the time it was built to find space for it in this crowded part of central Rome. Built on to the rear of the basilica were two libraries, one for Latin and the other for Greek literature, and between the two rose Trajan's victory column. Beyond this, at the end of the forum (between the two churches dedicated to the Virgin), was a temple of the deified Trajan. Only Trajan's column is left to represent this whole complex, much admired in ancient times, dedicated to honouring the Emperor under whom the Roman Empire reached the limits of its expansion.

Trajan's column, which was extensively cleaned and restored in the Eighties, is a magnificent monument to Roman Imperial power and the skill of Roman sculptors. The victory column, 38m/125ft high and in marble from the Greek island of Paros, is covered with a spiral frieze 200m/655ft long, with over 2500 figures depicting Trajan's wars with the Dacians in 101–102 and 105–106. This frieze, with its vivid images of battling soldiers, snorting horses and the whole panoply of Roman arms and war engines, is worth studying in detail – although this is more difficult for the modern visitor than for the ancients, who could examine the reliefs from the windows of the two libraries. A spiral staircase of 185 steps runs up inside the column, lit by 43 narrow slits in the column wall. The base of the column held a golden urn containing the Emperor's ashes, and on its top stood a golden statue of Trajan. This was lost during the Middle Ages and replaced by Pope Sixtus V in 1588 with a figure of the Apostle Peter with his key.

Colonna di Traiano

The three-tiered market halls of Trajan

Mercati di Traiano	North of Trajan's Forum in a semicircle stood his three-tiered market halls. These were used both for wholesale and retail trading and served as the distribution point for state food aid. Their red-brick ruins, with high vaulted roofs, impressively round off the group of Imperial fora, rising up the slopes of the Quirinal Hill to Via Quattro Novembre. The difference in level was skilfully exploited by the architect, Apollodorus of Damascus (early 2nd c.). By setting up his markets Trajan aimed to mitigate the tax burden with cheaper food supplies and to reduce social tension through the distribution of Imperial food rations. The buildings held over 150 shops and to get an idea of what these were like look down from the Via Quattro Novembre into a well preserved ancient street of shops, some of which still have the fishmongers' water tanks.

★Foro di Augusto

Entrance Piazza del Grillo 1	So far only parts of the Forum of Augustus have been excavated. The forum was surrounded by colonnades and its central feature was the temple of Mars Ultor (Vengeful Mars). This was consecrated by Augustus in 2 B.C. to commemorate the battle of Philippi, fought in 42 B.C. to avenge the murder of Julius Caesar. This podium temple, of which three columns remain, was originally a peripteros with eight 15.3m/50ft high Corinthian columns on each side. The interior held statues of Mars and Venus, of which the plinths can still be seen, while there were statues of famous people from Roman history in the portico and a gigantic statue of Augustus (14m/46ft high) in the Aula del Colosso. The temple precinct, protected against fire by a high wall, was the scene of many state functions under Augustus. Tiberius also commissioned a triumphal arch for Drusus and Germanicus in the forum. Around 1200 the Knights of St John (later of Rhodes and
Temple of Mars Ultor	

The last remains of the Temple of Mars in the Forum of Augustus

Malta) used the ruins of the forum for their palaces. Nowadays the Priory of the Knights of Malta can be found in the Antiquarium and a former exedra.

Foro di Cesare

The Forum of Caesar, or Forum Julium, lies opposite the Forum of Augustus at the foot of the Capitol hill, with part of it now occupied by the gardens and car parks of the Via dei Fori Imperiali. It was built between 54 and 46 B.C. for Julius Caesar who was seeking to enhance his own fame while at the same time meeting the needs of Rome's citizens for whom the old Forum Romanum no longer sufficed. What is left of the original complex, which covered an area of 170×75m/ 550×250ft, conveys little of its original scale. The edge of the forum was taken up by stalls and workshops on the Clivus Argentarius, the Basilica Argentaria, which held the money-changers and the bankers, and, above all, the temple to Venus Genetrix. Nothing has survived of the forum's ornamentation which included the equestrian statue of Caesar and was described in great detail by the authors of antiquity.

Basilica Argentaria, Temple of Venus Genetrix

Foro di Nerva

The long narrow Forum of Nerva (Caesar from A.D. 96 to 98), next to the Forum of Augustus, centred on a Temple of Minerva which was demolished by Pope Paul V in 1606 to provide the marble to build the fountain on the Janiculum. All that remains are two Corinthian pillars from the right colonnade, pieces of an entablature frieze with scenes of spinning and weaving (Minerva was patron saint of crafts), and fragments of a relief.

A large model in the Museo della Città Romana showing Rome in the time of Constantine the Great

Ancient Rome

**in the time of
Constantine the Great
(4th century A.D.)**

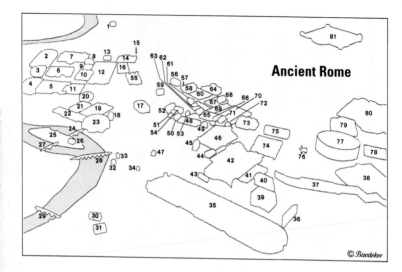

© Baedeker

Ancient Rome
in the time of Constantine the Great
(4th century A.D.)

1 Mausoleum of Augustus
2 Stadium of Domitian
  (Piazza Navona)
3 Odeon of Domitian
4 Theatre of Pompey
5 Portico of Pompey
6 Stagnum
7 Baths of Nero
8 Pantheon
9 Basilica of Neptune
10 Baths of Agrippa
11 Area Sacra
12 Saepta Iulia
13 Basilica of Matidia
14 Hadrianeum
15 Column of Marcus Aurelius
16 Shrine of Isis and Serapis
17 Temple of Jupiter Optimus
  Maximus
18 Temple of Bellona (?)
19 Portico of Octavia
20 Theatre of Balbinus
21 Portico of Philippus
22 Circus Flaminius
23 Theatre of Marcellus
24 Pons Fabricius
25 Tiber Island
26 Temple of Aesculap
27 Pons Cestius
28 Pons Aemilius

29 Pons Probi
30 Temple of Minerva
31 Temple of Diana
32 Temple of Hercules (?)
33 Temple of Portunus (?)
34 Temple of Hercules
35 Circus Maximus
36 Septizonium of
  Septimus Severus
37 Aqueduct of Claudius
38 Temple of Claudius
39 Palace of Flavier
40 Baths of Septimus Severus
41 Stadium of Domitian
42 House of Augustus
43 Paedagogium
44 Temple of Apollo
45 Temple of Cybele
46 House of Tiberius
47 Arch of Janus
48 Basilica Iulia
49 Temple of Castor
50 Temple of Saturn
51 Temple of Vespasian
52 Tabularium
53 Triumphal Arch of
  Septimus Severus
54 Temple of Concordia
55 Portico of the
  Twelve Gods

56 Temple of Trajan
57 Column of Trajan
58 Basilica Ulpia
59 Temple of Juno
60 Forum of Trajan
61 Temple of Venus Genetrix
62 Forum Iulium
63 Curia
64 Market of Trajan
65 Basilica Aemilia
66 Temple of Caesar
67 Forum of Augustus
68 Temple of the avenging Mars
69 Forum of Nerva
70 Temple of Antonio
  and Faustina
71 Forum of Peace
72 Temple of Vesta
73 Basilica of Constantine
74 Temple of Caesar (?)
75 Temple of Venus and Roma
76 Triumphal Arch
  of Constantine
77 Colosseum
78 Ludus Magnus
  Gladiator School
79 Baths of Titus
80 Baths of Trajan
81 Baths of Diocletian

Foro di Vespasiano

Next to the Forum of Nerva, at the point where Via Cavour now joins the Via dei Fori Imperiali, was the Forum of Vespasian (A.D. 69–79), in the centre of which was the Temple of Peace (after which it was also known as the Forum of Peace). The forum, of which only a few fragments remain, was built for Vespasian and financed with spoils from the Jewish War.

★★Foro Romano

D/E 6/7

Nowhere in Europe is as powerfully imbued with history as the Roman Forum. Although the surviving remains give little idea of the splendour of the Forum in ancient times, this area between the Capitol hill (see Campidoglio) to the west, the Palatine (see Palatino) to the south, and Quirinal and Viminal to the north, with its columns, some intact, others broken on the ground, its triumphal arches and ruined walls, is still immensely impressive, for it was here that for many centuries the fate of Europe was decided. For over a thousand years this great forum imposingly reflected the might of Rome and the magnificence of Roman art, the law of Rome and Rome's religion. The history of the Forum Romanum was for a long time the history of Rome and of the western world. Originally a marshy area between the hills of Rome and outside the settlement, it was later drained. The first buildings erected here were temples, one of the oldest being the Temple of Saturn, dedicated in 498 B.C. These were soon followed by various public buildings, so that this became the political centre of the city, the meeting-place of the Roman courts and the assemblies which took decisions on the internal and external affairs of the republic. This in turn led to the building of market halls where the citizens of Rome could conduct their business. The Forum thus developed into a complex of buildings serving the purposes of Rome's religious, political and commercial life, increasing in splendour as the city grew in power. Consuls and senators, Julius Caesar and subsequent Emperors vied with one another in developing and enhancing this centre of the Roman world which became the meeting-place of the peoples of Europe and the Empire. By the end of the Imperial period the Forum was a densely built-up complex in which buildings from many different centuries were mixed, which is why it is so difficult nowadays to distinguish the details of one from another.

The last monument erected in ancient times was the plain column set up in A.D. 608 for the Byzantine Emperor Phocas. After this the buildings became dilapidated and churches and fortresses were built between them. The site became a quarry for other buildings and land for grazing cattle (hence Campo Vaccino – cows' field). It was not until the 18th and 19th c. that systematic excavations brought the ancient buildings to light from under a layer of earth and rubble between 10 and 15m/30 and 50ft deep. It needs imagination (and small-scale plaster models) to summon up a picture of the Forum in Imperial times, but this in no way diminishes this place's evocative significance.

The entire area suffers considerably from the heavy traffic flowing around it, and there are therefore long-term plans for traffic-calming measures for this archaeological site and the subsequent closure of the adjoining Via dei Fori Imperiali.

Location
Via dei Fori
Imperiali

Underground station
Colosseo (line B)

Buses
11, 27, 81, 85, 87, 186

Opening times
Mon.–Sat.
9am–3pm
(6pm in summer),

The 100m/1094yds long Basilica Aemilia was extended by Consul Marcus Aemilius Paulus in A.D. 78 and renovated under Augustus after a fire. The basilica, which here probably served as a money market or court of justice, was a form of building which the Romans had taken

Basilica Aemilia

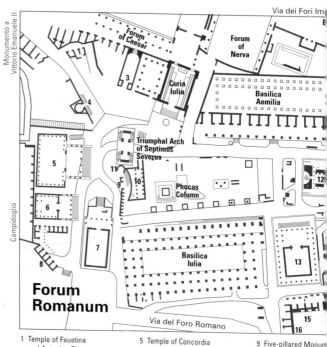

Via dei Fori Im

Forum of Caesar

Forum of Nerva

Curia Iulia

Basilica Aemilia

Triumphal Arch of Septimus Severus

Phocas Column

Basilica Iulia

Forum Romanum

Via del Foro Romano

1 Temple of Faustina and Antonius Pios
2 Lapis Niger
3 Santi Luca e Martina
4 Mamertine prisons
5 Temple of Concordia
6 Temple of Vestpasian
7 Temple of Saturn
8 Portico di Divi consenti
9 Five-pillared Monum of Diocletian
10 Rostra
11 Umbilicus Urbis
12 Temple of Caesar

over from the Greeks (basilica in Greek means something like "king's hall"). It was an oblong building with a roof and a central nave with aisles on either side. These were divided into three spaces by pillars, with an apse at the end where the judge or the hall overseer would be seated. This type of basilica, slightly amended, became the prototype of the early Christian churches.

Tempio di Antonino e Faustina

From the Via Sacra (Sacred Way) a broad flight of steps leads up to the temple of Antoninus Pius and his wife Faustina. The temple was built on the orders of the Senate in A.D. 141 in honour of the deified Empress, and was also dedicated, after her death, to Antoninus in 161. This is recorded in the inscription "Divo Antonino et Divae Faustrinae ex S(enatus) C(onsulto)". Six columns with Corinthian capitals survive from the temple along the front and a number of columns along the side. In the 12th c. the whole temple was converted into the church of San Lorenzo in Miranda, but when Emperor Charles V visited Rome in 1536 the walls built around the columns were taken down.

Curia

The Curia, west of the Basilica Aemilia and one of the best preserved ancient buildings in the Forum, was the meeting place of the Roman Senate. The first such building was erected in the time of the kings, and thereafter rebuilding was frequently necessary as a result of fires and other forms of destruction in the time of Sulla, Julius Caesar,

© Baedeker

Temple of the Dioscuri –	17 Santa Maria Antiqua	22 Santa Francesca
Castor and Pollux	18 Round Temple of Vesta	Romana
Spring of Juturna	19 Regia	23 Temple of Venus
Temple of Augustus	20 Temple of Romulus	and Roma
Horrea Agrippiana	21 Santi Cosma e Damiano	

Augustus, Diocletian, Julianus Apostata, etc. Finally in the 7th c. the Curia was converted into a church and thus preserved from further destruction. Borromini adapted its bronze doors to serve as the main doorway of St John Lateran (see San Giovanni in Laterano). The Curia, then as now a sober building and without ornament both inside and out, having been stripped in the Thirties of later additions, was for several centuries the setting for decisions governing the fate of the known world of the day. It is now used for occasional exhibitions.

The interior (27×18m/90×60ft) had seating along the sides for about 300 senators and still retains fragments of a coloured marble floor. Here, too, are displayed the Anaglyphs of Trajan, two travertine slabs with reliefs depicting the Emperor with the people.

In front of the Curia was the Comitium, the public square where the citizens of Rome assembled when political decisions were made. A black-paved area marks the place where the Lapis Niger, a block of black marble, was found. Underneath this there is a subterranean room (not open to the public) assumed in the Middle Ages to hold the tomb of Romulus. Close by is a stele, excavated in 1899, with the oldest known Latin inscription.

Lapis Niger

A prison has stood close to the Forum Romanum at the foot of the Capitoline hill since the 4th c. B.C. The Mamertine Prisons comprised two vaulted complexes, one above the other, with the lower one also called Tullianum from "tullus" – a water container. As the historians

Carcere Mamertino

The Temple of Antonius Pius and his wife Faustina

have verified, those imprisoned there included Jugurtha, King of Numidia (104 B.C., Vercingetorix, leader of the Gauls (46 B.C., and the Catiline conspirators. According to Christian legend this is also where the Apostles Peter and Paul were held and where Peter baptised the other prisoners with water from the spring in the Tullianum. This is why the church later built on this site was called San Pietro in Carcere, St Peter in Prison. The church above it, San Giuseppe dei Falegnami, is dedicated to Joseph the Carpenter.

Arco di Settimio Severo

The Senate and people of Rome could honour victorious Emperors and generals by erecting a triumphal arch, and this is precisely what they did in A.D. 203 when, opposite the church of Santi Luca e Martina, an arch was built for the Emperor Septimius Severus and his sons Caracalla and Geta after their victory over the Parthians and the desert tribes.

On the arch, 21m/69ft high and 23m/75ft wide, are four marble reliefs giving lively accounts of episodes from these wars, the figures standing out prominently from the background. Goddesses of victory with trophies and a large inscription proclaim the glory of the Emperor and his sons (though the name of Geta was later deleted).

Rostra

Umbilicus Urbis

Near the Septimius Severus arch can also be seen the remains of the Rostra, the antique orators' platform originally decorated with the prows (rostra) of captured enemy ships, and parts of a round pedestal in the ground marking the "Umbilicis Urbis", the symbolic centre (navel) of the city of Rome and the Empire.

Monument to Diocletian

The "tenth anniversary" plinth is the base of a five-column monument with reliefs of sacrificial rites celebrating the twentieth year of the reign of Diocletian and ten years of the Tetrarchy in 303 B.C..

A few yards further on are the remains of the foundations of the Altar of Vulcanus, a very old stone shrine.

Altar of Vulcanus

In front of the Rostra is the Colonna di Foca, a 13.8m/45ft high Corinthian column erected in A.D. 608 in honour of the Byzantine Emperor Phocas and in gratitude for his presentation of the Pantheon to Pope Boniface IV to be converted into a church.

Colonna di Foca

East of the column is the Lacus Curtius, the spot where myth has it that the young Roman knight Marcus Curtius saved his country by plunging into a chasm that had opened up and would only close if Rome's greatest treasure was cast in. The equestrian relief found there in 1553 could however equally well be the Sabine general Mettius Curtius who fell into a swamp here during the rape of the Sabines but was able to extricate himself.

Lacus Curtius

Only the foundations remain of the richly decorated Temple of Concord from the days of the republic but which already had been given a new appearance under Tiberius in 7 to 10 B.C. The temple commemorates the long drawn-out class war between patricians and plebeians. This was eventually settled by judicial means and the resulting concordat was finally expressed in a religious form with the building of the Temple of Concord in 366 B.C.

Tempio di Concordia

Three Corinthian pillars over 15m/49ft high mark the site of the Temple of Vespasian which the Senate had built in A.D. 79 and which was dedicated by Domitian. It held statues of the deified Emperors Vespasian and Titus.

Tempio di Vespasian

The Roman Forum's first temple was dedicated to Saturn, a god who was probably of Etruscan origin but was adopted by the Romans and

Tempio di Saturno

Triumphal Arch of Septimus Severus

The round Temple of Vesta

97

worshipped as the supreme god. Built about 498 B.C., soon after the expulsion of the Tarquins, the temple was one of the most important and most venerated of republican Rome. It was several times destroyed by fire (the last occasion being in the 3rd c. A.D.) but was repeatedly rebuilt. It is represented by eight columns with Ionic capitals, now much weathered. Under the Republic the state treasury was kept in this temple. The celebration of the Saturnalia, observed annually on December 17th, set out from this temple.

Miliarium Aureum

Adjoining the temple is a fragment of the Miliarium Aureum, the "Golden Milestone", which was the starting point of the Via Sacra and all the Roman consular roads. Beginning in 20 B.C. the stone gave, in golden letters, the distances from Rome to the various provinces of the Empire.

Portico of the Divi consenti

Nine fine columns with an entablature have been retained as fragments of a portico bearing figures depicting the twelve main Roman gods of Greek origin – Jupiter, Juno, Neptune, Minerva, Apollo, Diana, Mars, Venus, Vulcanus, Vesta, Mercury and Ceres.

Tabularium

The Tabularium, the state archive of Rome established by Consul Q. Lutatius Catulus in 78 B.C., stood at the entrance to the Capitol, with its façade of arches and Doric half-columns facing the Forum Romanum. Nowadays it forms the ground floor of the Palazzo dei Senatori (see Campidoglio).

Basilica Iulia

This large basilica 101m/331ft long and 49m/161ft wide was where the high court for civil cases was held in the three-storey middle section of the five parts of the building, based on a project of Caesar's from between 54 and 46 B.C. Augustus restored the building after a fire and then it was rebuilt again in 283.

Tempio di Castore e Polluce

The Dioscuri – Castor and Pollux – are the subject of numerous myths, partly of Greek and partly of Etruscan origin. The "Heavenly Twins" were originally thought to be the sons of the King of Sparta and Leda, and later even the offspring of Leda and Zeus. There are ancient tales of healing (along with the god Aesculapius), beautiful women (Helen of Troy was supposed to be their sister) and two young men appearing in battle on two white horses. The first temple of Castor and Pollux was built in 484 B.C. by the son of the dictator Aulus Postumius in thanksgiving for the defeat of the Tarquins at Lake Regillus, which was attributed to the help of the Dioscuri. According to legend, after their appearance on the battlefield Castor and Pollux rode to Rome and watered their horses at the spring of Juturna in the Forum, the Lacus Juturnae. In about 1900 archaeologists found actual statues of the Dioscuri and Aesculapius in the holy spring, named after the Italian water nymph Juturna, to the east of the temple. The temple was rebuilt in the reign of Tiberius (1st c. A.D.) as a peripteros and the three Corinthian columns left from this temple are popularly known as the "Three Sisters".

Juturna spring

Santa Maria Antiqua

The church of Santa Maria Antiqua to the south of the forum is the oldest (hence the name) and most important Christian building in the Forum Romanum. Nowadays badly damaged and rarely open to the public, it was converted from an Imperial building into a church in the 6th c. and richly furnished in the 8th c. by various Popes (John VII, Zacharias and Paul I). It then fell into a state of dilapidation before being restored in the 13th c. This extensive complex at the foot of the Palatine hill is of interest for its architecture and, above all, for its frescoes. These date from various periods in the 6th to 8th c. and include the Virgin as Queen of Heaven in the atrium, a series of Old Testament scenes in the left aisle and images of patrons and martyrs in the chapel left of the presbytery.

In ancient times the round Temple of Vesta in the Forum – there is another temple of Vesta in the Forum Boarium – contained the "Sacred Fire" which was guarded by the Vestals, six virgins chosen from Rome's most patrician families who served in the temple between the ages of 10 and 14. The Romans attached great importance to this "eternal fire"; on the first day of the new year (March 1st) they extinguished the fires in their houses and lit new ones from the flame in the temple of Vesta. The present remains date from the time of Septimius Severus (A.D.193–211) and still clearly show that the temple was circular with (20) slender columns supporting the roof which had an opening in the centre to let out the smoke from the sacred flame.

Tempio di Vesta

Adjoining the Temple of Vesta was the House of the Vestal Virgins, also built by Septimius Severus. It consisted of a large atrium, the rooms of the young guardians of the sacred flame, and various offices. The outline of the building can still clearly be seen, with remains of the foundations and many plinths for statues (those that have been preserved are on show in several of Rome's museums). According to Latin authors, the Palladium, an image of Pallas Athene which Aeneas was said to have brought from Troy to Latium, was kept in the House of the Vestals. The Vestal Virgins, who enjoyed high social esteem, could only leave their house on ceremonial occasions. If they crossed the path of someone who had been condemned to death that person would be pardoned. On the other hand, if a virgin broke her vow of chastity she would be buried alive in the Field of Villains.

Atrium Vestae

The Temple of Julius Caesar, which Augustus erected in memory of his adoptive father in 29 B.C. on the spot where Caesar's body had been burned, had already been started in 42 B.C. The little that is left is indicative of a simple Ionic Prostyle. The family dead were traditionally venerated as Divi (i.e. divine) by their descendants but, with the

Tempio di Caesare

The House of the Vestal Virgins, the young guardians of the sacred flame

Temple of Julius Caesar, Augustus for the first time combined private ritual with state ceremonial. Consequently thereafter the deification of the Imperial family by the Senate became the general rule. The nearby foundations of a triumphal arch for Augustus also date from 29 B.C.

Regia

This may well have been the official base of the Pontifex Maximus, the chief priest, where sacred artefacts and records such as the archives were kept.

Santi Cosma e Damiano

The church of the early martyrs Cosmas and Damian, supposedly twin brothers from Syria who dispensed free medicine, dates from the conversion in the 6th c. by Felix IV of the Templum Sacrae Urbis from Vespasian's forum (see Fori Imperiali); this accounts for it having just a single nave. It has a 17th c. Baroque interior; other interesting features include the wooden ceiling (1632), a medieval Easter lantern and above all Pope Felix IV's mosaics on the triumphal arch (scenes from Revelations) and in the apse where Christ in the centre is passing the scrolls of God's law to the Apostles Peter and Paul; they are flanked by the church's patron saints, Cosmas and Damian, St Theodore and Pope Felix himself. The Nativity in an adjacent room is one of Rome's finest. (Entrance: Via dei Fori Imperiali).

Basilica di Massenzio

The Basilica of Maxentius, or Constantine, was begun as courts of justice in A.D. 306–312 by Maxentius and completed in 330 by Constantine after considerable alterations. Even though only ruins remain they still give a good impression of what was once a most imposing building which, like other Roman basilicas, served both as a law court and a place of business. The central aisle, with a vaulted roof, measured 60×25m/220×80ft, and rose to a height of 35m/115ft;

View from the Via Sacra over the Forum to the Palatine

the lateral aisles were 24.5m/80ft high. The basilica was modelled on the enormous Baths of the Emperors Caracalla and Diocletian. The main piers were fronted by massive Corinthian columns, one of which, bearing a statue of the Virgin, now stands in front of the church of Santa Maria Maggiore (see entry). The ruin of the basilica was hastened when Pope Honorius I removed the bronze tiles in the 7th c. and used them to roof Old St Peter's; an earthquake in the 9th c. caused further damage. Fragments of a colossal statue of Constantine which once stood in the great west apse can be seen nowadays in the courtyard of Constantine's Palace.

To replace the church of Santa Maria Antiqua a new church dedicated to the Virgin, Santa Maria Nuova, was built in the second half of the 10th c. on the other side of the Forum, on what is now the Via dei Fori Imperiali. The church occupied part of the site of the temple of Venus and Roma. The tower, a characteristic example of a medieval Roman campanile, was added in the 13th c. The church received its present name when it was dedicated to the foundress of the Oblates, St Frances of Rome. Notable features of the interior, which is richly adorned with marble, stucco and pictures, are the Confessio, the apse mosaic and the 6th c. Madonna on the high altar. St Luke is supposed to have been prompted by the Virgin/to paint this first picture of her, which is why he is traditionally the patron saint of artists. (Entrance: Via dei Fori Imperiali).

Santa Francesca Romana

Ancient Rome's greatest temple is thought to have been designed by Hadrian. It was built as a twin shrine on a podium 145×100m/476×328ft surrounded by a portico of 150 columns. The western half of the temple was dedicated to Roma, patroness of the city, while the eastern half was for Venus, the mother of the Roman Emperors, with the two statues side by side in the apse.

Tempio di Venus e Roma

The arch of Titus, at the beginning of the Via Sacra, is the oldest of the remaining Roman triumphal arches. According to the dedication, it was erected after the death of Emperor Titus by his successor Domitian.

Arco di Tito

Titus, son of the Emperor Vespasian, was the Roman general who captured Jerusalem in the year 70, destroyed its temple and thus set in train the Jewish diaspora. The reliefs on the arch (15.4m/50ft high and 13.5m/44ft wide with a single arch), which served as a model for similar arches throughout the Western world, depict both this conquest and the victorious general's triumphal procession to the Capitol. Titus (who only became Emperor in 79) is shown in his war chariot, with the Goddess Roma and the Goddess of Victory with the laurel wreath, together with the spoils of the Jewish War – the seven-branched candlestick, the table with the shewbread and trumpets from the treasury of the Temple.

★Galleria Colonna (Palazzo Colonna)   D 5/6

The huge palace of the Colonnas, one of Rome's leading patrician families, which produced Pope Martin V (1417–31) and other notables, was begun in the 15th c. and completed after successive extensions in 1730. It also encompasses the church of Santi Apostoli (see entry) and the Galleria Colonna, built by Antonio del Grande and Girolamo Fontana in the 17th c.

The gallery contains some classical sculpture but its main feature is a famous collection of pictures first assembled by Cardinal Girolamo Colonna. This consists chiefly of works by 16th to 18th c. masters and includes works by Pietro da Cortona, Paolo Veronese's "Portrait of a

Address
Via della
Pilotta 17

Buses
56, 57, 60, 62, 64,
65, 70, 71, 75, 81
85, 88, 90, 95, 170

Opening times
Sat. 9am–1pm
(closed in Aug.)

Nobleman", Tintoretto's "Portrait of Onofrio Panvinio" and "Narcissus", the "Portrait of Lucrezia Tomacelli Colonna" attributed to Van Dyke and a ceiling painting by Sebastiano Ricci. There are also paintings recording the achievements of the Colonna family such as Marcantonio Colonna's victory over the Turks as commander of the European fleet at the battle of Lepanto in 1571.

Galleria Nazionale d'Arte Antica

See Palazzo Barberini
See Palazzo Corsini

★Galleria Nazionale d'Arte Moderna   D 4

Address
Viale delle Belle
Arti 131

Buses
13, 306, 926

Trams
19, 30, 225

Opening times
Tue.–Sat.
9am–7pm
Sun. 9am–1pm

The National Gallery of Modern Art, designed by Cesare Bazzani in 1911 and further extended in 1988, has a major collection of works by 19th and 20th c. Italian painters and sculptors. Only 25 of the massive building's 70 rooms are currently open to the public, and of these two are used for temporary exhibitions of mostly contemporary art. The gallery provides an overview of both Italian and international art since 1800, although some leading figures are missing and others are represented only by minor works.

The Italian artists include Canova, Induno, Caffi, Dalbono, Gigante, Morelli, Carrà, Maffai and Tozzi, while the rest of Europe is represented by Giacometti, Appel, Klee, Mirò and Max Ernst and, mostly from France, Degas, Cézanne, Monet, Rodin and Van Gogh. Of particular interest are works by the Macchiaioli, a group of al fresco painters who came together at Livorno in Tuscany and developed a style similar to the Impressionists. The sculpture on show includes pieces by Marino Marini, Giacomo Manzù, Giorgio de Chirico, Henry Moore and Tinguely. The gallery courtyard is a good place to relax and contemplate Antoine Bourdell's "Bowman" in a setting of trailing ivy and roses.

★Il Gesù   D 6

Location
Piazza del Gesó

Buses
46, 56, 60, 62, 64,
65, 70, 75, 81, 88,
90, 170

The impetus for building Il Gesó, the principal church of the Jesuits, came from Ignatius Loyola, founder in 1540 of the Society of Jesus, an order which spread quickly throughout the Catholic countries of Europe and organised the Counter Reformation. Adjoining the church is the house (now a Jesuit college) where Loyola was living at that time. Cardinal Alessandro Farnese, whose heraldic lilies are very much in evidence throughout the church, commissioned the architect Vignola to plan and execute the church, which was completed by members of the Society. The basic innovation of the design was to set a dome over the crossing of the nave and transepts of a basilica modelled on earlier Roman, Christian and medieval church buildings. Il Gesó was subsequently much copied both in terms of its design and its detail.

Façade

The façade by Giacomo della Porta, completed in 1575, shows both Renaissance and Baroque features. The two statues represent the order's founder, Ignatius Loyola, and St Francis Xavier, its much venerated missionary to Japan and the East Indies.

*The Galleria Nazionale d'Arte Moderne houses works by Italian ▶
and international artists of the 19th and 20th centuries*

Tomb of Ignatius of Loyola, founder of the Society of Jesus

Interior

The interior is notable for its unified effect. Flanking the nave are side chapels, which seem almost cut off from the body of the church, and beyond the spacious transepts is the choir, terminating in an apse. The decoration of the interior is of great richness, with variegated marble, sculpture, bronze statues, stucco ornament, gilding and frescoes. In the barrel vaulting of the nave is a painting of the "Triumph of the Name of Jesus", which glorifies the great missionary achievements of the Jesuits. The altars and tombs of the saints of the Jesuit order are particularly worth looking at. The south transept holds the altar of St Francis Xavier by Pietro da Cortona (1674–1678); to the right of the altar is the monument of St Robert Bellarmin, with a bust by Bernini (1622); the north transept has the magnificent altar and tomb of the order's founder, St Ignatius (1491–1556), by Andrea Pozzo (1696–1700). The present statue of the saint is a copy of the silver original by Pierre Legros, which Pope Pius VII was forced to melt down for the payment of reparations to Napoleon under the Treaty of Tolentino.

★Gianicolo (Ianiculum)   B/C 6/7

Bus
41

The Passeggiata del Gianicolo, the road running round the Gianicolo hill, begins at the Porta San Pancrazio and ends at the Piazza della Rovere on the Tiber near the Vatican (see entry). This road, lined with busts of patriots of the Roman Republic, offers probably the very best views over the inner city and beyond to the suburbs and surrounding hills.

In the middle of the Piazza Garibaldi stands the monumental statue of Giuseppe Garibaldi who led the struggle for the unification of Italy

(1870). A monument to his wife, Anita Garibaldi, her hair streaming behind her, can be seen a short distance to the north. Punctually on the stroke of twelve an Austrian cannon fires the shot that resounds far across Rome to mark midday. From the square's terraces there is a superb panoramic view of the city. The little Gianicolo beacon tower dates from 1911.

Isola Tiberina   D 7

Legend has it that a heavily laden ship once sank at the spot which is now Tiber Island; the island actually does look rather like a huge vessel in the middle of the river. The obelisk which once stood on the island must have seemed like a ship's mast. Another historical explanation is that the island was formed from mud built up from grain residues after the expulsion of the Tarquins. About 200 B.C. this was where they worshipped Aesculapius, the god of healing, and his sacred snakes – his boat is supposed to have landed here according to another legend.

Buses
15, 23, 26, 44, 56, 60, 65, 75, 170, 710, 718, 719, 774

The existence of the island made this the best place for bridging the Tiber. In 62 B.C. the consul Fabricius built the Ponte Fabrico, Rome's oldest surviving bridge, which links the island with the left bank of the river and the Capitol. It is popularly known as the Ponte dei Quattro Capi ("Bridge of the Four Heads") after two four-sided heads of Hermes on the bank side of the bridge.

Ponte Fabricio

On the island are the Fatebenefratelli Hospital – maintaining the tradition of healing associated with Aesculapius – and the church of San Bartolomeo, built at the end of the 10th c. by the Emperor Otto III on the ruins of the temple of Aesculapius and restored in the Baroque period. Notable features of the church are the beautiful Romanesque campanile and a marble font at the entrance to the chancel (probably over the spring belonging to the ancient sanctuary) carved with figures of Christ, St Adalbert of Bohemia, an Apostle (probably Bartholomew) and Otto III.

San Bartolomeo

The island is linked with the right bank of the Tiber (Trastevere) by the Ponte Cestio, built by Lucius Cestius in 46 B.C., and reinstated by various emperors.

Ponte Cestio

To the south of the Isola Tiberina, in the river, is the Ponte Rotto ("Broken Bridge"), all that remains of the Pons Aemilius, which was begun in timber by the censors Aemilius Lepidus and Fulvus Nobilior in 179 B.C. and completed as an arched stone bridge in 142, the first of its kind in Rome.

Ponte Rotto

Largo di Torre Argentina   D 6

In the centre of the Largo di Torre Argentina, a few feet below the level of this busy square with its heavy traffic, is the Largo Argentina temple precinct. The name Torre Argentina is derived from the tower of the house nearby at 44 Via del Sudario which was occupied by a certain Burckhardt of Strasbourg (Argentinensis) who was Papal master of ceremonies in the early 16th c. Another theory is that the square got its name from the shops of the local silversmiths (argentarii). The four temples which were excavated here in 1926–30 form one of the few such complexes from the republican period. They can be separated out as follows:

Buses
26, 44, 46, 56, 60, 62, 64, 65, 70, 75, 87, 94, 170, 710, 718, 719

Temple A (near the bus stops), which is rectangular, with 15 columns still standing, and which incorporated the medieval church of San Nicola dei Cesarini (since demolished).

The adjoining Temple B, circular and with six columns, which held a seated effigy of the goddess Juno.

Temple C, also rectangular but the smallest and oldest (4th or 3rd c. B.C.) of the four, and on a lower level than the others.

Lastly, Temple D, part of which is under the carriageway.

It is not known for certain which gods these temples were dedicated to.

Mausoleo di Augusto   D 5

Location
Piazza Augusto
Imperatore

Buses
2, 26, 81, 90, 90b,
115, 911

Opening times
Information:
tel. 67 10 20 70

The present appearance of the Piazza Augusto Imperatore gives little hint that for a long time this was at the centre of the history of Rome's history. Here, some years before his death, the Emperor Augustus constructed a mausoleum for himself and his family (the Julian-Claudians). This took the form of an enormous mound 89m/290ft in diameter, of the kind used for the burial of kings and princes in the Mediterranean area since prehistoric times.

In front of the entrance stood two Egyptian obelisks, now to be seen behind the church of Santa Maria Maggiore (see entry) and in the Piazza del Quirinale (see entry). By the entrance were the "Res Gestae", bronze tablets on which Augustus recorded the achievements of his reign. (The original tablets are lost, but their text has been preserved in inscriptions.) During the Middle Ages the mausoleum was used by the Colonna family as a fortress, but the bastion was demolished by Pope Gregory IX in 1241. Thereafter the mausoleum became a vineyard, a garden, an amphitheatre and even a concert hall, before being restored to its original state in 1936.

Monte Testaccio   D 8

★Lively artistic
and intellectual
quarter

Buses
27, 92

Between the Tiber and the Porta San Paolo is a small hill, 35m/115ft high and about 850m/930yds in circumference. This "heap of broken pottery" dates back to the Roman Republic when this was a site for rubbish made up mostly of earthenware shards from the warehouses on the Tiber waterfront. In ancient times this was the site of big shopping arcades with the Portus Aemilius (2nd c. B.C.), a street of shops 487m/530yd long. A wooden cross on the summit is a reminder that passion plays were staged here in the Middle Ages. Nowadays visitors to Rome will find that the hill appears to have little to recommend it: a dreary pattern of narrow streets, a view of the gasworks in the direction of Ostiense, big tenement blocks between here and the Tiber, and between the Ponte Testaccio and a railway bridge the less than appealing bulk of the Mattatoio, now closed down, but formerly the city's abbattoir which was praised as a successful example of functional aesthetics when it was opened in 1891. Despite all this many artists and intellectuals have been drawn to settle here, and the Testaccio quarter has become a popular place with visitors who can wander round the lively colourful market on the Piazza Testaccio, and at the weekend enjoy live music in establishments such as the Caffé Latino, the Caruso or the Alibi. And here on the hill, which is honeycombed with wine-cellars, are unassuming eating places with good plain food for the local workers side by side with refined nouvelle cuisine to suit the discriminating new bourgeoisie.

The large white National Monument on the Piazza Venezia commemorates Victor Emmanuel II and Italy's independence

★Monumento Nazionale a Vittorio Emanuele II   D 6

The great gleaming white National Monument to Victor Emmanuel II on the Piazza Veneziana (see entry) was designed by Count Giuseppe Sacconi and built between 1885 and 1911 to celebrate Italy's independence in 1870 and commemorate Victor Emmanuel II (d. 1878). As the first King of a united Italy, he is represented in the centre by Chiaradia's equestrian bronze. The enormous monument – on whose merits opinions differ – is 135m/440ft wide by 130m/425ft deep and reaches a height of 70m/230ft. Half-way up are the "Altar of the Fatherland" and, since 1921, the Tomb of the Unknown Soldier, with its eternal flame, banners and coats of arms. The eastern part of the Monument houses the Museo Centrale dei Risorgimento (entrance Via San Pietro in Carcere) which traces the history of Italy from the late 18th c. to the First World War (open. Tue.–Sun. 9am–1.30pm).

Location
Piazza Venezia

Buses
44, 45, 46, 56, 60, 62, 65, 70, 75, 90, 181, 186, 710, 718, 719

Museo Centrale
del Risorgimento

★Mosque   F1/2

Ten years after building commenced Rome's grand mosque, designed by top Italian architect Paolo Portoghesi, was consecrated in June 1995. This post-modern building, a blend of many styles, can hold around 2500 believers. It has a 26m/85ft tall lead-covered central dome, 16 other smaller domes, and the crescent-topped minaret rises to 30m/98ft. Western Europe's biggest mosque, at 30,000sq.m/32,292sq.ft, it also has a cultural centre and student hostel, and can be visited on weekdays from 10am to 1pm.

Location
Monte Antenne

Bus
230

Mura Aureliane   B 6/7– C 7

Aurelian
city walls

The city walls built by the Emperor Aurelius in A.D. 270–275 as a second line of defence for the city, which had expanded well beyond the Severian walls, was intended to protect Rome against new dangers from the Empire's northern provinces. Here the main threat came from the Goths who in A.D. 268 had pushed forward from the Po Valley into Umbria. The Aurelian city walls ran for some 20km/12½ miles. They were about 4m/13ft thick and originally stood 7.2m/24ft high, but were later raised by Stilicho, the great general to the Emperor Honorius (A.D. 395–423), to 10.6m/35ft and reinforced by 380 towers at intervals of about 30m/33yds; they contained 16 gates. The very length of the walls, however, meant that they were rarely called upon to serve their military function. They were kept in repair until the 19th c. and although parts were quarried in the last 100 years or so, some sections have been preserved and there are places where it is possible to walk along the top.

Museo della Mura

The history of the walls is recounted in the Museo della Mura (Via di Porta San Sebastiano 18; open Tue.–Sun. 9am–1.30pm).

Castro Pretorio
F/G 5

In A.D. 23 Sejanus, chief minister to Tiberius, built a barracks for the Praetorian Guard, the Emperor's personal bodyguards. This covered a 460×300m/1510×985ft site on what is now the Via Castro Pretorio and, along with its fortifications, was incorporated by Aurelianus into his city wall.

**Piramide di
Caio Cestio**
D 8

The Pyramid of Cestius on the Piazza di Porta San Paolo was also incorporated into the Aurelian Walls, together with the Porta San Paolo, the ancient Porta Ostiense. The pyramid was built in 12–11 B.C.

The Pyramid of Cestius built of Travertine and Carrara marble

as the tomb of Caius Cestius, who had been praetor, tribune of the people and one of the Septemviri Epulones, the committee of seven which organised religious festive banquets. The pyramid, 22m/72ft square and 27m/89ft high, is faced with Carrara marble and was built, as the incription records, within the space of 330 days. The tip of the pyramid is said to have originally been gilded. The tomb chamber inside the pyramid measures 6×4m/20×13ft. A similar tomb stood near the Castel Sant'Angelo (see entry) until the early 16th c.

The Cimitero degli Stranieri acattolico close to the Pyramid and within the Aurelian walls is Rome's Protestant cemetery. Also known as the English Cemetery it holds the graves of two celebrated English poets, John Keats who died in Rome in 1821 aged only 25, and his friend Percy Bysshe Shelley (1792–1822) who drowned a year later in a storm in the Gulf of La Spezia.

Cimitero degli Stranieri acattolico (Protestant cemetery)

The Porta Maggiore, now surrounded by the swirl of modern traffic on the Piazza Maggiore, was one of the most imposing structures in ancient Rome. It was built by the Emperor Claudius in A.D. 52 where the roads to Prenesta (Via Prenestina to Palestrina) and Labici (Casilina) forked and passed under two aqueducts, the Aqua Claudia and the Anio Novus (the River Aniene). The Great Gate only became part of the city wall under Aurelianus. Nearby is the tomb of master baker Virgilius Eurysaces and his wife.

Porta Maggiore

G 6/7

The Porta Pia, the city gate on the Piazza Porta Pia near the ancient Porta Nomentana, was built by Michelangelo for the Medici Pope Pius IV in 1561–64. It is particularly dear to Italian patriots because it was near here on 20 September 1870 that Italian troops entered the Papal city; for the Papacy, however, the memories are more painful since this heralded the end of the Pope's temporal authority in the Papal State.

Porta Pia

F 5

This gate in the Aurelian Walls on the Via Appia (see entry) was refortified by Emperor Honorius at the end of the 4th c. A.D. because of the increasing threat to Rome from the Germanic tribes, and then restored again in the 6th c. by Belisarius and Narses. The Porta Appia, later renamed after the church of St Sebastian outside the city on the Via Appia, was the main point of entry to Rome. The so-called Arch of Drusus (Arco di Druso) in front of the gate probably dates from the time of Trajan and was built under Caracalla to support an aqueduct.

Porta San Sebastiano (formerly Porta Appia)

F 8

The Porta Tiburtina, the city gate on the Via Tiburtina, the road to Tivoli (see entry), was originally built in the reign of Augustus as an arch supporting the Marcia, Tepula and Julia aqueducts. A gate flanked by towers was built in front of the arch in the reign of Honorius (early 5th c.).

Porta Tiburtina

G 6

Museo Barracco (Palazzo della Piccola Farnesina)   C 6

The Museo Barracco, housed in the Palazzo della Piccola Farnesina, was presented to the city by Baron Giovanni Barracco in 1902. It contains a small but very interesting collection of Assyrian, Egyptian, Babylonian, Greek, Etruscan and Roman sculpture, both originals and copies, illustrating the development of ancient art in the pre-Christian era. Particularly notable are some Assyrian reliefs of the 7th c. B.C., a sphinx with the head of Queen Hatshepsut (15th c. B.C.), Greek statues of the early Classical period and Etruscan cippi. Also of interest are the head of the Diadumenos (second half of the 5th c. B.C.) by Polycletus, the head of an Apollo (mid 5th c. B.C.) ascribed to Phidias, a bust of Epicurus (c. 270 B.C.), the head of the Lycian Apollo, the "Wounded Bitch" (Lysippus), and a head of Alexander Helios (late 4th c. B.C.).

Location
Corso Vittorio Emanuele II 168

Buses
46, 62, 64

Opening times
Tue.–Sat. 9am–2pm (Tue., Thur. also 5–8pm); Sun. 10am–1pm

Museo Capitolino

See Campidoglio

Museo della Civiltà Romana

See E.U.R.

★Museo Nazionale Etrusco di Villa Giulia D 4

Location
Piazzale di Villa
Giulia 9

Buses
225, 926

Trams
19, 30

Opening times
Tue.–Sat.
9am–7pm,
Sun. 9am–
1.30pm

The Villa Giulia, built by Vignola between 1551 and 1553 for Pope Julius III, has housed the national Etruscan collection since 1889. On display are finds from the Etruscan sites of Latium, south Etruria and Umbria. They give an excellent impression of the high standard of art and culture attained by this mysterious people, whose achievements the Romans deliberately obscured. The main area of Etruscan settlement was the northern part of present-day Latium.

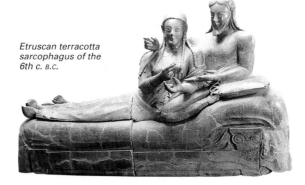

Etruscan terracotta sarcophagus of the 6th c. B.C.

★Museo Nazionale delle Paste Alimentari (Palazzo Scanderberg) E 6

Location
Piazza
Scanderberg 117

Underground station
Barberini (line A)

Buses
52, 53, 56, 58,
58b, 60, 61, 62,
71, 81, 85, 95,
116, 119, 160,
204, 492

Opening times
Mon.–Fri.
9.30am–12.30pm,
4–7pm, Sat.
9.30am–12.30pm

Situated only a few steps from the Fontana di Trevi (see entry), the National Pasta Museum, a foundation of the pasta makers Agnesi, opened in 1994. Here in a mecca for pasta lovers you can learn everything there is to know about Italy's favourite food.

Fifteen cleverly arranged rooms containing displays, models and pasta-related exhibits illustrate the story of pasta from a historical as well as a dietary point of view. In addition to having the difference between hard and soft wheat explained, visitors learn that the Etruscans in nearby Cerveteri were already familiar with "golden semolina", and that as early as 1154, a century before Marco Polo, there is a reference to pasta "in the shape of threads" in Norman Sicily. "Macaronis" are mentioned in Genoa in 1279, the super-thin vermicelli was prepared for the first time in Pisa in 1284, and in the 14th c. there was already a guild of pasta makers in Florence. In heavily-populated 16th c. Naples, the satisfying easily stored foodstuff became a staple of the diet. Its advantages were obvious. Rolled, cut and imaginatively moulded, the dough could simply be left to dry in the blazing sun. Salt-free to avoid attracting moisture, once dry it was easily stored, taking up little room. It could then be freshly prepared in boiling – and hence bacteria-free – water. In the process of cooking it regains its weight threefold, one part of pasta absorbing two parts of water; and of course the idea is that it remains "al dente", a firm texture to bite on being essential. In addition to tracing the development of pasta manufacturing and displaying hundreds of pasta creations, there are also some fascinating contemporary photographs of famous people enjoying pasta. Among them are film stars such as Ingrid Bergman, the comedian Toto and, of course, the luscious Sophia Loren. Who, after all, could be a better advert for Italian pasta?

★★Museo Nazionale Romano o delle Terme F 5

Founded in 1889, this museum of Greek and Roman art was previously accommodated in its entirety in the Baths of Diocletian (see entry). But as the collection has grown and the demands made on space by modern exhibitions have increased, it has had to expand into several different premises. Part is now housed in the Palazzo Massimo opposite, which opened its doors at the start of 1995; in the next year or two the Palazzo Altemps in the Via San Apollinare will become home to the Ludovisi Collection. The precise arrangement of the museum is still to be settled so it is impossible to do more here than draw visitors' attention to the most important exhibits.

Location
Piazza dei Cinquecento 68 and 79

Underground station
Termini

Opening times
Tue.–Sat. 9am–2pm, Sun. 9am–1pm

The nucleus of the museum in the Terme di Diocleziano comprises the collections of Prince Ludovisi and the German Jesuit Athanasius Kircher. Following rearrangement the emphasis will be on finds from the imperial thermae, together with reliefs, sarcophagi and

Terme di Diocleziano
Piazza dei Cinquecento 79

A collection of ancient sculptures in the Baths of Diocletian

epigraphs. Of particular note among the mosaics, stucco-work and frescoes is a mural from the Villa of Livia in Prima Porta. The Great Cloister of 1565, embellished by a fountain, contains marble sculptures, architectural fragments, elaborate mosaics and inscriptions.

Palazzo Massimo

Piazza dei
Cinquecento 79

Built in 1885–87 for Massimiliano Massimo, this palace is to house the main body of the museum. Exhibits are distributed over four floors. The basement contains a collection of medallions. Arranged chronologically on the ground and first floors are sculptures dating from the early Republic to the 4th c. A.D. The second floor is to be given over to mosaics, stucco-work and frescoes including the mural from the Villa of Livia currently displayed in the Baths of Diocletian.

Highlights of
the collection

Among the highlights of the collection are pre-Christian and Christian sarcophagi and a great range of Greek, Hellenistic and Roman sculpture, including an Apollo, a Nereid, the "Young Dancing Girl", the "Discus Thrower" from Castel Porziano, "The Wounded Niobe" from the Gardens of Sallust (5th c. B.C.), the Venus of Cyrene (4th c. B.C.), the Ephebe of Subiaco (3rd c. B.C.), a "Defeated Boxer" (3rd c. B.C.), the "Maiden of Anzio", the Lancellotti "Discus Thrower" (an excellent copy of the statue by Myron), and the Ostia Altar.

Of special interest from the Ludovisi Collection, earmarked for rehousing in a newly restored Palazzo Altemps probably by the end of the century, are the so-called "Ludovisi Throne" (5th c. B.C.) and statues of "The Dying Galatian", Ares, Athena Parthenos (a copy of Phidias' statue in the Parthenon), Juno, and Orestes and Electra.

Museo di Roma (Palazzo Braschi)   C 6

Location
Piazza San
Pantaleo 10

Buses
46, 62, 64

Opening times
Tue.–Sat.
9am–2pm
(Tue., Thur.
also 5–8pm),
Sun. 9am–1pm

The Palazzo Braschi, built from 1792 onwards for the Braschi family, relatives of Pope Pius VI, has since 1952 housed a collection of paintings, drawings, watercolours and prints illustrating the history of the city of Rome. There are also sculptures, terracotta figures, majolica, tapestries, costumes and a variety of other exhibits including Pope Pius IX's private train (of 1850) and two state carriages. The items in the museum's 51 rooms are intended to illuminate Roman life in medieval and modern times, as well as the city's development and history.

The remnants of a figural group including statues of Menelaus and Patroclus were erected on the instructions of Cardinal Caraffa to mark the site of an earlier building.

Museo Torlonia   C 6

Location
Via Corsini 5

Buses
23, 28, 65

The Museo Torlonia is one of the largest private collections of antiquities in Europe, with more than 600 pieces of sculpture. The collection was begun by Giovanni Raimondo Torlonia (1754–1829), a wealthy Roman, who acquired a number of private collections to which he added material found in excavations on his estate.

The museum can be viewed by appointment only; apply to the Amministrazione Torlonia, Via della Conciliazione 30.

Oratorio di San Giovanni in Oleo   F 8

Location
Via di Porta San
Sebastiano

The Oratory of St John "in the Oil" is a small octagonal chapel built originally by Bramante at the beginning of the 16th c. on the remains of an earlier building and later embellished by Borromini. Here, according to legend, St John was thrown into boiling oil but emerged unscathed, thereafter being banished to Patmos. (If the Oratory is closed, apply to the missionary college at No. 17.)

Ostia (Day excursion)

The once beautiful resort of Ostia remains a favourite outing for the Romans, and so must be reckoned among the most popular beaches and promenades of the Italian peninsula. Yet in recent times the seaside town of Ostia has grown to be almost a city in its own right, with a population approaching 55,000. Since most of its sewage is discharged into the sea, where it joins sewage from Rome carried down by the Tiber, sea bathing is not recommended.

Location
20km/13 miles
south of Rome

Train
Rome – Ostia
Lido (branch of
Metro line B)

★★Ostia Antica

No site in the neighbourhood of Rome gives such a vivid and comprehensive impression of an ancient city as Ostia Antica, the excavated ruins of Roman Ostia. According to Roman legend it was here at the mouth (ostium) of the Tiber that Aeneas, forefather of the Latins, landed in Italy and King Martius established a settlement in the 7th c. B.C. Archaeological investigation has shown however that it was only in about 335 B.C. that a little coastal harbour and fishing town grew up here on the Tiber. This settlement developed and flourished along with Rome, and under the Empire became one of its busiest and most important commercial and naval ports, with a population of some

Entrance
Viale dei
Romagnoli 717

Opening times
daily 9am–4pm
(in summer till
6pm)

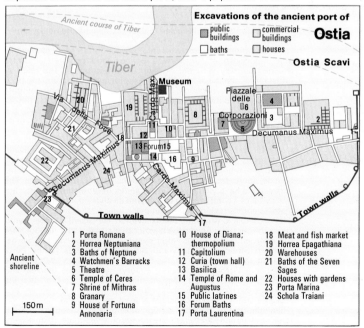

Excavations of the ancient port of Ostia

Ostia Scavi

- public buildings
- commercial buildings
- baths
- houses

1 Porta Romana	10 House of Diana; thermopolium	18 Meat and fish market
2 Horrea Neptuniana	11 Capitolium	19 Horrea Epagathiana
3 Baths of Neptune	12 Curia (town hall)	20 Warehouses
4 Watchmen's Barracks	13 Basilica	21 Baths of the Seven Sages
5 Theatre	14 Temple of Rome and Augustus	22 Houses with gardens
6 Temple of Ceres	15 Public latrines	23 Porta Marina
7 Shrine of Mithras	16 Forum Baths	24 Schola Traiani
8 Granary	17 Porta Laurentina	
9 House of Fortuna Annonaria		

Ampitheatre of Ostia Antica

50,000, a status clearly reflected in the extensive nature of the surviving remains.

In later centuries the town fell into oblivion for a variety of reasons. The importance of Rome as a political and commercial centre declined steadily with the division of the Empire in the reign of Constantine, the fall of the Western Empire in the 5th c. and the troubles of the medieval period. The Tiber deposited increasing amounts of silt around its mouth, so that the sea moved progressively further away from Ostia; the area was plagued by malaria and finally the construction of a canal at Fiumicino in 1613 deprived the town of its remaining maritime trade.

Excavations carried out since the 19th c. have brought to light more than half the town's area of 66ha/165 acres, revealing streets, dwelling houses, theatres, administrative buildings, temples, barracks, shops, workshops, tombs, warehouses, baths, city gates, inns, hostels, sports facilities, port installations, statues and mosaics. The excavations have yielded not just a series of unrelated remains, but the layout of a complete urban unit with its division into five wards or districts and its rectangular street plan.

It is possible to drive into the excavation site (scavi) and leave your car in the car park. Alternatively you can start your tour on foot from the main entrance. In the latter event you proceed via the Via dei Sepolcri (Street of Tombs) and the burial grounds to the Porta Romana, then past thermae, the Piazzale della Vittoria (with a statue of Minerva Victoria, goddess of victory), warehouses (horrea) and dwelling-houses on the Decumanus Maximus (part of the Via Ostiense, the road from Rome) to the theatre.

Even a brief visit should include at least the following:

First, the theatre. Built in the reign of Augustus, altered under Septimus Severus and Caracalla and restored some years ago, it can accommodate an audience of some 2700. Performances are given here during the summer. From the auditorium there is a view of the Piazzale delle Corporazioni behind the theatre, with the premises of 70 commercial enterprises and shipping agents, their particular line of business and place of origin being indicated by mosaics on the floor. In the centre of the square is the Temple of Ceres. To the right can be seen the Caserma dei Vigili (Watchmen's Barracks), a palaestra (gymnasium), and the Baths of Neptune (with mosaics). Further right still are the Horrea (warehouses) of Hortensius in front of an area not yet excavated.

Beyond the theatre are the handsome House of Apuleius (Casa di Apuleio), a mithraeum (shrine of Mithras) and more warehouses, and opposite, amid a densely-packed cluster of dwelling-houses, the Collegium Augustale and the House of Fortuna Annonaria. From here continue south to the temple of the Magna Mater (Cybele) before returning in the direction of the main street, passing on the way the Forum Baths, the Temple of Rome and Augustus, and the Casa dei Triclini. In the Forum, adjacent to the Temple of Rome and Augustus, is the Basilica, and at the far end of the Forum, dominating the scene, the towering Curia.

The tour of the site can be extended to take in the Tempio Rotondo, the Scuolo di Traiano, the Piazzale di Bona Dea, the Casa a Giardino (dwelling-houses, gardens and arcades), the Baths of Mithras, several temples of the republican period, the House of Amor and Psyche, the Little Market, the Casa dei Dipinti and the Casa di Diana. There is also an interesting museum containing finds from the site.

★★Palatino   D/E 7

The Palatine occupies a leading place among the seven hills of Rome. It is associated with the legend of the founding of the city by Romulus in 753 b.c. The earliest known settlement, strategically placed 50m/165ft above the Tiber, near the Isola Tiberina, dates from the 10th c. b.c.

Under the Empire, palaces (the word "palace" comes from the Palatine) were built here by the emperors and great aristocratic families of Rome; and although the remains of these buildings give only a very inadequate impression of their former magnificence, a walk over the Palatine nevertheless is a walk into the heart of Roman history.

Politicians such as Agrippa, the great patron of the arts, and writers, including Cicero, had houses on the Palatine. Augustus, who was born here, enlarged his father's mansion, and under Augustus and his successors, a whole series of splendid palaces, temples and public buildings were erected, reaching in the reign of Domitian the form in which we see their remains today. Since each generation carried out alterations and rebuilding, it is now difficult to disentangle the different periods of construction.

During the Middle Ages the splendours of the Palatine fell into eclipse. Numbers of convents and churches – the Oratory of St Caesarius, Santa Anastasia, Santa Lucia, San Sebastiano – were built over the remains of the pagan buildings, and the noble Frangipane family used them to establish a fortified stronghold. In the 16th c. wealthy families, including the Ronconi, Mattei, Spada, Magnani and Barberini, laid out gardens and vineyards on the hill, and Cardinal Alessandro Farnese commissioned famous architects to give the Palatine park its final form.

The Palatine began to attract archaeological interest in the 18th c. The names of many buildings on the Palatine were known from the works of Roman authors, but some buildings of major importance could not be located on the ground and even today have not been found. The Palatine was frequently ravaged by fire; as a result of these and other vicissitudes in its history it is now reduced, like the Forum, to a great field of ruins – but highly impressive and evocative ruins.

Underground station
Colosseo (line B)

Buses
11, 27, 81, 85, 87, 186

Trams
13, 30, 30b

Opening times
Mon.–Sat. 9am–3pm (in summer to 8pm), Sun. 9am–1pm

Ruins of the Imperial Palace on the Palatine

The most important and most interesting of the structures on the hill are described below.

Access

There are four routes of access to the Palatine. The first leads from the Via San Gregorio Magno through the gateway designed by Vignola as the entrance to the Farnese Gardens. The other three start from the Forum (see entry): the Clivus Palatinus, which leads past the Arch of Titus; the flight of steps at the House of the Vestals; and the large vaulted passage at Santa Maria Antiqua.

Criptoportico

To the north of the House of Livia are the remains of the Criptoportico (Cryptoporticus), a semi-subterranean barrel-vaulted corridor 130m/430ft long which linked the various imperial palaces (those of Tiberius, Livia and the Flavians). Tradition has it that it was here that the Emperor Caligula was murdered by conspirators in A.D. 41.

Orti Farnesiani

The Orti Farnesiani (Farnese Gardens) were laid out in the 16th c. by the architect Vignola for Cardinal Alessandro Farnese and were completed by Rainaldi at the beginning of the 17th c. Like the gardens of the Villa d'Este (see Tivoli), these gardens with their terraces and pavilions, their lawns and flowerbeds, their groves of trees and fountains, were designed to provide a kind of stage-setting for gatherings of like-minded people. The Arcadia literary academy met here in the late 17th c., leaving a small nymphaeum as its memorial. The stucco decoration is of interest as well as the fountains themselves. Beneath the gardens lie the remains of the palace of Tiberius. Excavations – still very far from complete – have brought to light remains of an atrium.

Tempio di Cibele (Magna Mater)

The Temple of Cybele (or of Magna Mater, the Great Mother) in the Farnese Gardens was built between 204 and 191 B.C. to house the "Black Stone" of the goddess, following the advice given in the Sibylline Books. In front of the temple, of which only the podium has

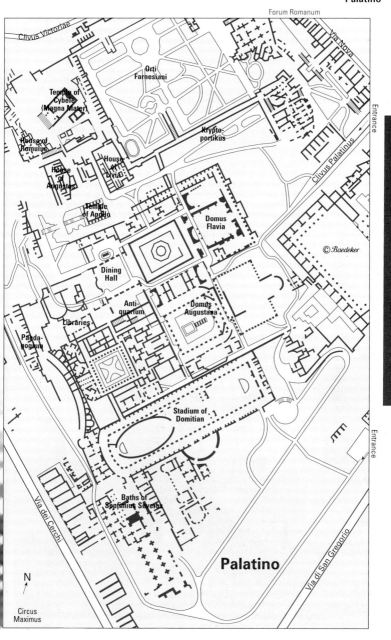

Forum Romanum

Clivus Victoriae

Via Nova

Entrance

Orti
Farnesiani

Temple of
Cybele
(Magna Mater)

Krypto-
portikus

Clivus Palatinus

House of
Romulus

House
of
Livia

House
of
Augustus

Temple
of Apollo

Domus
Flavia

© Baedeker

Dining
Hall

Anti-
quarium

Domus
Augustana

Libraries

Paeda-
gogium

Entrance

Stadium of
Domitian

Via del Cerchi

Baths of
Septimius Severus

Palatino

Via di San Gregorio

N

Circus
Maximus

survived, traces of hut foundations dating from the 9th and 8th c. B.C. have been found. These holes and lines cut in the rock represent the earliest evidence of human settlement on the Palatine and have been christened the "House of Romulus". To the east of them, old cisterns and parts of the Republican town wall have been uncovered.

Casa di Romulus

Casa di Livia

The Casa di Livia (House of Livia, Augustus' wife) was part of the palace of Augustus who in 36 B.C. acquired a complex of several houses which he altered. It is so-called because the inscription "Livia Augusta" was found on a lead pipe in one of the rooms. Augustus himself may have lived in these apartments. An atrium and four rooms reveal the comfortable lifestyle enjoyed by wealthy Romans of the time, with central heating conducted through ceramic pipes in the walls and elegant paintings in the Pompeian (second period) style with trompe l'oil architectural effects, figures – including Diana with attendants in a grove – and fantasy landscapes and creatures.

Domus Flavia

The ruins of the Palace of the Flavians lie in the centre of the Palatine hill. Built by an architect named Rabirius at the end of the 1st c. A.D. for the Emperor Domitian, a member of the Flavian dynasty, the Domus Flavia was intended to provide a setting for the increased splendour and display which the Roman emperors now demanded. This was the power centre of the Roman Empire in the imperial period. A large pillared courtyard (peristyle) with a spacious dining-room (triclinium) to the south and throne room (aula regia) to the north, a rectangular hall 30.5m/100ft by 38.7m/127ft with an apse at one end, a shrine to the domestic gods (lararium), and a basilica which probably served for affairs of state, all reflect the greatly enhanced importance and expanded circumstances of the imperial court. Beneath the lararium, the House of the Griffon (Casa dei Grifi) has been excavated, containing splendid murals, a vaulted stucco ceiling, and mosaic pavement from the 1st c. B.C.

One of the largest buildings on the Palatine – the massive Stadio Domitian

The Domus Augustana represents the remnants of the magnificent living quarters and state rooms of Domitian's imperial palace (augustana = imperial). Although by no means fully excavated, this building of two and three storeys, with its monumental yet harmonious dimensions, is still immensely impressive. Built, as was the Palace of the Flavians, in the reign of Domitian, it was at first the residence of successive Emperors; but later, right down to Byzantine times, it was occupied by high dignitaries of the Empire for whom it was both residence and place of work.

Domus Augustana

Among the principal buildings erected by Domitian (A.D. 81–96) on the Palatine was a running track 160m/525ft long and 47m/155ft across – the Stadio Domitian. It is not known whether the public were admitted to the contests and displays in the stadium, or whether it was reserved for the entertainment of the Emperor and his personal guests; indeed it is not even certain whether it was actually used for sporting contests at all or whether it was merely designed as a garden in the form of a stadium. According to tradition it was in this stadium that St Sebastian was martyred.

Stadio Domiziano

The ruins of the Baths of Septimius Severus are the most imposing on the Palatine. The piers and arches of the building were supported on massive substructures which have outlasted the centuries. Remains of the heating system can still be seen in some of the rooms and corridors.

Terme di Settimio Severo

★Palazzo Barberini   E 6

Pope Urban VIII (Maffeo Barberini), that great builder and patron of the arts, was fortunate indeed to have available to him, during his reign (1623–44), the talents of the two finest architects of the Baroque period, Borromini and Bernini. The bees which featured on the Barberini coat of arms are found on buildings all over Rome; and so many ancient buildings were destroyed to make room for these new creations that the epigram "Quod non fecerunt barbari, fecerunt Barberini" (What the barbarians did not destroy was destroyed by the Barberini) gained widespread currency in Rome.

The palace, rearing high above the Piazza Barberini (entrance in Via delle Quattro Fontane), was begun by Carlo Maderna, with the help of Borromini, in 1625, and completed by Bernini in 1633. The complex layout of rectangular and oval staircase halls, suites of rooms and state apartments can be more easily appreciated from a plan than on the ground.

The central feature of the palace is the Salone, two storeys high, with a ceiling painting of the "Triumph of Divine Providence" by Pietro da Cortona (1632–39), chiefly intended to glorify the papacy and the Barberini family.

Of great art historical importance is the fact that, with the Palazzo Barberini, the example of the palaces of northern Italy was introduced into Rome. Furthermore, in the palace, the High Baroque found its most complete expression.

Location
Via delle Quattro Fontane 13

Underground station
Barberini (line A)

Buses
60, 61, 62, 71, 415

★★Galleria Nazionale d'Arte Antica

The Palazzo Barberini now houses the National Gallery of Ancient Art. After the unification of Italy in 1870 the Italian state acquired many famous works of art by the expropriation of the Papal State, and also took over various private collections and acquired other works by gift and purchase, thus building up a great store of art treasures. Since the Second World War the National Gallery has acquired mainly works of the 13th–16th c. and also of the Baroque period.

Opening times
Tue.–Sat.
9am–2pm,
Thur., Sat. till 7pm;
Sun. 9am–1pm

Among the most notable are: in Room 1, Giovanni da Rimini's panel paintings of the Life of Christ (1345–62); in Room 2, Filippo Lippi's charming Madonna and Child (ca. 1437); in Room 4, Perugino's portrait of St Nicholas (ca. 1505); in Room 5, Bartolomeo Veneto's portrait of a nobleman (ca. 1512); in Room 6, Raphael's "Fornarina" (the portrait of a young woman baker, presumed to be the artist's mistress from Trastevere), Andrea del Sarto's "The Holy Family" (1529) and Beccafumi's "Madonna and St John as a Child", a picture flooded with light; two altarpieces by El Greco ("Adoration of the Shepherds" and "Baptism of Christ", 1596–1600) in Room 7; the exceptionally moving Pietà by the Master of Manchester in Room 9; Caravaggio's masterly paintings ("Narcissus" and "Judith beheading Holofernes", late 15th c.) in Room 13; landscapes by Nicolas Poussin in Room 16; Guido Reni's 1599 portrait of Beatrice Cenci, a Roman noblewoman condemned to death, in Room 17; Bernini's "David" (ca. 1625, probably a self-portrait) in Room 18; and in the chapel, Hans Holbein's famous portrait of Henry VIII on the day of his marriage (1540) to Anne of Cleves, fourth of his six wives.

★Palazzo Borghese   D 5

Location
Piazza Borghese

Buses
26, 28, 70

Opening times
Mon.–Sat.
10am–1pm,
3.30–8pm

Like other noble Roman families, the Borghese family, to which Pope Paul V (1605–21) belonged, had to have both a palace in the city and a summer or "weekend" residence in the country (see Villa Borghese). Cardinal Camillo Borghese accordingly bought a palace near the Tiber and on becoming Pope as Paul V presented it to his brothers Orazio and Francesco. The palace, begun by the architect Martino Lunghi, was completed for the Borghese family by Flaminio Ponzio to a plan which led to its being dubbed the "cembalo" (harpsicord), with the "keyboard" towards the Tiber.

An elegant Roman palace on the banks of the Tiber – the Palazzo Borghese

The sumptuous appointments of the palace reflected all the magnificence of a Papal family. The courtyard with its double row of arcades is a haven of peace for anyone entering from the noise and bustle of the streets, the pleasure being heightened by the elegant setting with its ancient statues, garlands and figures of youths and putti. Today temporary exhibitions are held in the palace's majestic rooms.

Opposite the Palazzo, where once the carriages stood, are the former servants' quarters.

★Palazzo della Cancellaria   C 6

In the 15th c. the leadership of Italy in the fields of art and culture was at first held by Florence under the Medici. Rome suffered during this period from the troubles afflicting the Papacy (the Pope's exile at Avignon, the schism during which various Cardinals contested the Papal throne), and only gradually recovered its dominant position as the city of the Popes and the centre of Christendom during the second half of the century – in spite of a further setback when the Eastern churches broke away from Papal control in 1452.

Location
Piazza della
Cancellaria

Buses
46, 62, 64

The magnificent Palazzo della Cancellaria (originally the palace of Cardinal Riario, later the Papal Chancery and seat of the government of the Papal State) marked a major step in this development. It was built between 1483 and 1513, partly with blocks of travertine from the Colosseum (see entry), for Cardinals Scarampo and Mezzarota and Raffaelle Riario (the latter of whom used on the project the 60,000 scudi he won in gaming from Franceschetto Cybo, nephew of Pope Innocent VIII). The architects were Andrea Bregno (Montecavallo) and Bramante. Fortune, however, turned against Cardinal Riario: having taken part in a conspiracy against Pope Leo X, he lost his wealth and the palace was confiscated.

The external elevations of the palace are very characteristic of Renaissance architecture, with their clean, geometrical lines and uniformity of pattern; the stone work is plain and uncluttered, without superfluous ornament.

The most notable feature of the interior is the large Hall of a Hundred Days, with paintings (1546) commissioned by Cardinal Alessandro Farnese and completed by Vasari and a team of assistants in a hundred days (drawing from Michelangelo the sarcastic comment "Anyone can see that").

Sala dei Cento
Giorni

The square inner courtyard, surrounded by three-storeyed ranges of rooms, is also notable for the clarity and regularity of its structure. Excavations in 1988 revealed the front of a sarcophagus (4th c. A.D.), remains of walls and pillars from a basilica, tombs (4th/5th c.) and late medieval wall paintings.

Palazzo Cenci   D 6

The Palazzo Cenci was built in the 16th c. on the site of the ruined Circus Flaminius (221 B.C.) According to popular tradition Francesco Cenci embellished the palace chapel in 1575 to house the tombs of his children, Giacomo and Beatrice, whom he had resolved to have killed. But it was the children who murdered their father, for which crime they were beheaded on the Ponte Sant'Angelo on 11 September 1599.

Location
Piazza Cenci

Buses
23, 26, 44, 56, 60,
65, 75, 170, 710,
718, 719, 774

Palazzo Corsini   C 6

The Palazzo Corsini was built in the 15th c. for Cardinal Domenico Riario, a nephew of Pope Sixtus IV. In the 17th c. it was occupied by Queen Christina of Sweden after her conversion to the Roman Catho-

Location
Via della
Lungara 10

Buses
23, 28, 28b, 65

Opening times
Tue.–Sat.
9am–2pm,
Sun. 9am–1pm

lic faith and subsequent abdication. Here she brought together artists and men of learning in an academy which later became the famous Arcadia. After coming into the possession of the Corsini family the palace was completely rebuilt by Ferdinando Fuga (1723–36). It now houses part of the collection of the Galleria Nazionale d'Arte Antica (the former Corsini Gallery) mainly comprising European painting of the 17th and 18th c. Much of the Corsini collection is now in the main part of the Galleria Nazionale in the Palazzo Barberini (see entry).

★Palazzo Doria Pamphili   D 6

Location
Via del Corso
(entrance to
Gallery at Piazza
del Colleggio
Romano 1a)

Buses
46, 56, 60, 62, 64,
65, 71, 75, 81, 85,
88, 90, 90b, 95,
170

Opening times
Fri.–Tue.
10am–1pm

The Palazzo Doria Pamphili, one of Rome's largest palaces, is bounded by the Via del Corso, Via del Plebiscito, Via della Gatta, Piazzo del Collegio Romano and Via Lata. In the course of three centuries of existence the palace with its varied facades and courtyards, has been fashioned by a number of different architects and owner-builders and in the possession of different families – the della Rovere, then the Aldobrandini and finally the Pamphili, from whom it descended to the Doria family.

★★Galleria Doria Pamphili

The Galleria Doria Pamphili contains a collection of paintings, mainly from the private collections of the Pamphili and Doria families. They include works by Tintoretto ("Portrait of a Prelate"), fragments of an

In the Galleria Doria Pamphili: "Rest on the Flight into Egypt" by Caravaggio

altarpiece, probably by Titian, Corregio ("Virtue"), Raphael ("Double Portrait"), Caravaggio ("Magdalena" and the masterly early work "Rest on the Flight into Egypt"), Velázquez (the famous portrait of Pope Innocent X), Lippi, Lotto, Bordone and Pamphili, landscapes by Lorrain and works by Pieter Breughel the Elder ("Sea Battle off Naples"), Jusepe Ribera ("St Jerome"), Domenichino and Solimena. There are also some fine marble sculptures including a bust of Innocent X by Bernini.

Visitors are also shown the private and state apartments, again with valuable pictures and sculptures. Guided tours between 10am and noon.

At the end of the Via del Corso nearest the Piazza Venezia stands the Palazzo Bonaparte, a 17th c. palace which still bears its name on its facade. It was the home of Napoleon's mother Letizia Ramorino until her death in 1836.

Palazzo Bonaparte

★Palazzo Farnese   C 6

The effect of the Palazzo Farnese is heightened even further by its being viewed across an open square. In this palace, the most handsome of all the 16th c. Roman palaces, Renaissance architecture, which had begun in Rome with the Palazzo Venezia (see entry), reached its magnificent culmination.

In 1514 Cardinal Alessandro Farnese, later Pope Paul III (1534–49), commissioned Antonio da Sangallo the Younger to build the palace. After Sangallo's death it was continued by Michelangelo (from 1546) and completed by Giacomo della Porta in 1580. The palace later passed into the hands of the Bourbons of Naples and is now the French Embassy.

The exterior is of majestic effect with its massive structure of ashlar masonry and its restrained articulation, mainly based on simple geometric forms. The facade, 46m/150ft long, has three storeys of contrasting design, almost completely dominated by the fenestration. The rows of windows with their different surrounds, the main entrance doorway, and the central window on the first floor, create a total harmony, so that nothing could be altered, added or taken away without reducing the perfection of the whole.

The side elevations repeat the structure of the main front, but the narrowness of the street deprives them of their full effect. The rear facade faces the Tiber. Stones from the Colosseum (see entry) were used in the construction of the palace.

The interior courtyard follows ancient precedent in having Doric columns and pillars on the ground floor, Ionic on the first floor and Corinthian on the second.

A further notable feature is the first-floor gallery, 20m/65ft long and 6m/20ft wide, with frescoes by Annibale Caracci ("The Triumph of Love in the Universe", 1597–1604).

Location
Piazza Farnese

Buses
23, 28, 28b, 46, 62, 64, 65

Gallery

Palazzo Massimo alle Colonne   C/D 6

Built in 1532–36 the Palazzo Massimo alle Colonne, a master work by Baldassare Peruzzi, lies between the Piazza Sant'Andrea della Valle and Piazza Pantaleo. The residences of the Massimo which had previously stood here were destroyed in 1527 during the notorious Sack of Rome, the plundering of the city by the troops of Charles V.

The palace is a fine example of the Mannerist school of architecture (between the Renaissance and Baroque), which typically relieves the

Location
Corso Vittorio Emanuele II

Buses
46, 62, 64

weight of the masonry by breaking up and transforming the basic geometric forms and giving them an elegant and playful effect. The portico, supported by six Doric columns, enhances the unique character of the palace.

Palazetto
Massimi

Standing behind the palace, towards the Piazza Navona (see entry), is the three-storeyed Palazzetto Massimi bearing traces of the graffiti decoration used in the 16th c. for some 50 Roman palaces. Here in 1467 the papal post-stage and the first printing works in Rome were established by the Germans Pannartz and Sweynheym.

★Palazzo Pallavicini-Rospigliosi   E 6

Location
Via XXIV
Maggio 33

Buses
57, 64, 65, 70,
71, 75, 81, 170

Opening times
Casino: first day
of the month,
10am–noon and
3–5pm

This palace, on the way up to the Quirinal hill, was built in 1611–16 by Vasanzio and Maderna for Cardinal Scipione Borghese and later enlarged for the French statesman Cardinal Mazarin, who was of Italian origin. It now belongs to the Pallavicini-Rospigliosi family. A gallery on the first floor houses the Pallavicini picture collection, which includes early works by Rubens and works by Botticelli, Poussin, Lotto, Signorelli, Van Dyck and Ribera (viewing by appointment only: tel. 4 74 40 19).

In the small garden is the Casino Pallavicini, the principal room in which boasts a famous ceiling painting of Aurora (1514) by Guido Reni.

Palazzo della Sapienza   D 6

Location
Corso del
Rinascimento

Buses
26, 46, 62, 64,
70, 81, 88, 90

The dome with its airy lantern and the white spiral campanile of Sant'Ivo, the church in the Palazzo della Sapienza, are quite unmistakable from wherever in the city they are seen. From its foundation by Pope Boniface VIII in 1303, the "Sapienza" was the seat of the University of Rome until the latter was moved to the Città Universitaria in 1935. The present spacious three-storeyed palace, now housing the state archives, was built in 1587 by Giacomo della Porta for Pope Sextus V.

★Sant'Ivo

The church of Sant'Ivo, the palace chapel, its façade enlivened by concave and convex forms, stands to the rear of the courtyard between the palace's massive wings. Using a combination of semicircles and trapezoids, the architect Borromini designed the interior in the shape of a bee – an allusion to the arms of Pope Urban VIII, a member of the aristocratic Barberini family. The church represents a masterly example in Rome of the art of Borromini, who was architect to the Barberini family.

Palazzo Spada   C 6

Location
Piazza Capo di
Ferro 13

Buses
23, 28, 28b, 65

The Palazzo Spada was built by Giulio Mersi da Caravaggio in 1540–50 for Cardinal Girolamo Capo di Ferro. Later it passed into the hands of Cardinal Spada and was restored by Borromini. It is now the seat of the Italian Council of State and also contains the Galleria Spada.

The most notable feature of the palace is the trompe l'oil colonnade built by Borromini in about 1635 to link two courtyards. By progressively reducing the size of the structural elements from one end to the other, the apparent length of the passage, with its twin rows of columns and coffered ceiling, is increased.

The four-storeyed façade is embellished with elegant stucco decoration (by Giulio Mazzoni, 1556–60) and eight statues of famous Romans (from left to right: Trajan, Pompey, Fabius Maximus, Romulus, Numa Pompilius, Marcellus, Caesar and Augustus). The rooms have rich stucco ornament, and in one room is a statue said to be the statue of Pompey beside which Caesar was murdered.

This gallery consists mainly of the private collection of paintings assembled by Cardinal Bernardino Spada (1594–1661). Among the many fine pictures displayed in rooms with graceful stucco decoration, are sketches in oil by Baciccia for the ceiling in Il Gesó (see entry), portraits of Cardinal Spada by Guido Reni and Guercino, Andrea del Sarto's "Visitation", Titian's unfinished "Musician", and a "Landscape with Windmill" by Jan Breughel the Elder.

★Galleria Spada

Opening times
Tue.–Sat.
9am–7pm,
Sun. 9am–
1.30pm

Palazzo (Casa) Zuccari — D/E 5

The Palazzo or Casa Zuccari, built by the painter Federico Zuccari about 1600 as a residence and studio, is situated on the Piazza Trinità dei Monti at the point where the Via Sistina and Via Gregoriana branch off. Later occupied by the widowed Queen Maria Casimira of Poland, it today houses the Biblioteca Hertziana, the art history arm of the Max Planck Institute (not open to the public). The windows and garden doorway of the palace (at Via Gregoriana no. 30) are in the form of monsters' jaws.

Location
Via Gregoriana

Underground station
Piazza di Spagna
(line A)

Bus
115

★★Pantheon — D 6

The architecture of the Pantheon, the largest and best preserved monument of Roman antiquity, is so simple in concept, that the structure has survived the hazards of the ages almost intact. The name of its builder is inscribed above the entrance: Marcus Agrippa, son-in-law of the Emperor Augustus. It was in 27 B.C. that he dedicated the temple to the "most holy (Greek "pantheon") planetary gods – hence the dome representing the firmament with its opening for the sun – not actually to all the gods as the name seems to imply.

The Pantheon was damaged by fire in A.D. 80 and was rebuilt in the reign of Hadrian (120–125). The brickwork of this period demonstrates the extraordinarily high standard of technical mastery achieved by the Romans. In the course of the centuries the building suffered further damage and plundering – Pope Gregory III removed the gilded bronze roof-tiles from the dome, while Urban VIII used the bronze roofing of the porch (weighing 25 tonnes) in the construction of Bernini's Confessio in St Peter's (see Vatican). The building was however regularly restored, and also received some structural additions, since removed.

The first Christian Emperors forbade the use of this pagan temple for worship, and it remained in disuse until Pope Boniface IV dedicated it to the Virgin and all the Christian martyrs on 1 November 609 – the origin of the feast of All Saints.

From the Piazza della Rotonda, from where the Pantheon is seen hemmed in by buildings and the semicircular dome appears much flatter than it really is, steps lead down into the porch: formerly there were steps up to the entrance, but the ground level has risen considerably since then. The porch, 33m/108ft wide and 13.5m/44ft high, has 16 granite columns with Corinthian capitals (12.5m/41ft high, 4.5m/15ft apart) and two massive ancient bronze doors.

Location
Piazza della
Rotonda

Buses
28, 87, 94, 119

Opening times
Tue.–Sat.
9am–4.30pm
(in summer
till 6pm),
Sun. 9am–1pm

Tour of the
building

The mighty dome of the Pantheon was the supreme achievement of Roman interior architecture. The overwhelming effect of the interior results from the harmonious proportions of the whole vast structure: the height is the same as the diameter (43.2m/142ft), while the walls of the cylinder supporting the dome measure half the diameter (21.6m/71ft). In the walls of the cylinder (6.2m/20ft thick) are semi-circular and rectangular niches. The interior of the dome is coffered. The only lighting comes from a circular opening, 9m/30ft across, in the roof of the dome.

The restrained decoration of the interior enhances the effect of the architecture. The harmony and perfect proportions of the Pantheon – built in the image of the earth with the vault of the firmament above – have profoundly impressed artists and visitors down the centuries.

The Pantheon is the burial place of the Italian kings Victor Emmanuel II (second niche on the right) and Umberto I (second niche on the left). The great Renaissance painter Raphael is also buried here (between the second and third niches on the left), as also is the greatest Cardinal Secretary of State of modern times, Enrico Consalvi (tomb by Thorvaldsen, 1824, third niche on the left).

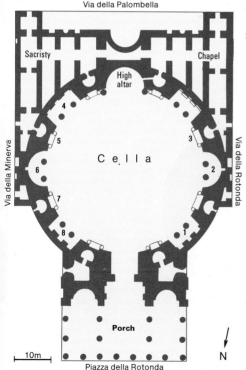

Pantheon
St Maria ad Martyres

1 "Annunciation", a fresco by Melozzo da Forlì (15th c.)
2 Tomb of Victor Emmanuel II, first king of Italy (1820–78)
3 "St Anne and the Virgin", sculpture by Lorenzo Ottoni (?: 17th c.)
4 Monument to the Papal diplomat Cardinal Ercole Consalvi (1757–1824: tomb in San Marcello)
5 Tomb of Raphael (Raffaello Santi or Sanzio, 1483–1520)
6 Tomb of Umberto I, second king of Italy (1844–1900: assassinated at Monza); below it the tomb of Queen Margherita (d. 1926)
7 Tomb of Baldassare Peruzzi (1481–1536), architect and painter
8 On the altar "St Joseph with the Boy Jesus" by Vincenzo de' Rossi; on either side the tombs of the painters Perin del Vaga (1501–47) and Taddeo Zuccari (1529–66) and the architect and sculptor Flaminio Vacca (1538–1605); on the walls "Joseph's Dream" and "Flight into Egypt", stucco reliefs by Carlo Monaldi (*c.* 1720)

◄ *The perfect proportions of the Pantheon have impressed artists and visitors throughout the centuries*

Pizza della Bocca della Verità

★Piazza della Rotonda

The Piazza della Rotonda in front of the Pantheon, the heart of the Centro Storico, is a popular meeting place for all ages, particularly in the summer months. The pleasant cafés, bars and tearooms encircling the square with its fountain, guarantee a lively atmosphere late into the night. After visiting the Pantheon, energy can be recouped by ordering one of those delicious "bignes", a kind of cream puff, at Di Rienzo's, or a tramezzini. Around the corner the Tazza d'Oro in the Via degli Orfani serves the best coffee in Rome.

★Piazza della Bocca della Verità   D 7

Buses
15, 23, 57, 90,
92, 94, 95, 716

The Piazza della Bocca della Verità occupies the site of the ancient Forum Boarium or cattle market, situated conveniently close to the Tiber which provided a ready means for the disposal of refuse. From the square there is a view scarcely to be equalled anywhere else in Rome, taking in both ancient and Christian buildings: the church of Santa Maria in Cosmedin, a Romanesque building with a modestly proportioned porch and graceful campanile; the Arch of Janus and beyond it the handsome church of San Giorgio in Velabro (see entry) and the Arco degli Argentari, the arch of the merchants and bankers; the church of San Giovanni Decollato (see entry); the Casa dei Crescenzi, the residence of the most powerful family in Rome during the early medieval period; and two ancient temples, the Tempio della Fortuna Virile and the Tempio di Vesta, with the Baroque Fountain of the Two Tritons.

★Santa Maria in Cosmedin

On the south side of the Piazza stands the church of Santa Maria in Cosmedin (probably so christened by Byzantines after a square in their city). This is one of the finest examples of medieval church architecture in Rome. Begun in 772, during the reign of Pope Adrian and completed in about 1124 under Calixtus II, it is an architectural gem (suggesting an alternative derivation for the name Cosmedin from the Greek "cosmos", meaning "perfect order" or "ornament").

The noble harmony of the church's proportions begins with the seven-storey campanile and is continued in the wide two-storey porch with its projecting canopy; it reaches even more sublime heights in the interior, with its tall nave and carefully structured layout to meet liturgical needs, and is infinitely repeated in the intarsia (inlaid marble) work.

Bocca della Verità (mouth of truth)

The alternation of columns and piers, the irregular dimensions, the three apses in front of the nave, the aisles with their famous frescoes, the Cosmatesque in the floor and the marble screens of the schola cantorum (the area reserved for the clergy); the marble ambos (reading pulpits), the bishop's throne with its two lion's heads and the ornamental disc behind it, the twisted Easter candlestick, the ciborium over the altar; all these details combine to make Santa Maria in Cosmedin one of the most beautiful of the smaller churches in Rome.

In the crypt are early Christian tombs and the foundations of a pagan temple.

At the left-hand end of the porch is the large stone mask known as the

Warm Mediterranean colours give a special atmosphere to the Campo dei Fiori

Bocca della Verità, the "Mouth of Truth". According to popular belief the Romans, when taking an oath, would put their right hand into the mouth of the mask. It is said it would close and hold them fast if they perjured themselves. There's nothing to stop visitors trying too!

★Piazza di Campo dei Fiori   C 6

Nowhere in Rome is more truly Roman than the Campo dei Fiori (field of flowers) with its colourful array of flower, fruit and vegetable stalls every weekday morning. Leaves of dark green spinach stand tall alongside deep red tomatoes – tomatoes which taste every bit as good as they look. On nearby stalls fishmongers offer giant tuna, spiny lobsters and mussels, and there are fresh chickens and sizeable turkeys. In the early afternoon the square is swept clean and becomes the preserve of flower sellers and strolling visitors. Even if not wanting to buy a glorious bouquet of bright flowers, visitors can sit at a table in one of the welcoming cafés or a trattoria and soak up the atmosphere: the Mediterranean light, the warm hues of the old palazzi with their distinctive roof gardens, and a cornucopia of fresh southern fruit and vegetables from the countryside around Rome.

Buses
46, 62, 64

In the centre of the square, commemorating all those put to death here during the period of papal rule, stands a bronze statue of the Dominican monk Giordano Bruno, burned at the stake on 17 February 1600. Convicted of heresy by the Inquisition and refusing to recant, after seven years of imprisonment he was condemned to death. Beneath the statue are a series of medallions bearing the names of other heretics condemned by the Catholic Church, including Erasmus of Rotterdam, Wycliffe and Hus.

Statue of
Giordano Bruno

Piazza Colonna   D 6

Buses
52, 53, 56, 58,
58b, 60, 61, 62,
71, 81, 85, 88,
90, 90b, 95, 115

Palazzo Chigi

★**Colonna di
Marco Aurelio**

Dominating the Piazza Colonna, where the Italian prime minister's official residence, the Palazzo Chigi, stands, is the column erected in honour of the Emperor Marcus Aurelius (see Prominent Figures in Roman History). Following his victories over the Marcomanni, Quadi and Sarmatians, the Roman Senate sanctioned the erection of the column in the centre of the square between the Temples of Hadrian and Marcus Aurelius and other public buildings. The inscription on the base of the column mistakenly attributes it to the Emperor Antonius Pius, which is why it is sometimes seen described as his. The 29.6m/97ft column (42m/138ft including the base and capital), with a diameter of 3.7m/12ft, is formed from 29 blocks of Carrara marble. On the shaft an ascending spiral of bas-reliefs depict scenes from the Germanic (171–73) and Sarmatic (174–75) wars. The figures of soldiers and horses stand out further from the background than those on Trajan's Column and reveal much about the weapons, uniforms, equipment and customs of the time.

A staircase of 190 steps within the column leads to the top, crowned originally by a statue of the Emperor. In 1589 this was replaced by a bronze statue of the Apostle Paul by Domenico Fontana.

★★Piazza Navona   C/D 6

Buses
26, 46, 62, 64,
70, 81, 88, 90

The picturesque Piazza Navona with its enchanting back-drop of ochre-coloured buildings and magnificent central fountain symbolising four rivers, is a real favourite with the Romans and a magnet for tourists until late into the night. Lively crowds permanently throng the Baroque square,

A favourite meeting place of the Romans – the broad Piazza Navona

The Baroque square is a stage for instant portrait painters

a colourful arena for musicians, instant portrait artists, magicians, fire-eaters and souvenir sellers – plenty of kitsch, a bit of show and fairground atmosphere, but sometimes also a concert stage or the venue for a demonstration. Chocoholics can sample the legendary "tartuffo" at Tre Scalini, others the equally special ice-cream at the Café di Colombia.

The buildings around the square still mark out the area of the stadium (240m/790ft long and 65m/215ft across) constructed here by Domitian. In the Middle Ages the arena was used for water festivals and horse racing. It was rebuilt during the Baroque period by Borromini who embellished it with a series of superb palaces and churches. To these were added Bernini's marvellous waterscape.

Three fountains adorn the square. The most eye-catching is the Fountain of Four Rivers (1647–51), by which Bernini gained favour with Pope Innocent X, a member of the Pamphili family. It displays all the mastery of this brilliant architect-sculptor. The centrepiece, in the form of sculpted rocks rising from the waters of the large basin, is crowned by an obelisk and embellished with carvings of animals and plants. Figures at the four corners personify the Nile, Ganges, Danube and Plate, considered the greatest rivers of the four known continents, each with typical flora and fauna. The statues have often been the butt of Roman humour. Why does the Nile figure hide his head? Maybe because the river's source was hidden too! Or, alluding to the fierce and not always honourable rivalry between the two great architects Bernini and Borromini, is it that the figure covers his eyes to avoid seeing the faults in Borromini's church of Sant'Agnese opposite!

★★Fontana dei Fiumi

The Fontana del Moro in front of the Palazzo Pamphili, and the Fontana del Nettuno, were erected by Giacomo della Porta in 1575–76. The figure of the Moor was executed by Bernini in 1654; those of Neptune and the nereids are 19th c.

★Fontana del Moro,
★Fontana del Nettuno

131

★Sant'Agnese The church of Sant'Agnese, dominating the west side of the Piazza Navona, is dedicated to the Roman martyr St Agnes. It is built on the foundations of one side of the Stadium of Domitian, on the spot where in 304, so legend has it, the saint was about to be exposed naked before the populace when her hair suddenly and miraculously grew long, covering her nakedness. It is believed that the martyrdom of St Agnes by beheading actually took place where the church of Sant'Agnese fuori le Mura (see entry) now stands.

Sant'Agnese was founded by Pope Innocent X, a member of the Pamphili family, who is commemorated in a monument by G. B. Maini over the entrance. The church was built by a succession of architects – first Girolamo Rainaldi (1652), then Borromini (1653–57) and finally Carlo Rainaldi (1672). The façade, campanile and dome (heightened by Borromini) present a lively interplay of convex and concave forms, gables, canopies, windows, columns and piers.

The interior shows the same sense of movement and yet of unity. The crypt contains Alessandro Algardi's portrayal of "The Miracle of St Agnes" (1653) and the remains of a Roman mosaic pavement.

★Piazza del Popolo   D 4/5

Underground station
Flaminio (line A)

Buses
2, 90, 90b, 115

Before the demolition of the city walls visitors arriving in Rome from the north on the Via Cassia or Via Flaminia, two of the old Roman consular highways, received their first impression of the magnificence of the city when they passed through the Porta del Popolo into the Piazza del Popolo. On the east under the Pincio hill, and on the west above the Tiber, the square is enclosed by semicircular walls built by Giuseppe Valadier in 1809–20. The square was enlarged in the 16th c. during the reign of Pope Sixtus V and the Via di Ripetta and Via

The Flaminio Obelisque stands in the centre of the Piazza del Popolo

del Babuino were laid out. Some decades later the twin churches of Santa Maria dei Miracoli and Santa Maria in Monte Santo were built flanking the end of the Corso.

On the east side of the square the Café Rosati, traditionally the meeting place of artists, and the Canova opposite, offer many of the famous Italian sweet delicacies.

In the middle of the square rises the Obelisco Flaminio, an Egyptian obelisk from the Circus Maximus (see entry), which Emperor Augustus had brought to Rome. Weary sightseers can often be seen enjoying a rest beside the four lions spouting water at the foot of the obelisk.

Obelisco
Flaminio

Beyond the pines of the Pincio Gardens (see entry) stands the church of Santa Maria del Popolo, with its fine Renaissance façade, dome and campanile. Legend has it that there was once a chapel here, built to drive away the evil spirits of Nero, which Pope Sixtus IV enlarged into a church in the 15th c. This was extended by Bramante in 1505, occupied by Augustinian canons and later restored by Bernini. Martin Luther, an Augustinian, lived in the Augustinian house during his visit to Rome in 1510–11; after the Reformation the altar at which he had celebrated mass was shunned by other members of the order.

★Santa Maria
del Popolo

As a parish church Santa Maria del Popolo, built on a Latin cross plan with three aisles and many side chapels, contains numerous tombs including, in the choir, those of Cardinal Ascanio Sforza (d. 1505) and Cardinal Girolamo Basso della Rovere (d. 1507), both by Andrea Sansovino. On the vaulting of the choir are frescoes by Pinturicchio depicting the Coronation of the Virgin, with Evangelists, Sibyls and Fathers of the Church. The side chapels are particularly fine. The first on the right was built for the della Rovere family, the second (by Carlo Fontana, 1682–87) for Cardinal Cybo, and the second on the left (designed by Raphael, 1513–15) for the Chigi family. The Cesari Chapel in the north transept contains two famous pictures by Caravaggio, the "Conversion of St Paul" and the "Crucifixion of St Peter".

★Piazza del Quirinale

E 6

The square in front of the Quirinal Palace, official residence of the President of Italy, is one of the most beautiful in Rome, offering a panoramic view of the city extending westwards to St Peter's (see Vatican).

Buses
57, 64, 65, 70,
71, 75, 170

In the centre of the square is the famous Dioscuri Fountain, with the 14m/46ft-high obelisk which formerly stood at the entrance to the Mausoleum of Augustus, and the 5.6m/18ft-high figures of the Dioscuri (Castor and Pollux as horse-tamers) from the nearby Baths of Constantine.

Dioscuri
Fountain

In Roman times the Quirinal hill, which had legendary association with Romulus, was occupied by a residential district of the city with numerous handsome mansions. In the 16th c. Pope Gregory VIII chose this as the site for a Papal summer residence. Begun in 1574 it was later extended stage by stage (such famous architects as Fontana, Maderna and Bernini being involved in the work), until by the time of Pope Clement XII (1730–40) it formed a gigantic complex with long ranges of buildings surrounded by gardens. From 1870 to 1946 the Quirinal was the official residence of the king: it is now occupied by the President of Italy.

Palazzo
del Quirinale

The Quirinal Palace – today the residence of the President of Italy

Palazzo della Consultà	Opposite the Palazzo del Quirinale stands the superbly ornamented mansion built in 1734 during the reign of Pope Clement XII by the architect Ferdinando Fuga for the Papal court (Tribunale della Sacra Consultà). Today it houses the "Corte Costituzionale", Italy's supreme court.

Piazza San Giovanni in Laterano   F 7

Underground station San Giovanni (line A) **Buses** 16, 85, 87, 88, 93, 93b, 93c, 218, 650 Obelisk	The Piazza San Giovanni in Laterano, at the end of Via Merulana, is bounded by the Lateran Palace, the side entrance to the church of St John Lateran, and the baptistery of San Giovanni in Fonte. It is dominated by an Egyptian obelisk, at 31m/102ft (47m/154ft including the base) the tallest and also the oldest in Rome. It was brought from Thebes to Rome in a specially constructed ship in A.D. 357, and was set up in the Circus Maximus (see entry). In 1587, during the reign of Sixtus V, it was transferred to its present site. The equestrian statue of Marcus Aurelius which previously stood here was moved to the Capitol (see Campidoglio).
★★San Giovanni in Laterano Main entrance: Via Vittorio Emanuele Filiberto; side entrance: Piazza San Giovanni in Laterano 4	The inscription on the façade of St John Lateran claims for it the status of "Mater et caput omnium ecclesiarum urbis et orbis" (Mother and head of all the churches of the city and the world). A beginning was made in A.D. 313 with the building of a large church dedicated to the Saviour, on the ruins of the palace of the Laterani (hence the name) and of a barracks. This was accordingly the first of the four "patriarchal" basilicas – the others being St Peter's (see Vatican), San Paolo fuori le Mura and Santa Maria Maggiore (see entries) – and the most venerable of the seven pilgrimage churches of Rome (the four patriarchal churches together with Santa Croce in Gerusalemme,

134

San Sebastiano and San Lorenzo fuori le Mura (see entries). This status was confirmed by the holding of five General Councils of the Church in St John Lateran, in 1123, 1139, 1179, 1215 and 1512.

Before the Popes established their residence in the Apostolic Palace in the Vatican after their return from exile in Avignon, they lived mainly in the Lateran; and St John Lateran has remained the episcopal church of the Pope. Various additions and alteration were carried out in the 5th, 8th, 10th, 13th and 15th c., and in the 16th and 17th c. the church was almost completely rebuilt. The west porch, the interior and the main façade were entirely refashioned at this period. During medieval times the church was put under the patronage of St John the Baptist and St John the Evangelist.

The basilican plan of the church, with its porch, narthex, five-aisled nave, transept with altar, and apse, was established in the original Constantinian church and respected in the Baroque rebuilding. The wide façade with its huge statues by Alessandro Galilei (ca. 1735) is a masterpiece of late Baroque architecture. Note also the bronze doors of the main doorway which came from the ancient Curia in the Forum (see entry), and the Holy Door (far right). The interior, 130m/427ft long, was refashioned by Borromini on the occasion of Holy Year 1650, with massive piers along the nave and huge, 4.25m/14ft-high figures of Apostles by various sculptors in the niches. The magnificent timber ceiling dates from the 16th c.

Above the Papal altar (Altare papale) is a tabernacle-like baldachin in which the heads of the Apostles Peter and Paul are preserved. The altar itself is said to be the one at which Peter's immediate successors, the earliest Roman bishops, celebrated mass. In the Confessio at the foot of the altar is the bronze tomb of Pope Martin V (on which it is the Roman custom to throw a coin) – one of the numerous tombs of the famous, both ecclesiastical and lay, which the church contains. — Papal altar

In the apse, which was widened by Pope Leo XIII (1878–84), are some very fine mosaics, faithful copies of early Christian originals renewed by Torriti in the 13th c., depicting Christ surrounded by angels and (below, on either side of a jewelled cross) various saints, including St Francis of Assisi and St Anthony of Padua. — Apse

The cloister (chiostro: entrance in left-hand aisle), the work of the Vassalletti, a family of Roman artists, is a masterpiece of 13th c. architecture and should not be missed. — Cloister

San Giovanni in Laterano

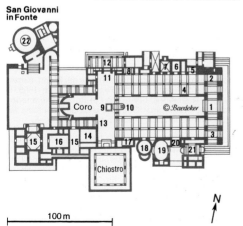

1 Bronze doors (Roman)
2 Holy Door
3 Statue of Constatine the Great
4 Frescoes by Giotto (Boniface VIII)
5 Orsini Chapel
6 Torlonia Chapel
7 Massimo Chapel
8 St John's Chapel
9 Papal altar
10 Tomb of Pope Martin V (crypt)
11 Baroque organ
12 Side door
13 Monument of Pope Leo XIII. Entrance to Portico of Leo XIII
14 Choir chapel
15 Sacristies
16 Chapterhouse
17 St Hilary's Chapel. Entrance to cloister
18 Chapel of St Francis of Assisi (monument of 1927)
19 Santorio Chapel
20 Chapel of Assumption
21 Corsini Chapel
22 Baptistery

★Battistero San Giovanni in Fonte	The Baptistery of St John was built on the instructions of the Emperor Constantine and stands over a nymphaeum of the Lateran Palace. The circular, or more accurately, octagonal, structure, one of the oldest baptismal churches in Christendom, became the architectural model for all later baptisteries.
Palazzo Laterano	The Lateran Palace was the residence of the Pope from the time of Constantine until 1309 when Clement V was compelled to transfer the seat of the Papacy to Avignon. After the Pope's return from exile in France, the Apostolic Palace in the Vatican was enlarged and took its place. The original palace dating from the time of Constantine was destroyed on a number of occasions, and in 1556 it was completely rebuilt by Sixtus V. Today it is occupied by the episcopal administration.
Scala Santa	Diagonally opposite the main façade of San Giovanni in Laterano is the church of the Scala Santa, on the site of the banqueting hall (triclinium) of the old Lateran Palace. Within the church are the Capella Sancta Sanctorium, the private Papal chapel of the old palace (with 13th c. mosaics), and the Scala Santa (Holy Stairs), a flight of 28 marble steps, now clad in wood for protection, which tradition has it came from Pilate's house in Jerusalem and were brought to Rome by St Helena in the 4th c. It is the custom for worshippers, in remembrance of Christ's suffering, to ascend the stairs on their knees.

★★Piazza di Spagna/Scalinata della Trinità dei Monti   D 5

Underground station Piazza di Spagna (line A)	Essential for every visitor to Rome is a stroll round the ever busy Piazza di Spagna, one of the favourite meeting places for young people in the heart of the historic centre. On the west side of the large square, horse-drawn carriages wait patiently for custom, ready to take tourists on an atmospheric drive through the Eternal City – a real experience in fine weather. The irregularly shaped square takes its name from the Spanish legation to the Holy See which has been housed here since the 17th c.
★★Scalinata della Trinità dei Monti (Spanish Steps)	First to catch the eye in the square are the elegant Spanish Steps, a landmark of the capital, restored most recently in 1995–96. This impressive flight, a bewildering arrangement of steps and landings, now wide, now narrow, now twisting this way, now that, with a terrace half-way up on which to pause and enjoy the view, was constructed by Francesco de Sanctis in 1723–25. The steps were paid for by the French ambassador, Gueffier – hence the fleurs-de-lis from the coat of arms of the Bourbons.
Trinità dei Monti	At the top of the steps is the French church of Trinità dei Monti, begun by Louis XII in 1502 and consecrated by Pope Sixtus V in 1585. It was restored after the Napoleonic occupation of Rome. The interior still preserves some of the original Gothic arches and contains an "Entombment" by Daniele da Volterra, a pupil of Michelangelo.
Palazzo di Spagna Palazzo di Propaganda Fide	Diagonally opposite the Palazzo di Spagna, which houses the Spanish legation to the Holy See, stands the Palazzo di Propaganda Fide, built for Popes Gregory XV and Urban VIII by Bernini and Borromini. This is the headquarters of the Congregation for the Propagation of the Faith, an organisation established in the 16th c. to promote the missionary activities of the Church.

Visitors resting on the Spanish Steps enjoy the view of the ▶
Piazza di Spagna and La Barcaccia Fountain

Piazza Venezia

Column of the Immaculate Conception

In front of the two palaces is an ancient column bearing a figure of the Virgin, the Column of the Immaculate Conception, around the base of which are the prophets Isaiah and Ezekiel, together with Moses and David. Every year on December 8th the Pope comes to the column to commemorate the proclamation of the dogma of the Immaculate Conception in 1854.

★★Shopping district

Like the Via del Corso which runs roughly parallel, the Via del Babuino and Via Margutta between the Piazza di Spagna and Piazza del Popolo (see entry) are busy shopping streets with a panoply of art galleries, antique shops and elegant boutiques – just the place for a leisurely shopping expedition.

★★Via Condotti shopping mile

★Caffè Greco

From the Piazza di Spagna the Via Condotti runs south-west to the Corso. The Via Condotti is Rome's most fashionable shopping street, famed for haute couture and a place where shoes and leather goods, stylish accessories and extravagant design can all be found. Ever since the 18th c. the Antica Caffè Greco (no. 86) has been frequented by celebrated international artists and writers. Patrons have included such great names as Goethe, Gogol, Schopenhauer, Mendelssohn, Berlioz, Wagner and Liszt.

★Fontana La Barcaccia

The fountain at the foot of the Spanish Steps, in the shape of a boat, is known as the Barcaccia. It is said that Pietro Bernini, Gian Lorenzo's father, who created the fountain in 1627, came upon the idea after the Tiber had overflowed its banks, leaving a boat stranded in the square.

Piazza Venezia   D 6

Buses
44, 45, 46, 56, 60, 62, 65, 70, 75, 90, 181, 186, 710, 718, 719

From the Piazza Venezia, an incessantly busy traffic intersection, roads lead off in five directions: along the Via del Corso, Rome's main thoroughfare, to the Piazza del Popolo (see entry); along the Via del Plebiscito in the direction of the Vatican (see entry); to the piazza in Aracoeli on the Campidoglio (see entry); along the Via dei Fori Imperiali (see Fori Imperiali), past the imperial fora to the Colosseum (see entry); and by way of the Via Battista to the Piazza del Quirinale (see entry).

★Museo di Palazzo Venezia

Via del Plebiscito 118

Opening times
Tue.–Sat. 9am–1.30pm, Sun. 9am–12.30pm

On the west side of the square stands the Palazzo Venezia, begun in its present form in 1451 by Cardinal Pietro Barbo, later Pope Paul II; a number of architects were involved before the building was completed in 1491. The palace is now occupied by the museum of the Istituto Nazionale d'Archeologia e Storia dell'Arte (National Institute of Archeology and Art History). It is also frequently used for temporary art exhibitions.

This elegant and harmoniously proportioned palace belonged between 1594 and 1797 to the Republic of Venice – hence its name – and then became the Austrian Embassy. During the Fascist period it was the official residence of Mussolini, who used to deliver his rhetorical speeches from the centre balcony. Adjoining the Palazzo Venezia, with its massive façade and tower, is the smaller Palazzetto Venezia, which was moved to its present site when the National Monument to Victor Emmanuel II (see Monumento Nazionale a Vittorio Emanuele II) was built.

The museum collection in the Palazzo Venezia is extremely varied – sculptures in wood and marble, weaponry, pictures, tapestries, busts, terracotta models, applied arts, printed books and, in the Sala del Mappamondo, a map of the world.

The Basilica di San Marco, founded by Pope Mark in 336

Basilica di San Marco

This church, now partly incorporated into the Palazzo Venezia, is traditionally believed to have been founded by Pope Marcus (Mark) in honour of the Evangelists in 336. Its present form results from restoration and rebuilding in about 800 and in the 15th and 16th c. Appropriately, since St Mark is the patron saint of Venice, the Palazzo Venezia was from 1564 to 1797 the residence of the Venetian ambassador to the Holy See.

Notable features of the church are the two-storey portico, the campanile adjoining the tower of the Palazzo Venezia, and the mosaic in the apse of Christ transmitting the Law. Dating from the time of Pope Gregory IV (827–44), it shows Christ on a dais surrounded by the Apostles and saints (Gregory, being still alive, is depicted with a square nimbus), above a frieze with symbolic representations of the Lamb of the Apocalypse amid twelve other lambs, and of two cities.

★Pincio   D 4/5

The Pincio Gardens, lying above the Piazza del Popolo below the park of the Villa Medici (see entries), were laid out at the beginning of the 19th c. by the architect Giuseppe Valadier, in an area occupied by gardens belonging to old Roman families, including the Pincio after whom they were named. .

The paths in the gardens are lined with busts of Italian patriots. The views from the terraces, looking down on the Piazza del Popolo and across the whole of central Rome to St Peter's and the Vatican (see entry), are among the finest in the city, particularly at sunset. To this glorious view a meal in the Casino Valadier adds gastronomic delight.

Underground station
Flaminio (line A)

Buses
1, 2b, 90b, 95, 115, 202, 203, 205, 490, 492, 495

Ponte Milvio (Ponte Molle)   C 2

Buses
1, 32, 201, 202,
203, 204, 205,
220, 301, 391,
446, 911

This bridge, to the north of the city and on a direct line from the Forum
(see entry) and Piazza del Popolo (see entry) by way of the Via
Flaminia, was originally constructed over the Tiber during the republican period. The first reconstruction of the bridge was undertaken in
109 B.C. and in the 3rd c. A.D. a tower was added as part of the city
defences. Pope Pius VII ordered further reconstruction in the early
19th c. Subsequently the bridge was blown up by Garibaldi's troops
to halt the advancing French army. A year later, under Pope Pius IX,
the present bridge was constructed.

Also popularly known as the Ponte Molle, it was the scene on 28 October
A.D. 312 of the fateful battle in which Constantine defeated his imperial rival
Maxentius, a victory he attributed to "the God of the Christians".

On weekdays a colourful local market is held on the Piazzale di Ponte
Milvio on the north side of the bridge. It supplies the restaurants in the
area with fish, fruit and vegetables and is well worth a visit.

Portico di Ottavia   D 6

Location
Via del Progresso

Buses
15, 23, 57, 90,
90b, 92, 94, 95,
716, 774

The Portico of Octavia was originally built by Quintus Metellus
Macedonius in 149 B.C., and dedicated to his sister Octavia, whose name it
now bears; it was later rebuilt by Septimus Severus and Caracalla. The
portico once covered an area some 115m/375ft by 135m/445ft enclosing
the temples of Juno and Jupiter. It is now represented by a number of
columns and remains of the entablature incorporated into the porch of the
church of Sant'Angelo in Peschiera. The church takes its name from a fish
market held in the neighbourhood until 1888.

San Carlo ai Catinari   D 6

Location
Piazza Benedetto
Cairoli

Buses
26, 44, 46, 56,
60, 65, 75, 87,
94, 170, 710,
718, 719

St Charles Borromeo, to whom this church is dedicated, was born at
Arona in 1538. In 1560 he was made Cardinal Archbishop of Milan by
his uncle Pope Pius IV. He died in 1584 and was canonised in 1610.
Soon after his canonisation this church, built by Rosato Rosati, was
dedicated to him by the Barnabite order.

San Carlo ai Catinari (named after the washtubs *catinari*, which
were manufactured near here) has an imposing travertine façade
added by G. B. Soria in 1636–38. The lavish interior furnishings
include, in the four pendentives of the cupola, "The Cardinal Virtues"
(1628–30) by Domenichino, and on the high altar the moving portrait
of St Borromeo (1667) by Pietro da Cortona.

San Carlo alle Quattro Fontane   E 5

Location
Via del Quirinale

Buses
57, 64, 65, 70,
71, 75, 170

This church, a masterpiece by Borromini, is situated only a short distance away from the church of Sant'Andrea al Quirinale, a masterpiece by Bernini. San Carlo alle Quattro Fontane takes its name from
the four Baroque fountains close by, with reclining figures representing the Tiber, Anio, Fidelity and Valour.

The building shows a lively interplay of convex and concave lines
with no attempt at regular form. "Harmony and dissonance, symmetry
and asymmetry, passion and serenity blend here into an inexhaustible
play of forms" (Anton Henze). The two-storeyed Baroque façade is
strongly articulated, with columns, niches and a portal flanked by two

One of the four fountains in front of the church of San Carlo alle Quattro Fontane

angels. In the domed interior, an elongated oval, the richness of the decoration largely conceals the underlying architecture.

Borromini died in 1667, shortly before the façade was completed.

★San Clemente   F 7

San Clemente is one of the most venerable and beautiful of Rome's churches. On a site previously occupied by a house containing a shrine of Mithras – now far below street level – an early Christian church was built some time before A.D. 385 and dedicated to Clement, third bishop of Rome after Peter. Following the destruction of this church by the Normans in 1084, a new basilican church was built over its ruins at the beginning of the 12th c.

Location
Via San Giovanni in Laterano

Buses
85, 88

The upper church reflects the old basilican structure with its sequence of entrance porch, atrium with a fountain, nave, where the congregation worship, and schola cantorum, the area reserved for the clergy with the high altar and apse. Notable features in the interior are the ancient columns, the intarsia work by the Cosmati family in the marble pavement, the screens, the Easter candlestick, the tabernacle and the bishop's throne. The triumphal arch and apse are decorated with mosaics of Old and New Testament scenes ("The Triumph of the Cross"), the most richly decorated in Rome. Here the Tree of Life and the Cross, saints and Christian symbolism – animals (including doves on the Cross representing the Apostles, likewise twelve sheep, drawn to the Lamb of God) and plants (the vine: "I am the vine and ye are the branches") – appear interwoven in intricate patterns.

Upper church

In the little St Catherine's Chapel at the west end of the north aisle are early Renaissance frescoes by Masolino (pre 1431) depicting

141

The triumphal arch and apse of the upper church of San Clemente

scenes from the life of St Catherine of Alexandria. As the earliest manifestation of perspective painting in Rome, they are of particular art historical interest.

Lower church

The lower church, a three-aisled pillared basilica of the 4th c., has frescoes dating from different centuries in the Romanesque period. Notable among them are an Ascension in the centre aisle (the donor, Pope Leo IV, appearing with a square nimbus, indicating that he was still alive), episodes from the Passion, and scenes from the life of St Clement.

A passage leads underground to the excavated foundations of a 2nd c. Roman dwelling with a shrine of Mithras in a long barrel-vaulted chamber. The altar, in the middle of the shrine, has a relief depicting Mithras (the Persian sun-god) killing a bull.

San Giorgio in Velabro   D 7

Location
Via del Velabro

Buses
15, 23, 57, 90,
90b, 92, 94, 95,
716, 774

The name Velabro refers to the marshy area on the banks of the Tiber where according to Roman legend Faustulus found the twins Romulus and Remus. The first church on the site was built by Leo II (682–83), the second by Gregory IV (827–44); the campanile and porch were added in the 12th c. The present church, a handsome Romanesque building, incorporates ancient elements such as columns and capitals. In 1933 the church was partly destroyed in a bomb attack by the Falange Armata.

Arco degli
Argentari

Adjoining the church is the Arch of the Moneychangers, erected in honour of Septimus Severus, his wife Julia Domna and their sons Caracalla and Geta, by merchants and bankers of the Forum Boarium, and later incorporated into the church of San Giorgio. It has reliefs, some of them remarkably well preserved, depicting the Imperial family attending a sacrifice, and barbarian prisoners. Some of the names in the original dedication were later erased.

The marble Arch of Janus (Ianus Quadrifrons), in the centre of the Via del Velabro in front of the church, was for a long time believed to have been part of a temple of Janus. In fact it was a covered crossroads (janus) with four exits (quadrifrons) at a busy point in the commercial quarter of ancient Rome. The so-called arch was built using stone from other structures during the reign of Constantine. In the Middle Ages the Frangipani family had a base here.

Arco di Giano

San Giovanni Decollato · D 7

There was in Papal Rome a Fraternity of Mercy (Confraternità della Misericordia), established in 1488 (and of which Michelangelo was a member), which undertook responsibility for accompanying condemned prisoners to execution and had the right, once a year, to secure the pardon of a prisoner. This Fraternity erected the church of San Giovanni to commemorate the beheading (decollation) of St John the Baptist. Begun in 1535, the church was completed in 1555. The handsome mannerist altar paintings and the frescoes in the oratory adjoining the cloister, depict scenes from the life of the saint, the "Beheading of John the Baptist" in the reign of King Herod being the principal theme.

Location
Via di San Giovanni Decollato

Buses
15, 57, 90, 90b, 92, 94, 95, 716

San Giovanni dei Fiorentini · C 6

Pope Leo X, a member of the Florentine ruling dynasty of the Medici, being desirous of providing a church for his "fellow countrymen" in Rome, held an architectural competition in which both Michelangelo and Raphael took part. The competition was won, however, by Sansovino, who enlisted other architects in the building of the church – Sangallo, Michelangelo (in an advisory capacity), della Porta, Maderna, and Alessandro Galilei who was responsible for the façade. The church is impressive particularly on account of its size, the exactly contrived spatial effect of the interior and the rich Baroque decoration and furnishings, including the apse designed by Pietro da Cortona and the high altar by Borromini. Interred within the church are the famous architects Francesco Borromini (memorial tablet, third pillar on the left) and Carlo Maderna (memorial slab beneath the dome).

Location
Via Giulia

Buses
23, 28, 28b, 41, 42, 46b, 62, 64, 65, 98, 98c, 881

San Giovanni in Laterano

See Piazza San Giovanni in Laterano

San Giovanni a Porta Latina · F 8

This early Romanesque church lies hidden behind the ancient city walls in the Via di Porta Latina. The basilica of St John at the Latin Gate was founded in the 5th c., rebuilt about 720 and restored in 1191 during the reign of Pope Celestine III. It is in the familiar form of the Roman basilica, with a simple portico supported on columns and a tall campanile of classical design.

Location
Via Porta Latina

Bus
118

The church contains an important cycle of early 13th c. frescoes depicting 46 scenes from the Old and New Testament; they are among the finest medieval frescoes in Rome.

San Girolamo (degli Illirici o degli Schiavoni)   D 5

Location
Via di Ripetta/
Via Tomacelli

Buses
2, 26, 28, 70,
81, 88, 90, 115

Following the Turkish victory at Kosovo in 1387, many refugees from Dalmatia and Albania fled to Rome. Thereafter this church, built during the reigns of Sixtus IV and V and completed in 1588, became known as the church "degli Illirici" or "degli Schiavoni". The Baroque building, restored during the reign of Pius IX, is now the Croatian national church and has a seminary attached to it.

San Gregorio Magno   E 7

Location
Via di San
Gregorio

Buses
11, 15, 27, 118,
673

Trams
13, 30, 30b

Starting at the Arco di Constantino (see entry), the wide tree-lined Via San Gregorio, once the Via triumphalis of victorious Roman generals but today a broad main thoroughfare, runs between the slopes of the Palatino (see entry) and Celio, past the church of San Gregorio Magno – from which it takes its name – to the southern end of the Circus Maximus (see entry).

The church of San Gregorio, which is approached by a large flight of steps, was founded in 575 – before he became Pope – by Gregory the Great, a member of the Antiti family, who converted his family house on this site into a convent. It was rebuilt in medieval times, and completely refashioned in the Baroque period by Giovanni Battista Sorià (1629–33), on the model of the church of Sant'Ignazio, though on a smaller scale. The interior was remodelled by Francesco Ferrari in the mid 18th c.; the ceiling painting "St Gregory and Romuald in Glory" (1727) is by Placido Constanzi.

The atrium, the church itself, the oratory, and the three chapels – of St Andrew (frescoes by Guido Reni and Domenichino, 17th c.), St Silvia (fresco of angels by Reni, 1608) and St Barbara (wall painting by Antonio Viviani, 1602) – combine to form a unity of impressive effect.

San Lorenzo in Lucina   D 5

Location
Piazza di San
Lorenzo in Lucina

Buses
52, 53, 56, 58,
60, 61, 62, 71,
81, 88, 90, 95,
115

The church of San Lorenzo in Lucina, dedicated to the martyr St Lawrence who is much venerated in Rome, has had an eventful history. Originally built in the 4th and 5th c. over the house of a Roman woman called Lucina, it was rebuilt in the 12th c. and acquired its present form in 1650.

On the high altar (by Carlo Rainaldi, 1675) is a "Crucifixion" by Guido Reni, one of his finest works. The first chapel in the north aisle has an altar-piece by Carlo Saraceni; the Fonseca family chapel (south aisle, fourth chapel) was designed by Bernini.

★San Lorenzo fuori le Mura   H 5

Location
Piazza San
Lorenzo

This early Christian basilica, one of the seven pilgrimage churches of Rome, is dedicated to St Lawrence, who was martyred in A.D. 328 by being roasted on a gridiron. (The other pilgrimage churches are San Giovanni in Laterano, San Pietro in Vaticano, San Paolo fuori le Mura, Santa Maria Maggiore, San Sebastiano and Santa Croce in Gerusalemme; see entries). The church was founded by Constantine the Great and thereafter frequently rebuilt and restored – most recently after having suffered damage during an Allied air raid on Rome in July 1943.

San Lorenzo, situated "outside the walls" beside the Campo Verano (see entry), Rome's largest cemetery, has preserved through all rebuildings (particularly in the 13th c.) the structure of an early Christian basilica, with its porch (containing ancient sarcophagi), its wide, high nave with narrow lateral aisles, its chancel on a higher level and its handsome columns. Lower down, on the level of the first basilica, is the tomb of Pope Pius IX (1846–78). Also of particular note are the Cosmatesque work (coloured stones inlaid in marble) on the two marble ambos (pulpits from which the Gospels and Epistles are read: the one on the right for the reading of the Epistle is the finest in Rome), the Easter candlestick, the floor, the tabernacle, the bishop's throne and the tomb of Cardinal Fieschi.

The mosaics on the triumphal arch depict Christ surrounded by saints, with elaborate representation, to the left and right, of Jerusalem and Bethlehem. There is a plain cloister dating from the late 12th c.

The extensive catacombs off the cloister contain a columbarium and interesting early Christian paintings including the fresco "The Wise and Foolish Virgins".

Buses
11, 71, 109, 111, 309, 311, 411, 415, 492

Trams
19, 19b, 30, 30b

Catacombe di Santa Ciriaca

★San Luigi dei Francesi   D 6

San Luigi dei Francesi, dedicated to St Louis (Louis IX of France), is the French national church in Rome. It was begun by Cardinal Giulio

Location
Piazza di San Luigi dei Francesi

Buses
26, 70, 81, 87, 88, 90, 94

"St Matthew with an Angel" a masterpiece by Caravaggio

dei Medici, later Pope Clement VII, in 1518, but the work was suspended and not resumed until 1580 (under the direction of Domenico Fontana and possibly also Jean de Chenevières). The church was finally dedicated in 1589. The monumental Renaissance façade was probably the work of Giacomo della Porta (ca. 1540–1602).

A three-aisled basilica, the church contains three important paintings of scenes from the life of St Matthew by Caravaggio; from left to right: the Summons, the Evangelist and the Martyrdom (ca. 1597). Masterpieces of realistic painting, with Caravaggio's new composition of light and shade and striking chiaroscuro effects, they were not universally admired at the time. A self-portrait of the artist can be seen to the left of the executioner in the martyrdom scene.

★San Paolo fuori le Mura   D 10

Location
Piazzale di
San Paolo

**Underground
station**
San Paolo (line B)

Buses
23, 123, 170, 223,
673, 707, 766

Few remains have so far been found of the early Christian chapel built in the time of Constantine (4th c.) over the grave of St Paul, well outside the city walls on the road to Ostia; but it seems certain that Paul – who according to tradition was beheaded in A.D. 67 and buried by the Via Ostiensis – was venerated in early times at the site of the present church. In order to do honour to the Apostles the Emperors of the 4th and 5th c. built a basilica which until the rebuilding of St Peter's (see Vatican) was the largest in the world. This church was damaged on various occasions by earthquake and fire, and eventually completely destroyed by fire on 15 July 1823 as a result of the carelessness of a plumber. Thereafter it was rebuilt, with financial assistance from many countries, and reopened in 1854. San Paolo is one of the four patriarchal churches of Rome (the others being San Giovanni in Laterano, St Peter's/San Pietro in Vaticano, and Santa Maria

One of the four patriarchal churches of Rome: San Paolo fuori le Mura

Maggiore) and one of the seven pilgrimage churches (the patriarchal churches together with Santa Croce in Gerusalemme, San Lorenzo fuori le Mura and San Sebastiano; see entries).

Subsequent to its 19th c. rebuilding, San Paolo is notable particularly for its basilican plan, following the early Christian model, and for a number of fine works of art. The church is entered by way of a colonnaded forecourt which leads into a porch (19th c. mosaics high up on the façade), with the Holy Door, on the inner side of which can be seen the old bronze door cast in Constantinople in the 11th c. The interior of the church is dark, since the alabaster windows admit little light. The nave (120m/395ft long, 60m/195ft wide and 23m/75ft high) is divided into five aisles by a forest of 80 columns leading into a triumphal arch (5th c. mosaic), the altar with its ciborium and the apse (mosaics). High up on the walls of the church are 265 portrait medallions of all the Popes from Peter onwards. Apart from the 13th c. mosaics by Venetian artists, commissioned in 1220 by Honorius III, which were extensively restored, the decorations in the apse, including the bishop's throne, are copies dating from the 19th c.

Particular features of note are the ciborium (by Arnolfo di Cambio, 1285, commissioned by Abbot Bartolomeo) over the Papal altar, which like the altar in St Peter's, probably marks the spot where the Apostle was buried; the 5.6m/18ft-high Easter candlestick to the right of the altar, a magnificent medieval sculpture by Nicolò di Angelo and Pietro Vassalletti; the Chapel of the Crucifix; and the baptistery.

In the sacristy is the entrance to the cloister of the Benedictine abbey, decorated with mosaics by the Vassalletti family (1204–41). The variety of form of the columns and the colour of the mosaics make this one of the most attractive cloisters in the West.

San Pietro in Montorio   C 7

The church of St Peter on the Golden Mountain, an early Renaissance building of the late 15th c., owes its foundation to the medieval legend that the Apostle Paul was crucified on this spot.

The hall-like church was built for King Ferdinand IV of Spain by Baccio Pontelli (after 1481). The chapels on the left-hand side contain notable pictures, including the "Scourging of Christ" (by Sebastiano del Piombo, (ca. 1519), a Madonna by Pomarancio, and the "Conversion of St Paul" by Giorgio Vasari. The second chapel on the left was designed by Bernini in about 1640. The "Crucifixion of St Peter" in the apse is a copy of a work by Guido Reni; the original is in the Pinacoteca of the Vatican Museum (see Vatican).

Location
Via Garibaldi

Buses
41, 44, 75, 710

In a court to the right of the church is the famous Tempietto di Bramante, a small round pillared temple built as a chapel by Bramante in 1502 to commemorate the crucifixion of St Peter. It is considered a classic of High Renaissance architecture, demonstrating the characteristic return to antiquity and the revival of Greco-Roman architectural forms. The harmony of its proportions and symmetry of its forms makes this little temple an architectural delight.

★Tempietto di Bramante

★San Pietro in Vincoli   E 6

The church of Saint Peter in Chains is one of the oldest in Rome, having been begun in 431. It was originally dedicated to St Peter and St Paul, but when Pope Leo the Great was presented with the chains traditionally believed to be those worn by Peter while in the Mamertine Prison – in his famous Stanzas in the Vatican (see entry), Raphael depicted an

Location
Piazza San Pietro in Vincoli

San Pietro in Vincoli

Underground station
Cavour (line B)

Buses
11, 27, 81

angel setting him free – St Peter became the sole patron of the church. The chains are now preserved as a precious relic in the high altar. The gold decoration on the tabernacle is attributed to Christoforo Caradossa. The impressive portico is the work of Meo da Caprino and the marble porch bears the coat of arms of the architect Giuliano della Rovere. The most notable features are the 20 columns with Doric capitals in the nave and the tomb of Cardinal Nicholas of Cusa (d. 1465) in the north aisle (with a relief by Andrea Bregno showing St Peter flanked by the liberating angel and the cardinal).

Even more precious however is the magnificent monument of Pope Julius II (east end of the south aisle). This monument to the great Pope of the della Rovere family (1503–13) was originally conceived by Michelangelo on a larger scale for erection in St Peter's. Of the sculpture originally planned Michelangelo himself executed only three figures – the central figure of Moses, together with Rachel and Leah, the two wives of Jacob. The figures of Rachel and Leah, symbols of the active and contemplative life, are late works of outstanding quality; but the figure of Moses (1513–16), intended also to celebrate the great Pope and Prince of the Renaissance, ranks among the finest achievements of this brilliant sculptor. Moses, leader of the Israelites, is depicted at the moment when, having received from God the tablets of the Law (inscribed with the Ten Commandments) which he holds beneath his right arm, he watches his people dancing around the golden calf. His face expresses both divine illumination and wrath over the faithlessness of his people. (The horns on his forehead reflect a mistranslation of the Biblical text.)

The Moses Statue created by Michelangelo for the monument of Pope Julius II

San Sebastiano

The church of St Sebastian on the Via Appia is one of the seven pilgrimage churches of Rome (the others being San Giovanni in Laterano, San Pietro in Vaticano, San Paolo fuori le Mura, Santa Maria Maggiore, Santa Croce in Gerusalemme, and San Lorenzo fuori le Mura; see entries). The church was built in the 4th c. on the site of old cemeteries and catacombs.

Location
Via Appia Antica
136

Bus
118

It is believed that the remains of Peter and Paul were brought here for safe keeping during the Christian persecutions in the reigns of Decius and Valerian, and that St Sebastian, a Christian officer of the Praetorian Guard martyred in the reign of Diocletian, was also buried here.

Behind the apse, stairs lead down to the so-called Platonia, the crypt of the martyr St Quirinus; to the left is the "Domus Petri", a cell with wall paintings dating from the 4th c.

In the 13th and early 17th c. three Roman tombs and a series of Christian catacombs were brought to light. Also uncovered were the foundations of the Constantine basilica and remains of Roman houses. Beneath the centre of the church was found a meeting-hall (triclia) in which services of remembrance were held, with large numbers of scratched inscriptions dating from the turn of the 3–4th c. They include numerous examples of the symbolism used by the early Christians – the fish (Greek "ichthys", from the initial letters of the words "Jesus Christ, Son of God, Saviour"); the lamb, referring to Christ's sacrificial death; the anchor, a sign of trust; and the dove, the symbol of peace.

★Catacombe di
San Sebastiano

Here too are tomb chambers on several levels (1st c. A.D.) with fine paintings, stucco decoration and inscriptions (open: Mon.–Wed., Fri.–Sun. 8.30am–noon, 2.30–5pm, in summer until 5.30pm).

★Sant'Agnese fuori le Mura

According to legend, Agnes was a young [girl?] who steadfastly refused to marry the son of [a prefect of the?] city and was martyred for her faith. In the 4[th c. Emperor] ter Constantia erected a church in her hon[our outside the] walls, on the Via Nomentana.

36, 37, 60, 136,
137, 310

The present church was built by Pope Honorius I (625–38) but has undergone much alteration through the centuries. A basilica with a high narrow nave, among its notable features are the sixteen antique columns, the richly decorated wooden ceiling (17th c.), and the marble candelabra and bishop's throne in the chancel. Finest of all, however, is the 7th c. mosaic in the apse, depicting St Agnes with Popes Honorius and Symmachus against a gilded background. The martyred girl wears a garment bearing a phoenix risen from the ashes, symbol of immortality. Relics of St Agnes and her sister, St Emeritiana, are preserved in the high altar.

Beneath the church are the Catacombs of Sant'Agnese (3rd c. A.D.). Extending over three levels, they have a total length of 7km/4 miles (open: Mon.–Sun. 9am–12.30pm, Tue.–Sun. 4–6pm; visits on application to the verger).

Catacombe di
Sant'Agnese

Close to the church of Sant'Agnese is another – Santa Costanza – with one of the most delightful interiors of all the Roman churches. A round church, it was built at the beginning of the 4th c. as a mausoleum for Constantine's daughter Constantia (or Constantina) and

★Santa Costanza

Helena, wife of Julian the Apostate. This little architectural master-piece, measuring 22.5km/74ft in diameter, is simple in conception, with an unpretentious brick-built exterior; but the internal construc-tion incorporates costly and valuable materials (12 double columns with capitals). The mosaics depict both sacred and pagan figures, with animals playing amid vines. In this small church, Roman archi-tecture, the mosaic art of late antiquity, and early Christian symbol-ism, are blended into a harmonious whole.

★Sant'Agostino   D 6

Location
Piazza di Sant'
Agostino

Buses
26, 70

Sant'Agostino, situated near the Piazza Navona (see entry), is noted for its image of the Madonna del Parto (Madonna of Childbirth) who is invoked by pregnant women seeking a safe delivery and by married couples wanting a child. The church, built between 1479 and 1483 (probably by Giacomo da Pietrasanta) and rebuilt in 1750, has a severe travertine façade, one of the earliest Renaissance façades in Rome.

The interior, with a tall nave scarcely wider than the side aisles, is dominated by the dome flanked by transepts. In addition to the Madonna del Parto (by Jacopo Sansovino, 1521), the church boasts a painting of the prophet Isaiah by Raphael (1512; third pillar on the left) and Caravaggio's "Madonna of the Pilgrims" (1605; first chapel in the left aisle).

To the right of the church is the Biblioteca Angelica (state-owned since 1873), a library specialising in philology.

★Sant'Andrea al Quirinale   E 6

Location
Via del Quirinale

Buses
64, 65, 70,
75, 170

Sant'Andrea al Quirinale, built by Bernini (1658–71) for Cardinal Camillo Pamphili as the church of the Jesuit missionary, is a jewel among the smaller churches of Rome, and forms a counterpart to the nearby church of St Carlo alle Quatro Fontane (see entry), built by Bernini's great rival Borromini.

Sant'Andrea, which was the court chapel of the Italian royal house from 1870 to 1946, is notable both for the consummate perfection of its design and the richness of its decoration. The circular ground plan typical of the Renaissance is here extended into the oval favoured by Baroque architects, and this, opened out still further by eight lateral chapels, creates the sense of space and movement which appealed to the Baroque taste.

The lively architectual pattern is matched by the lavish interior decoration with its pilasters and friezes, arches and recesses, coffered domes, cornices, windows, and marble and stucco of many colours (old rose, white, gold). There are also fine frescoes and panel paint-ings, mainly of the Baroque period.

Sant'Andrea della Valle   D 6

Location
Corso Vittorio
Emanuele II

Buses
46, 62, 64, 70,
81, 88, 90

The full beauty of the façade and dome of the church of Sant'Andrea della Valle is best appreciated from the Corso del Rinascimento; a dis-tinctive feature is the angel with outspread wings on the left-hand side, taking the place of a volute (there is no corresponding feature on the right-hand side). Sant'Andrea, served by the Theatines (a preach-ing order), is very popular with the people of Rome – as is evidenced by the fact that Puccini sets the first act of "Tosca" in the Cappella Allaventi, the first chapel in the south aisle of the church.

The architects responsible for Sant'Andrea (Francesco Grimaldi, Giacomo della Porta, Carlo Maderna and Carlo Rainaldi) followed the model of Il Gesó (see entry), some 500m/550yds away. Many features are clearly reminiscent of that church – the two-storey travertine façade with its plastic structure, the nave, tall and wide but yet creating an effect of harmony and unity, with its side chapels, transept, choir and apse, and the mighty dome, the second largest in Rome after the dome of St Peter's (see entry); indeed the ground plan of Sant'Andrea is almost indistinguishable from that of Il Gesó.

The side chapels contain some fine paintings and statues, but the most notable feature of the interior are the monuments to two Popes belonging to the Piccolomini family of Siena which were brought here from St Peter's in 1614 and can now be seen in the nave near the north transept: the humanist Pope Pius II (Aeneas Silvius Piccolomini, d. 1464) on the left and Pope Pius III (Francesco Todeschini Piccolomini, d. 1503) on the right. Both tombs were the work of Paolo Taccone and Andrea Bregno.

The magnificent frescoes in the dome and the semi-dome of the apse were painted by Domenichino (1624–28).

Sant'Ignazio   D 6

The Society of Jesus, founded by Ignatius Loyola in 1540, soon attracted an increasing following and a large membership in Rome and throughout Europe. To honour the memory of their founder, who died in 1556 and was canonised in 1622, the Jesuits built the church of Sant'Ignazio – the second Jesuit church in Rome, following Il Gesó (see entry) – between 1626 and 1650, with financial assistance from Cardinal Ludovico Ludovisi, a nephew of Pope Gregory XV. Both the architect, Orazio Grassi, and the painter, Andrea Pozzo, were Jesuits.

Location
Piazza di
Sant'Ignazio

Buses
26, 56, 60, 62,
71, 81, 85, 87,
88, 90, 90b, 94,
95

Like the square in which it stands, which has something of the air of a stage set, the imposing façade of the church is very much in the Baroque spirit; the interior even more so. The broad and spacious nave, equally suited to preaching or to conducting the service from one central spot; the linked side chapels; the sumptuous decoration and furnishings with their use of precious materials and elaborate ornamental patterns; all were calculated to draw the faithful back to the Church (this was the period of the Counter-Reformation). The harmony of the interior suffers not at all from the omission of the central dome originally planned; instead, on the ceiling, Andrea Pozzo created a trompe l'oil painting celebrating St Ignatius's triumphant entry into Paradise and the four missionary quarters of the world. The illusion created is of the false dome breaking asunder to reveal a glimpse of Heaven above. (A marble disc in the floor marks the spot from which the illusion is most effective.) In Sant'Ignazio architecture, sculpture and painting merge into one another; the eye of the believer was to be caught and held by art, his heart to be opened to the teaching of the Church.

In the south transept is the tomb of St Aloysius (Luigi Gonzaga, 1568–91); in the north transept that of St John Berchmans, both Jesuits.

Santa Croce in Gerusalemme   G 7

Santa Croce in Gerusalemme is one of the seven pilgrimage churches of Rome, the others being San Giovanni in Laterano, San Pietro in Vaticano, San Paolo fuori le Mura, Santa Maria Maggiore, San Sebastiano and San Lorenzo fuori le Mura (see entries). Pilgrims like to attend services at these churches on the eve of important Catholic festivals.

Location
Piazza Santa
Croce in
Gerusalemme

Underground station
San Giovanni, (line A)

Buses
3, 9, 15, 81

The church was built in the reign of Constantine for the purpose – so legend has it – of housing the relics of Christ's Passion which Constantine's mother Helena had brought from the Holy Land. It was given its present Baroque form in the 18th c. (architect, Domenico Gregorini).

Santa Maria dell'Anima   C 6

Location
Via di Santa
Maria dell'Anima
(entrance:
Piazza della
Pace 20)

Buses
26, 70, 81, 88, 90

Pilgrims to Rome expected to find a hospice where they could stay and a church of their own nationality. Santa Maria dell'Anima, situated near the Piazza Navona (see entry), was built in 1501–14 for German pilgrims, or rather, pilgrims from the Holy Roman Empire. It is still the church of the German Catholic community in Rome.

Soon after the church was built, Pope Adrian VI (1522–23), a native of Utrecht and the last non-Italian Pope before John Paul II, was buried here. His tomb in the choir is flanked by allegorical figures representing the four cardinal virtues, Prudence, Justice, Fortitude and Temperance. The experience of this sorely tried Pope, who reigned during the early days of the Reformation, is summarised in a Latin inscription referring to the effect on a man's life of the age into which he is born. The interior of this tall, three-aisled hall-church, its vaulting supported by square pillars, is richly decorated in the Renaissance style.

Santa Maria in Aracoeli   D 6

Location
Via di Teatro
di Marcello

Buses
57, 90, 90b, 92,
94, 95, 716, 718,
719

Santa Maria in Aracoeli bathes in the reflected glory of the Capitol. The church occupies a most venerable and sacred site, having been built by Franciscans in the 13th c. on the foundations of the ancient temple of Juno Moneta, probably dating from the 6th c. B.C. The steep flight of 124 steps leading up to the church (which young couples like to climb after their wedding) was constructed in 1348. In the Middle Ages the church was at the centre of Roman political life, being the meeting place of the municipal parliament. The interior was redecorated after the defeat of the Turkish fleet at Lepanto in 1571.

The majestic flight of steps ascends steeply from the Piazza d'Aracoeli on the Via di Teatro di Marcello, to a bare brick façade, which makes the interior appear all the more sumptuous despite its simple basilican plan (with side chapels added later). Notable features of the church are the 16th c. wooden ceiling, the Cappella Bufalini at the near end of the south aisle, which has frescoes of San Bernardino by Pinturicchio (1485), and numerous grave-slabs and monuments in the floor and on the walls. The tomb of Pope Honorius IV (d. 1287) in the south transept is of outstanding artistic quality.

In the north transept is an elegant aedicula (miniature temple) marking the place where a Tiburtine Sibyl prophesied to Augustus that a virgin would bear a divine child who would overthrow the altars of the gods. Whereupon the Emperor set up an altar on the same spot with the inscription – now on the triumphal arch – "Ecce ara promogeneti Dei" (Behold the altar of the firstborn of God). Beneath the aedicula are interred the remains of St Helena, Constantine's mother, who went to the Holy Land in search of the True Cross and relics of Christ's Passion and brought them back to Rome.

Santo Bambino

Before its theft in 1994, the "Santo Bambino", a figure of the Child Jesus which legend says was carved from the wood of an olive-tree in the garden of Gethsemane and which was popularly credited with miraculous qualities, stood in the sacristy. At Christmas the image would be set up in the nave and children preached "sermons" in front of it.

★★Santa Maria Maggiore — F 6

Santa Maria Maggiore is the largest of the 80 Roman churches dedicated to the Virgin. It is also one of the four patriarchal basilicas (after San Giovanni in Laterano, San Pietro in Vaticano and San Paolo fuori le Mura; see entries) and one of the seven pilgrimage churches (the patriarchal churches together with Santa Croce in Gerusalemme, San Lorenzo fuori le Mura and San Sebastiano; see entries). It is the only church in Rome in which mass has been celebrated every day without interruption since the 5th c.

According to legend, on the night of the 4th/5th August in the year 352, the Virgin appeared to Pope Liberius and a Roman patrician named John and told them to build a church on the spot where snow would fall the following day (in August of all months!). Snow did fall on the following morning on the Esquiline hill, outlining the plan of a basilica; since then the feast of Our Lady of the Snow has been celebrated on August 5th.

Archeological research has been unable to establish however, whether the church was erected in the 4th or the 5th c. The original church was added to in later centuries; a new apse was built in the 13th c.; the campanile (75m/245ft high; the tallest in Rome) in 1377. Alexander VI built the golden coffered roof using the first gold from America; two side chapels, the Cappella Sistina and Cappella Paolina were added, and between the 16th and 18th c. the church was surrounded by a whole series of extensions (prelates' quarters).

There is an entrance on the apsidal facade, gained by means of an imposing flight of steps from the Piazza dell'Esquilino (with its 15m/49ft-high obelisk from the Mausoleum of Augustus; see Mausoleo di Augusto). The main entrance (façade by Ferdinando Fuga, 1743–50) is

Location
Piazza di Santa Maria Maggiore

Underground station
Termini
(lines A, B)

Buses
3, 4, 16, 27, 70, 71, 93, 93b, 93c

Trams
14, 516, 517

Opening times
7am–noon, 4–7pm

The largest of the Santa Maria churches in Rome – Santa Maria Maggiore

153

Crypt of Santa Maria Maggiore, with relics of the crib of Bethlehem

from the Piazza Santa Maria Maggiore, itself adorned with a column from the Basilica of Maxentius, now crowned with a figure of the Virgin.

The interior is perhaps the finest and most majestic church interior in Rome; 86m/282ft long, three-aisled, with 36 marble and four granite columns, mosaics (4th or 5th c., the oldest in Rome) on the upper part of the walls, Cosmatesque work in the floor (mid 12th c) and a coffered ceiling by Giuliano da Sangallo (15th c.).

The Cappella Sistina on the right and the Cappella Paolina on the left are in effect transepts. The Cappella Sistina, built by Domenico Fontana (1584–90) for Pope Sixtus V and embellished with late 16th c. mannerist frescoes, contains a bronze tabernacle and the tombs of Sixtus V and his predecessor Pius V. The Cappella Paolina was built for Pope Paul V by Flaminio Ponzio; the richly decorated altarpiece was designed by Girolamo Rainaldi.

On the canopied high altar, by Ferdinando Fuga, is a much venerated image of the Virgin (the "Salus Populi Romani"), traditionally attributed to St Luke but in fact a 13th c. work. The Confessio contains a glass case displaying relics of the manger in Bethlehem, in front of which is the kneeling statue of Pius IX by Ignazio Iacometti (1880). The capopy over the Papal altar is supported on four porphyry columns from Hadrian's villa at Tivoli (see entry).

Further contributing to the magnificence of the decoration are the mosaics on the triumphal arch and in the apse, depicting scenes from the Old and New Testament and from the life of the Virgin. They include the story of Abraham, Isaac and Jacob, the Annunciation, the Three Wise Men, the Flight into Egypt and the Coronation of the Virgin. This late 13th c. masterpiece by Jacopo Torriti represents the supreme artistic achievement of the Roman mosaic-workers (best light early in the morning).

★Santa Maria sopra Minerva   D 6

The square in front of the church of Santa Maria sopra Minerva is
graced by a charming monument, a marble elephant by Bernini (1667)
supporting a small Egyptian obelisk (6th c. B.C.) The inscription on the
plinth is to the effect that great strength is required to bear wisdom.

Location
Piazza della
Minerva

Buses
26, 87, 94

The church is built over the ruins of a temple of Minerva; hence
"sopra Minerva". It was begun, in Gothic style, about 1280 but was
completed only in 1453 with the vaulting of the nave. It is thus the
only Gothic church building of any size in Rome.

Situated in the centre of the city and served by St Dominic's preach-
ing order (the Dominicans's headquarters are to the left of the building), the church was popular with the people of Rome. The large
number of grave-slabs and memorials in the floor and on the walls
of the three-aisled basilica, as also in the side chapels adorned with
pictures, bear witness to the part it played in the religious life of the
city. The best known of the funerary chapels is the Caraffa Chapel
at the end of the south transept, also known as the Chapel of the
Annunciation of St Thomas, which contains the tomb of Cardinal
Oliviero Caraffa and is renowned for its frescoes by Filippo Lippi
(1489). These glorify both the Virgin (Annunciation and Assumption)
and St Thomas Aquinas, a member of the Dominican order (the
triumph of the saint and scenes from his life).

The high altar contains the relics of St Catherine of Siena (1347–80),
author of numerous letters to the exiled Popes at Avignon, urging
them to return to Rome. In front of the altar, on the left, is a figure of
the Risen Christ by Michelangelo (1521), a statue unfairly found
wanting in comparison with his other works. It was criticised
during Michelangelo's lifetime for looking more like a youthful
pagan god than the founder of Christianity, and later a loincloth
was added to cover the figure's nakedness. Quiet contemplation
is needed to appreciate the full expressiveness of the statue, but
the masterly skill with which the marble is fashioned is evident at
first glance. Michelangelo's genius so impressed other artists that
the painter Sebastiano del Piombo, for example, maintained that
Christ's knees were worth more than all the buildings in Rome. In
a passageway to the left of the presbytery is the tomb of the painter
Fra Angelico, a member of the Dominican order.

*The Elephant
Obelisk*

Santa Maria di Monserrato   C 6

About the same time as the church of Santa Maria dell'Anima was built
for pilgrims from Germany, this church was built by Antonio da
Sangallo the Elder (1495 onwards) for the Catalans and Aragonese.
The initiative came from the famous (or notorious) Pope Alexander VI
(see Famous People), a member of the Spanish Borja family (Italian:
Borgia), who is buried in the church. Named after the renowned
Marian pilgrimage centre of Monserrat near Barcelona, Santa Maria di
Monserrato has been since 1875 the Spanish national church in Rome.

Location
Via di
Monserrato/
Via Giulia 151

Buses
23, 28, 28b, 65

Notable features of the church are the tombs of the two Borgia
Popes, Calixtus III and Alexander VI, and a marble bust of Cardinal
Pietro Molto by Bernini (1621).

★Santa Maria della Pace   C 6

Santa Maria della Pace, one of Rome's most beautiful churches,
reached its present form in a number of stages. In 1482 Pope Sixtus IV
rebuilt an earlier church of the Virgin on this site in thanksgiving for

Location
Via della Pace

Buses
26, 70, 81, 88, 90

the peace of Milan. The architect is thought to have been Baccio Pontelli, who created a rectangular building to which another architect, perhaps Bramante, afterwards appended a domed octagon. In 1656 Pietro da Cortona restored the church, adding the façade and a semicircular porch (pronate). This delightful entrance gives access to the nave and octagon, containing famous frescoes (1515) by Raphael depicting the ancient Sibyls; figures of prophets and saints were later added by other painters.

The admirably proportioned cloister was built by Bramante for Cardinal Oliviero Caraffa in 1504.

★Santa Maria della Vittoria E 5

Location
Via XX Settembre

Underground stations
Repubblica,
Barberini, (line A)

Buses
60, 61, 62, 415

Santa Maria della Vittoria commemorates the Emperor Ferdinand II's victory at the battle of the White Mountain near Prague in 1620 during the Thirty Years War, a victory attributed to the intervention of the Virgin. The church, previously dedicated to St Paul, then received an image of the Virgin, found at Pilsen and reputed to be miraculous, and was re-dedicated under its present name.

This attractive Baroque church, built by Carlo Maderna in 1608–20, is of imposing effect with its finely contrived decoration of coloured marble, rich stucco ornament and paintings. The most impressive part of the church, however, is the altar of St Teresa of Avila (fourth chapel on the left), created by Bernini for Cardinal Cornaro. St Teresa (1515–82), authoress and mystic, who refounded the order of Carmelite nuns, is depicted in a state of ecstatic rapture, pierced by the love of God which is symbolised by the arrow of the angel who hovers over her.

The sacristy contains standards from the Battle of Prague and pictures of the battle.

The rich mosiac decoration in the Chapel of Zeno in Santa Prassede

★Santa Prassede   F 6

A legend relates that Pudentiana (see Santa Pudenziana) and
Praxedes, two daughters of a Roman senator named Pudens, were
converted to the Christian faith by St Peter. The church, dedicated to
St Praxedes, has gone through a number of different building stages,
but has preserved the spatial character of an early Christian basilica,
its high nave rising into the presbytery with its triumphal arch and
apse mosaics (9th c., in the reign of Pope Paschal I) which are among
the finest in Rome. On the triumphal arch is a representation of the
heavenly Jerusalem; in the apse is the apocalyptic Lamb of the Revelation, and in the conch of the apse, above a frieze of lambs, SS Peter
and Paul leading Praxedes and Pudentiana, accompanied by Pope
Paschal as the donor and by St Zeno. In addition to glorifying the
saints, the representations had a didactic purpose: the object, as in
other religious painting, was to instruct the worshippers, who in the
Middle Ages were mostly illiterate, in the doctrines of the faith. The
chapel of St Zeno (in the south aisle), built by Pope Paschal I to house
the tomb of his mother Theodora, is like a medieval picturebook,
every part of the walls and vaulting being covered with mosaics
depicting saints and Biblical symbols.

Location
Via Santa
Prassede

Buses
16, 93, 93b, 93c

★Santa Pudenziana   F 6

Santa Pudenzia church, originally built in the reign of Pope Siricius
(384–99), is said to occupy the site of the house of the Roman
senator Pudens (see above). It has undergone much subsequent
alteration, but the original apse with its mosaic decoration has been
preserved.
   The church, now lying below the present street level, is entered
from Via Urbana. Externally its most notable features are the
campanile and the remains of a Romanesque doorway. The finest feature of the interior is the mosaic in the apse (late 4th c.), now rather
cramped by later building. It shows Christ surrounded by Apostles
and women against a lively background based on ancient scenes,
with a skilful use of perspective. Above the central group are the
buildings of a city, a cross and the (partly obliterated) symbols of the
four Evangelists, the man, the lion, the bull and the eagle.

Location
Via Urbana

Buses
27, 70, 71, 81

★Santa Sabina   D 7

Both externally and internally the church of Santa Sabina has preserved the character of an early Christian basilica. Built by Peter of
Illyria in 425–432 over the house of a Christian woman named Sabina,
it was embellished with marble by Pope Eugenius II in 824. In 1222
Pope Honorius II presented the church to the Dominicans.
   The central doorway in the porch has the oldest carved wooden
doors in Christian art (432), made of African cedar-wood with delicate
and expressive reliefs by unknown artists depicting Old and New
Testament scenes. Of the original 28 panels 18 have survived, though
not in their original positions. The scenes can be readily identified
(from top to bottom and left to right):
   1st row: Crucifixion, Healing of the Blind Man, Miracle of the Loaves
and Fishes, Marriage in Cana, Doubting Thomas, Moses and the
Burning Bush, Christ before Pilate.
   2nd row: Resurrection, Miracles of Moses, Christ's Appearance to
the Women.

Location
Piazza Pietro
d'Illiria

Buses
23, 57, 92, 94, 95,
716

3rd row: Three Kings, Ascension, Peter's Denial, Crossing of the Red Sea, Miracle of the Serpent.

4th row: Christ between Peter and Paul, Triumph of Christ, Assumption of Elijah. Moses before Pharaoh.

The nave (20m/65ft high) is flanked by 20 Corinthian columns of Parian marble. On the wall above the entrance is one of the oldest mosaics in Rome – two female figures symbolising the Church of the Gentiles (pagans) and the Church of the Circumcision (Jews), with an inscription commemorating the erection of the church. The choir has fine marble screens with intarsia ornament.

Adjoining the church is a Dominican monastery in which St Thomas Aquinas was a monk, with a beautiful Romanesque cloister.

From the broad terrace next to the church there is a magnificent view across the Tiber towards Trastevere, Piazza Venezia and the Vatican City (see entries).

★Santi Apostoli   D/E 6

Location
Piazza
SS Apostoli

Buses
56, 57, 60, 62, 64, 65, 70, 71, 75, 81, 85, 88, 90, 95, 170

The Church of the Apostles in the Palazzo Colonna, originally dedicated to SS Philip and James, was probably founded by Pope Pelagius I (556–561) after the expulsion of the Goths from Rome. It was altered and renovated by later Popes and finally rebuilt by Francesco and Carlo Fontana (1702 onwards) as the last basilica church erected in Rome. In the porch, which lies at an angle to the church, are examples of ancient and medieval art. Notable features of the interior (63m/207ft long) are the ceiling frescoes (Triumph of the Franciscan Order), the tomb of Pope Clement XIV, a masterpiece by Caravaggio (1787), and the tomb of Cardinal Pietro Riario (d. 1474).

Santi Giovanni e Paolo   E 7

Location
Piazza dei Santi
Giovanni e Paolo

Buses
11, 15, 27, 118, 673

Trams
13, 30, 30b

A church was built on this site in the 5th c. by a Roman senator named Byzantius and his son Pammachius in honour of the martyrs John and Paul, officers in the Roman army who were executed in the time of Julian the Apostate. The church was said to have been built over the remains of the house on the Caelian hill in which they were killed. Around 1150 it was completed by Cardinal Giovanni di Sutri, with the addition of the porch, the campanile and the dwarf gallery in the apse. During the Baroque period the interior was redecorated.

Excavations in the present century have revealed the Roman house under the church. so it is now possible to follow the history of the site in an unbroken line from the original Roman house with its fine brick masonry and lively frescoes (one of the best preserved wall-paintings in Rome, depicting Venus with a male divinity), the antique columns and the two lions in the porch, by way of the medieval building, with its marble columns and the campanile built over the walls of the large temple of Claudius on the Caelian hill, to the basilica we see today.

Santi Quattro Coronati   F 7

Location
Via dei Santi
Quattro Coronati

Buses
15, 81, 85, 87, 88, 118, 673

The first church on this site was built in the 4th c. in honour of four martyrs. According to one legend they were Roman soldiers who refused to bow down before a statue of Asesculapius; another version states that they were sculptors of Pannonia who refused to carve a pagan idol. The martyrs are said to have been killed by having an iron crown driven on to their heads; hence the name of the "four crowned" martyrs.

The present church was erected in the time of Pope Paschal II (c. 1100) after the destruction of an earlier church by the Normans in 1084. The principal features include the tall campanile; the Capella di San Silvestro, with scenes from the life of Constantine (13th c.), selected for their relevance to the conflict between the Pope and the Emperor in the Middle Ages; frescoes depicting the discovery of the Cross by Empress Helen; and the famous early 13th c. cloister.

Trams
13, 30, 30b

Santo Stefano Rotondo   F 7

This church was originally a most imposing structure, with its ground plan of a Greek cross set within a circle. It dates from the 5th and 7th c. (Popes Simplicius and Adrian I). Of the two original ambulatories only the inner one is preserved. The 34 pillars which used to divide them can be seen today in the outer wall. On the ambulatory wall is a cycle of frescoes depicting the cruel martyrdom of the saints. In addition to St Stephen the Protomartyr (feast December 26th), St Stephen of Hungary is honoured here. The chapel of St Stephen of Hungary and Paulus Ermita, built in 1778 by Pietro Damporese, forms one of the transepts of the church.

Location
Via di Santo Stefano Rotondo

Buses
85, 88, 673

★Sinagoga (synagogue)   D 6

There was a Jewish community in Rome in the 2nd c. B.C.. By an edict issued by Pope Paul IV in 1555, the district on the left bank of the Tiber bounded by the Ponta dei Quattro Capi, the Portico di Ottavia (see entry), the Piazza Mattei and Via Arnula was declared a ghetto.

Location
Lungotevere di Cenci

The 1904 synagogue in Lungotevere di Cenci

Buses
717, 774, 780

Museo Ebraico

Osvaldo Armanni and Vincenzo Costa designed the synagogue (1904), while the paintings in the interior of the aluminium-domed building are the work of Annibale Brugnoli and Domenico Bruschi.

Adjoining the synagogue is a Jewish museum with a valuable collection of Torah scrolls as well as 18th c. gold and silver-work (open: Mon.–Thur. 9.30am–2pm, 3–5pm, Fri. 9.30am–2pm, Sun. 9.30am–12.30pm).

Teatro di Marcello   D 6

Location
Via del Teatro di
Marcello

Buses
15, 23, 57, 90,
90b, 92, 94, 96,
716, 774

The Romans had seen in Greece how theatres with a semicircular auditorium could be built against the slope of a hill, thus avoiding the necessity of a costly building operation to provide support for the tiers of seating. The same technique could well have been used in Rome, which had plenty of hills.

The desire to display Roman power, artistic pride and technical skill, however, led Pompey to erect a free-standing theatre in 61 B.C., and Augustus followed his example with a theatre with seating for 15,000, which was used from 17 B.C. onwards and was dedicated between 13 and 11 B.C. to the memory of his nephew Marcellus, predestined to be the Emperor's successor had he not predeceased him. The two massive arcades supporting the auditorium were originally 33m/108ft high. Constructed of travertine blocks, the Theatre of Marcellus was once adorned with pilaster columns in the Doric, Corinthian and Ionic styles. The massive arches of the external facade are still very impressive, in spite of the fact that the theatre was converted into a fortress and residence by the Fabi, Savelli and Orsini families during the Middle Ages.

In the 16th c. a new palace was built by Baldassare Peruzzi for the Savelli family on the ruins, but preserving the form of the original structure; today it houses luxury apartments. The restoration of the theatre, begun in 1989, is still not complete.

Temple of
Apollo Sosianus

On a high platform in front of the Theatre of Marcellus (on the right) stand three corner columns from the Temple of Apollo Sosianus, originally built in 431 B.C. and dedicated to the god Apollo. It was restored in 179 B.C. and rebuilt in 32 B.C. by the consul Sosianus (thus its name). In ancient Rome the Theatre of Marcellus was adjoined on the south-east by the Foro Oblitorio (fruit and vegetable market), providing the link to the cattle market (Forum Boarium) on what is now the Piazza Bocca della Verità (see entry).

★Terme di Caracalla   E 8

Location
Via delle Terme di
Caracalla

**Underground
station**
Circo Massimo
(line B)

Buses
11, 27, 90, 90b,
94, 118, 673

The Baths of Caracalla to the south of the city, begun by Septimus Severus in A.D. 206 and completed by Caracalla in 216, were much more than public baths. Nowadays they would be called a "leisure centre", containing as they did a whole system of baths (hot and cold baths, a swimming pool, "Turkish baths" with both dry and damp heat), facilities for gymnastics and sport, pleasant rooms for social activities, gardens to walk in, lecture rooms and libraries, hairdressers and shops.

These various needs were met in a massively imposing structure covering an area of 330sq.m/3550sq.ft, a complex of gigantic halls with huge columns and piers, domes and semi-domes, barrel vaulting and cross vaulting, which could accommodate 1500 people at

Remains of the floor mosaics in the cooling room of the Baths of Caracalla

a time. The floors and walls were covered with marble, mosaics and frescoes. The leisure needs of the population have never been catered for with such magnificence as in the Roman baths; even in ruin their splendour is still apparent (open: Tue.–Sat. 9am–3pm, in summer to 6pm; Sun. 9am–1pm).

★Terme di Diocleziano   F 5

Diocletian built these baths to serve the northern districts of the city, the southern districts having been catered for by the Baths of Caracalla. (For the functions of Roman baths, see Terme di Caracalla.) The Baths of Diocletian, built between A.D. 298 and 305 and measuring 356×316m/1170×1035ft, were even larger than those of Caracalla. Their huge scale can be appreciated when it is seen how widely separated from one another are the surviving parts of the structure, many of them now incorporated into later buildings – the Museo Nazionale Romano o delle Terme (see entry), with a collection of Greek and Roman art; the church of Santa Maria degli Angeli with vaulted ceilings by Michelangelo, the round church of San Bernardo, the Planetarium, the Piazza Esedra (formerly an exedra of the baths); and the cloister and other structures belonging to a Carthusian monastery. The baths could no longer be used after the Acqua Marcia was cut in A.D. 536, and thereafter fell into decay.

Location
Piazza dei Cinquecento, Piazza della Repubblica

Underground stations
Repubblica, Termini

Buses
3, 4, 16, 36, 37, 38, 57, 60, 61, 62, 63, 64, 65, 170, 319, 910

The Museu Nazionale Romano o delle Terme (see entry) in a section of the Baths of Diocletian boasts the most important collection of ancient works of art after that of the Vatican Museum.

★★Museo Nazionale Romano o delle Terme

In a rotunda in the west of the Baths on the Piazza di San Bernardo is the church of San Bernardo alle Terme, built at the end of the 16th c. The dome is similar to that of the Pantheon, but at 22m/72ft in diameter it is only half its size.

San Bernardo alle Terme

The central complex of the Baths was preserved by being incorporated into this church, built on the Piazza della Repubblica in the 16th c. and dedicated to the Virgin and her attendant archangels. It was designed by Michelangelo, taking in parts of the ancient structure, in particular the tepidarium (warm bath), a hall 90m/295ft long, 27m/90ft

Piazza della Repubblica

Santa Maria degli Angeli

wide and 30m/100ft high. The church is in the form of a Greek cross (with arms of equal length), with chapels attached, In order to keep the building dry its floor was raised 2m/6½ft above ground level, so that the bases of the ancient columns were buried. The building of the church was continued after Michelangelo's death, and thereafter restored and redecorated on a number of occasions. Many well-known personalities are buried in the church, which is also used by the State for solemn services on special occasions.

Fontana delle Naiadi

The Fountain of the Naiads in the Piazza della Repubblica – also known as the Piazza Esedre since it was laid out on the exedra of the Baths – was erected between 1885 and 1914. It consists of four groups of female figures playing with marine animals, with a figure of "Man Victorious over the Hostile Forces of Nature" in the middle.

★Tivoli

Excursion

Location
31km/19 miles east of Rome

Buses
Buses to Tivoli from Stazione Rebibbia of underground line B

Tivoli, the ancient Tibur, situated on the Via Tiburtina, is now a town of 52,000 inhabitants. In Imperial times it was a favourite summer residence of Roman aristocrats, including Emperors Augustus and Maecenas. Tivoli has two main tourist attractions – the Villa d'Este and the Villa Adriana, the latter situated a short distance from the town. Also worth seeing are the Villa Gregoriana with its impressive park and the Templo di Vesta, a round temple with Corinthian columns, dating from the 2nd c. B.C.

Decoration on one of the fountains at the Villa d'Este

The Villa d'Este, situated in beautiful gardens and originally owned by the Este family of Ferrara, ranks as the "Queen of Villas". Initially laid out by Pirro Ligorio for Cardinal Ippolito d'Este in the 16th c., the whole complex blended the gently sloping hillside of the natural landscape, the play of water in fountains and cascades and the architectural form of the buildings into a harmonious and refreshing whole. The villa was completed in the early 17th c. by Luigi and Alessandro d'Este. It later passed into the hands of the Habsburg family and in 1918 was taken over by the State.

★★Villa d'Este

Opening times:
Tue.–Sun. 9am
to one hour
before sunset

From the villa itself a series of terraces and flights of steps leads down into the spacious gardens, in which hundreds of fountains, cascades and basins toss water into the air, collect it or allow it to pass on its way downhill; as a result the gardens are filled with the sound of splashing and running water. The whole system, with its playful sculptural forms, was designed with a single purpose in mind – to please the eye and delight the senses.

The mighty ruins of Hadrian's Villa give an overwhelming impression of Imperial grandeur and the splendour of the Roman Empire in its heyday. In the extensive grounds (0.75sq.km/180 acres) of the villa (5km/3 miles south-west of Tivoli) Hadrian built small-scale copies of the places and buildings which had particularly impressed him on his wide travels through the Empire, including the Vale of Tempe in Thessaly, a canal from the Egyptian Canopus valley near Alexandria, and the Academy of Athens. Here, too, everything was provided to meet the needs of the Imperial court. Visitors can now walk about the site and see the remains both of the reproductions of famous buildings and the summer residences of the Emperor and his court. Of particular interest are the Greek Theatre (at the entrance); the "garden room" of a small palace showing the restless architectural style of the period with its interplay of convex and concave lines; the Piazza d'Oro (Golden Square), which was surrounded by 60 columns; the Teatro Marittimo (Maritime Theatre); a small villa with a marble colonnade and the "Island of Solitude"; small and large baths; the Canopus, a 240m/790ft long structure in the open, with the Temple of Serapis and the Academy; the Stadium; the Caserma dei Vigii (Watchmen's Barracks); the Library for Greek and Roman authors; and the Imperial palace proper.

★★Villa Adriana

Opening times:
Tue.–Sun. 9am
to one hour

A general impression of the whole complex is provided by a model housed in a building near the entrance.

★Torre delle Milizie   E 6

The Torre delle Milizie is one of the oldest and strongest fortified towers in Italy, and the largest in Rome. It is popularly believed that Augustus is buried under the tower and that Nero watched the burning of Rome from the top.

Location
Via Quatro
Novembre

The tower was built by Pope Gregory IX in the 13th c. and probably takes its name from a nearby barracks of Byzantine militia. It belonged to a succession of different noble families and played a part in their endless feuds. In 1312 the German king Henry VII used it as his base during his successful attempt to secure his coronation as Emperor in spite of the hostility of the Roman nobility. The tower began sinking on one side soon after its erection, so that Rome, like Pisa, has its "leaning tower". From the top there are magnificent views of central Rome and the ancient remains. Some excellent temporary exhibitions are held in the tower, and from here one can visit the Forum of Augustus (see Fori Imperial).

Buses
46, 56, 57, 60, 62,
64, 65, 70, 71, 75,
81, 88, 90, 95, 170

★Trastevere C/D 6/8

★A district full of character

Buses
26, 28, 44, 60, 75, 97, 170, 710, 718. 719

Trastevere (from trans Tiberini), the district of Rome beyond the Tiber, has preserved much of the character of old Rome, with its narrow streets, romantic little squares and venerable churches. Even though the well-to-do citizens of the city have "discovered" Trastevere and prices have risen accordingly, time should be allowed for a stroll through the little streets. In the evenings especially there is a very lively atmosphere in the Viale Trastevere and in the little lanes and squares opening off it where visitors can chose between simple Italian eating-houses, public houses and high-class restaurants such as that of Alberto Ciarlas – it is best to take a taxi, as parking places are very hard to find at this time of day.

Santa Maria in Trastevere

Santa Maria in Trastevere is the oldest church of the Virgin Mary in Rome. According to legend, it stands on the spot where a spring of oil flowed 38 years before Christ's birth as an intimation of the future Saviour. This may also be the place where Christians were able for the first time to hold services in public. The building of the church began between 221 and 227, under Pope Calixtus I, and was completed in 340, during the time of Pope Julius I. It was rebuilt by Innocent II (1130–43), who came from the Trastevere district, and redecorated in the Baroque period.

The church has a façade decorated with mosaics (the Virgin with ten female saints) and a portico containing early Christian sarcophagi and examples of medieval art. Notable features of the interior include the cosmatesque (marble intarsia) work in the floor, the coffered wooden ceiling, partly gilded by Domenichino (1617), the 22 massive Ionic columns in the large nave, and a 15th c. tabernacle by Mlno del Reame on the right at the west end of the nave. The mosaics in the apse are masterpieces of medieval art. In the conch (c. 1140) can be seen Christ, the Virgin and saints above a frieze of lambs, and below scenes from the life of the Virgin – her Nativity, Annunciation, Nativity of Christ, Three Kings, Presentation in the Temple, Assumption (by Pietro Cavallini, c. 1291). The mosaics at the exit of the church were to remind worshippers of the glory of Heaven, portraying the saints against a celestial background of gold.

San Crisogono

Situated in the busy Piazza Sonnino at the end of the Viale di Trastevere, the church of San Crisognono was originally built before 499 in honour of St Chrysogonus, martyred in the reign of Diocletian; it was rebuilt in 1129. The two porphyry columns of the triumphal arch are the largest in Rome.

San Francesco a Ripa

The present church of San Francesco a Ripa was built in 1231, replacing an earlier chapel belonging to the pilgrim hospice of San Biagio, in which St Francis was said to have stayed when visiting Rome. The church was completely rebuilt by Mattia di Rossi in 1682–89. In the fourth chapel in the north aisle is a famous statue of the Blessed Ludovica Albertoni, a major late work by Bernini (1674).

Santa Cecilia

Cecilia or "Coeli Lilia" (Lily of Heaven) was one of the early Christian female martyrs who were deeply revered in Rome and who gave rise to many legends, one of which says that the house of her husband Valerianus stood on the square. A church was built over it in the 5th c., and this was later rebuilt and extended. It is basilica in form with a forecourt, portico – the façade being the work of Fernando Fuga (1725 –, a Romanesque campanile, a wide nave with rows of pillars, choir and apse. In the choir note the marble ziborium (1283) by Arnolfo di Cambio and the statue of St Cecilia by Stefano Maderno dating from 1600, the year in which the corpse of a young girl was found in this position in a grave. The apse is decorated with a mosaic laid out during the time of Pope Paschali. From the crypt visitors can view the excavated foundations of an old Roman dwelling. Special permission is required to visit the nuns' convent in which Pietro Cavallini created the "Last Judgement", a magnificent portrayal of the end of the world dating from 1293.

★★Vatican City Città del Vaticano   A/B 5/6

The papal residence near St Peter's is named after Monte Vaticano (Vatican Hill). From modest beginnings – until the 15th c. the bishops of Rome resided mainly in the Lateran Palace – it developed to become the prime authority of the Catholic church and today is the centre of the Vatican State. The extensive territories of the Papal States in central Italy, originally presented to the Pope by the Frankish king Pippin the Short, were incorporated into the new kingdom of Italy in 1870. The Pope thereafter regarded himself as deprived of his rights and as a prisoner in the Vatican. In 1929 Mussolini concluded the Lateran Treaty with the Holy See under which the Pope regained full sovereignty over the more restricted territory of the Vatican State.

Underground station
Ottaviano
(line A)

Buses
23, 49, 51, 64, 81, 907, 990, 991

Trams
19, 30

The Vatican State thus formed is the smallest independent state in the world with an area of 0.44sq.km/110 acres and a population of 750. It consists essentially of the Vatican palace and gardens, St Peter's and St Peter's Square, most of the area being enclosed by the Vatican

Stato della Città del Vaticano

The Papal Bodyguard: members of the Swiss Guard in Renaissance uniforms

165

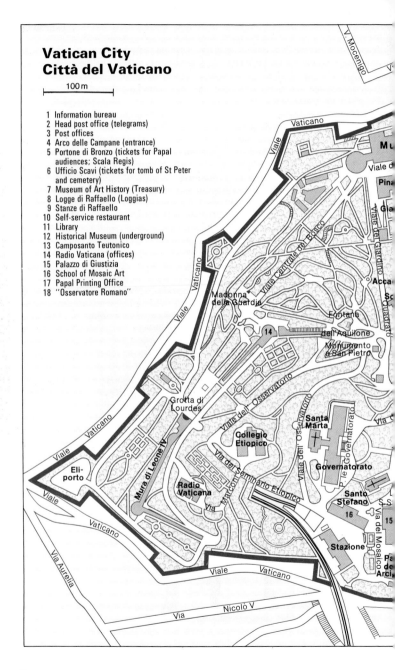

Vatican City
Città del Vaticano

|— 100 m —|

1 Information bureau
2 Head post office (telegrams)
3 Post offices
4 Arco delle Campane (entrance)
5 Portone di Bronzo (tickets for Papal audiences; Scala Regis)
6 Ufficio Scavi (tickets for tomb of St Peter and cemetery)
7 Museum of Art History (Treasury)
8 Logge di Raffaello (Loggias)
9 Stanze di Raffaello
10 Self-service restaurant
11 Library
12 Historical Museum (underground)
13 Camposanto Teutonico
14 Radio Vaticana (offices)
15 Palazzo di Giustizia
16 School of Mosaic Art
17 Papal Printing Office
18 "Osservatore Romano"

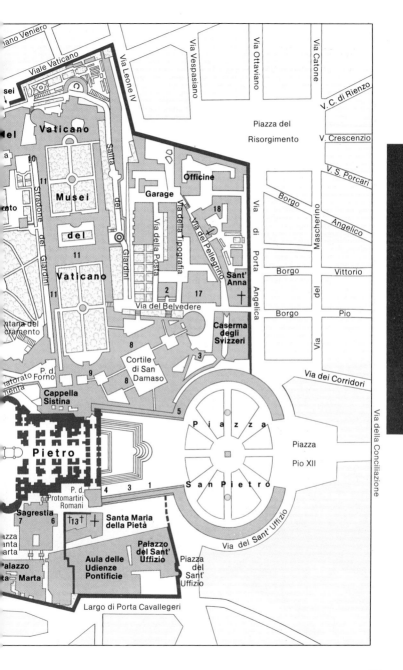

167

walls, with a white strip across St Peter's Square marking the boundary on that side. (During the period of German occupation in the Second World War this line was of some significance).

Papal possessions outside Vatican City – including the basilicas of San Paolo fuori le Mura, San Giovanni in Laterano and Santa Maria Maggiore (see entries), the Papal administrative offices and the Pope's summer residence at Castel Gandolfo (see Colli Albani) – enjoy extra-territorial status and are not subject to Italian law.

The territory of Vatican City, with the exception of certain permitted areas (St Peter's, the museums, Camposanto Teutonico, etc.) can be entered only with special permission. Visitors who desire a Papal audience or who wish to take part in one of the religious ceremonies should write to the Prefetto della Casa Pontificia (Città del Vaticano, 1–00120 Roma, tel. 69 88 32 73).

State flag of the Vatican

The Vatican flag has vertical stripes of yellow and white, with two crossed keys below the papal tiara (triple crown) on a white ground.

The Vatican has its own currency (1 Vatican lira = 1 Italian lira), postal service, newspapers and periodicals (in particular the "Osservatore Romano", with a circulation of 60,000–70,000), radio station (Radio Vaticana: transmissions on medium and short waves in 35 languages to some 170 countries), a fleet of about 100 vehicles (registration letters SCV or CV for those resident in Vatican City) and its own railway station and helicopter pad.

Holy Father

The Pope (Holy Father; since 1978 the Polish Cardinal Karol Wojtyla as John Paul II), supreme head of the Roman Catholic Church (membership some 860 million), is invested with legislative, executive and judicial powers. In external affairs he is represented by a Cardinal Secretary of State, while the administration is headed by a Governor responsible only to the Pope.

Vatican City: View of the Governor's Palace from the dome of St Peter's

Since the dissolution of the Guardia Nobile and Guardia Palatina in 1970 and the Gendarmerie in 1971, the Pope's bodyguard consists of the "Vigilanza" police corps (plain uniforms without insignia of rank) and the Swiss Guard. Membership of the Swiss Guard is restricted to Roman Catholic citizens of Switzerland aged between 18 and 25, single and of a minumum height of 1.8m/5ft 8¹/₂in. The period of service lasts from 2 to 20 years. In accordance with the Papal decree of 1979 the Swiss Guard consists of exactly 100 men (4 officers, 1 chaplain, 25 NCOs and 70 halbadiers. Members of the Guard wear Renaissance uniforms in the colours of the Medici Popes.

Papal bodyguard

★★Musei Vaticani

The Vatican Museums, which occupy much of the Vatican Palaces on Viale Vaticano (where the entrance also is) contain some of the world's greatest art collections. The history of the museums goes back to 1506, when Pope Julius II, pursuing the ideals of the Renaissance, began to collect ancient works of art. The collections were increased over the centuries from the territories of the Papal States, works of art presented to the Popes and items related to the work of the Roman Catholic Church. In addition there are works of art created specially for the Vatican Palace, including the wall and ceiling paintings in the Sistine Chapel and the Stanze di Raffaello. There are four tours of the museums marked with signs in different colours (A, B, C, D, according to the extent and duration of the tour, varying from 1¹/₂ to 5 hours; one-way is indicated). Visitors should be correctly attired (i.e. bare shoulders covered; shorts not permitted).

Information
Tel. 69 88 33 33

Opening times
June–Aug.,
Nov.–Mar. daily
8.45am–1.45pm;
Apr., May., Sept.,
Oct. Mon.–Fri.
8.45am–4.45pm,
Sat., Sun. 8.45am
–1.45pm;
(free entry on
last Sun. in the
month)

★★Pinacoteca

The Pinacoteca, founded by Pius VI and later robbed of many of its treasures by Napoleon, contains in its sixteen rooms paintings ranging in date from the Middle Ages to the present day, giving an excellent survey of the development of religious painting. The order of the pictures may change as they are moved around.

Panels from the 11th to the 13th c. (Sienese, Umbrian and Tuscan), including an outstanding circular panel of Benedictine origin (11th c.) depicting the Last Judgement.

Room I

Works by Giotto and his pupils, including the Stefanaschi triptych (c. 1300) from Old St Peter's with Christ on His throne surrounded by angels on the centre panel and the martyrdom of St Peter and St Paul on the side panels. Other important panels are by the Sienese artists Simone Martini and Pietro Lorenzetti.

Room II

15th c. Florentine Renaissance painting including "St Nicolas of Bari" (1437) by Fra Angelico, "Coronation of the Virgin" by Filippo Lippi and work by Benozzo Gozzoli.

Room III

The fresco "Sixtus IV founds the Vatican Library" by Melozzo da Forii (1477). Seated on his throne, the Pope is surrounded by secular and religious family members, and kneeling before him is the librarian and humanist Bartolomeo Platina pointing to a Latin inscription describing the Pope's building achievements. Charming, too, is the fragment of a fresco by Melozzo showing an angel playing a lute.

Room IV

A pietà by Lucas Cranach the Elder, and "The Miracle of St Vincent of Ferrara" by Francesco del Cossa.

Room V

Altarpieces by the Venetians Carlo Crivelli and Antonio Vivarini.

Room VI

The Umbrian school is represented by Pinturicchio ("Coronation of the Virgin", ca. 1502) and Perugino, pupil of Raphael, with a very expressive "Madonna with Saints" (1483–95).

Room VII

Magnificent tapestries from cartoons by Raphael – the originals of 1516/17 are in the Victoria and Albert Museum in London – produced

Room VIII

in the Brussels studio of Pieter van Aeist, who at one time decorated the lower parts of the walls of the Sistine Chapel. Raphael's early worh "Coronation of the Virgin" (c. 1503) shows the influence of his teacher Perugino. The "Madonna of Foligno" (c. 1512) was painted by Raphael for Sigismondo de'Conti, historian, secretary and friend to Pope Julius II. The donator is kneeling on the right in his offical robes and is being commended to the Virgin by St Hieronymus. Raphael's last work, completed by Giuilio Romano, is the "Transfiguration of Christ" (1520). The Son of God floats in the upper part of the picture between Elijah and Moses, while below the disciples Jacob, Peter and John bow down before Him on Mount Tabor. In the foreground a man possessed of the devil is miraculously cured. Raphael succeeded magnificently in linking the various groups in the picture by the use of dramatic colour and light and evocative gestures, combined with the skilful use of circular and triangular composition.

Room IX   Most striking is the incomplete picture of St Hieronymus (ca. 1480) by Leonardo da Vinci, who portrays most impressively the psychological experiences of the penitent. The pietà (ca. 1470) by Giovanni Bellini is masterly in the way it reflects the facial expression and gestures of the bereaved.

Room X   In his picture of the Madonna painted in 1528 for San Niccolò dei Frari in Venice, Titian produced a group of figures on two levels, in which the saints standing at the feet of the Virgin are drawn by the direction of their gaze into a triangular composition, the peak of which is formed by the Virgin floating on clouds. Paolo Veronese is represented by an allegory, and Paris Bordone by a painting of St George and the Dragon.

Room XI   Works by artists from the second half of the 16th c., including Georgio Vasary ("The Stoning of St Stephan") and Frederico Barocci ("The Stigmatizing of St Francis").

Room XII   Paintings by Domenichino ("Communion of Hieronymus", 1614), Guercino ("Doubting Thomas"), Nicolas Poussin ("The Martyrdom of St Erasmus", ca. 1630) and Guido Reni ("St Peter's Crucifixion").

Room XIII   Carvaggio's stark realism and the employment of powerful body-language and an effective light and dark technique represents a bold step forward in art, as shown in the "Entombment of Christ"" (1602–4). Other works here include Pietro da Cortona's "Coronation of St Theresa", van Dyck's "St Francis Xaver", painted in 1622 during a stay in Rome, and José Ribera's "Martyrdom of St Lawrence".

Room XIV   Works by Dutch and Flemish Baroque artists.

Room XV   Portrait collection with works by Titian, Carlo Maratta and Thomas Lawrence.

Museo Gregoriano Egizio

The Egyptian Museum in the Cortile della Pigna, re-founded by Pope Gregory XVI (the first collection having been assembled by Pius VII), contains a small but high quality collection of Egyptian art from the 3rd millenium B.C. to the birth of Christ, found largely in Rome and its environs as well as from the period of the Roman occupation of Egypt up to the 3rd c. A.D. It includes basalt and wooden sarcophagi, heads of gods and pharaohs, mummified heads, stelae, heads and statues of gods and animals, and papyri.

★★Museo Pio Clementino

The Vatican Museums boast the largest collection of ancient sculptures in the world, mainly found in Rome and the surrounding areas. The collection was arranged on a systematic basis by Popes Clement XIV (1769–74) and Pius VI (1775–99). Among outstanding items are the following:

Vatican Museums
Musei Vaticani

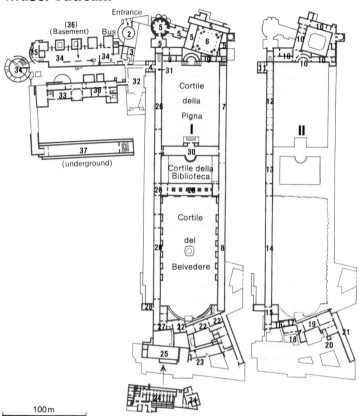

1 Lift
2 Stairs
3 Vestibule (tickets, information)
4 Atrio dei Quattro Cancelli
5 Museo Pio-Clementino
6 Cortile Ottagono
7 Museo Chiaramonti
8 Galleria Lapidaria
9 Museo Gregoriano Egizio (Egyptian Museum)
10 Museo Gregoriano Etrusco (Etruscan Museum)
11 Sala della Biga
12 Galleria dei Candelabri
13 Galleria degli Arazzi (Tapestry Gallery)

14 Galleria delle Carte Geografiche (Map Gallery)
15 Pius V's Chapel
16 Sala Sobieski
17 Sala dell'Immacolata
18 Urban VIII's Chapel
19 Stanze di Raffaello
20 Nicholas V's Chapel (Beato Angelico)
21 Logge di Raffaello (Loggias of Raphael)
22 Appartamento Borgia
23 Salette Borgia
24 Collezione d'Arte Religiosa Moderna (Museum of Modern Religious Art)

25 Sistine Chapel
26 Vatican Library
27 Museo Sacro della Biblioteca
28 Sala delle Nozze Aldobrandine
29 Salone Sistino
30 Braccio Nuovo
31 Museo Profano della Biblioteca
32 Cortile della Pinacoteca
33 Pinacoteca (Picture Gallery)
34 Museo Gregoriano Profano (Museum of Secular Art)
35 Museo Pio Cristiano
36 Museo Missionario Etnologico
37 Museo Storico (Historical Museum)

Vatican City

Sala Rotonda

In the middle of this room, which has mosaic floors from Otricoli, stands a giant porphyry bowl 13m/43ft in circumference from the domus aurea of the Emperor Nero. In the niches and in front of the pillars are colossal statues of gods and heroes, including a head of Zeus of Otricoli, a copy of a work by Braxis (4th c. B.C., a bust of Antinus, a favourite of the Emperor Hadrian who was drowned in the Nile, a head of Hadrian and a statue of Hercules in gilded bronze (2nd c.).

Sala a Croce Greca

Two valuable dark red porphyry sarcophagi: that of Constantia (Constantine's daughter, d. 354) was brought here from the church of Santa Costanza. It is embellished with relief decoration showing winged Cupids at wine-harvesting time, surrounded by vine twigs and tendrils, a motif which can symbolize both Dionysian revels and Christian concepts linking wine with the blood of Christ and redemption from sin. The sarcophagus of St Helen (mother of Constantine, d. 336) shows relief decoration portraying victorious Romans and captured barbarians. It is possible that the monument was originally intended for Constantine himself.

Sala delle Muse

The Belvedere Torso, a powerful male figure seated on a rock and, according to the inscription, the work of Apollonius of Athens (1st c. B.C.); it was admired by Michelangelo because of the skilful depiction of anatomy which is found reflected in the figures in the Sistine Chapel. Statues of Apollo and the Muses based on 3rd c. A.D. Greek originals. Also a Mithras group (3rd c. A.D. showing the Persian god of light at the slaying of the bull which was then sacrificed in defiance of the malicious snake and stinging scorpion. The Mithras cult was particularly popular among Roman soldiers during the Empire period.

Sala degli Animali

Numerous realistic marble and alabaster statues of animals; statue of Meleager with a dog and a wild boar's head (Roman copies of 4th c. B.C. Greek originals) and Minotaur bust (copy of 5th c. B.C. original).

Galleria della Statue

Apollo Sauroctonus (Apollo the Lizard Killer; Roman copy of a bronze original by Praxiteles, 4th c. B.C.); a reclining figure of Ariadne (2nd c. A.D. Roman copy of Greek original); the Candelabri Barberini (the finest ancient candelabras known), from the Villa Adriana at Tivoli (see entry); a wounded Amazon, a Roman copy of a sculpture by Phidias, created c. 430 B.C. for the Temple of Artemis in Ephesos. The head is probably a replica of an Amazon head by Polyklet.

Gabinetto delle Maschere

The Cabinet of Masks contains mosaic paving of theatrical masks from the Villa Adriana in Tivoli (see entry); a Cnidian Aphrodite (Venus) preparing to bathe (one of the best copies of a famous work by Praxiteles from the 4th c. B.C.).

Galleria dei Busti

Lunette frescoes by Pinturicchio; numerous ancient portraits of Emperors; a Roman statue of Jupiter Verospi, seated with a sceptre in the left hand and a sheaf of faggots in the right; a married couple from a 1st c. B.C. grave monument.

Cortile del Belvedere

One of the most famous statues in the Vatican is the Apollo Belvedere: of great presence, the dancing form of the deity in all his youthful beauty holds a bow in his outstretched left hand, an arrow from which could bring sickness and death, while in his right hand he carries a healing laurel twig. The figures represents the epitome of classical beauty as best expressed in Greek art (Roman copy of an original bronze by Leochares, ca. 330 B.C.). Also to be seen are Perseus by Canova (1757–1822) and a Hermes from the Hadrianic period (copy of an original by Praxiteles, 4th c. B.C.). The highlight is the Laocoön Group, discovered in 1506 when Michelangelo was present, which depicts the Trojan priest and his sons in a mortal battle with two huge

snakes which – according to Greek legend – had been sent by the goddess Athena because the priest had warned of the wooden horse. According to Plinius the Elder (d. A.D. 79), who had seen the group in the palace of the Emperor Titus, it was the work of the sculptors Hagesander, Polydoros and Athanodoros of Rhodes. It resembles a bronze original from Pergamon which probably dates from the time of Tiberius. The right arm of the Trojan priest was originally missing and wrongly copied; however, the original arm was found in 1905 and correctly substituted by L. Pollak in 1906.

The Laocoön Group

The Athlete Apoxyomenos, a Roman copy of a Greek original by Lysippus (ca. 320 B.C.), was found in Trastevere in 1849. It shows a world champion athlete, happy but exhausted, shaving the dirt from his oiled body with a "striglis".

Gabinetto del Apoxyomenos

★Museo Chiaramonti

The Museo Chiaramonti, founded by Pope Pius VII (1800–23), a member of the Chiaramonti family, is housed in a long gallery leading to the Papal palace and contains numerous works of Greek and Roman art of varying quality. There are also examples of Greek and Roman sculpture in the Galleria Lapidaria (not normally open to the public) and the Braccio Nuovo, which links the two long wings extending from the entrance to the museums in the Palazzi vaticani.

The most notable item in the Braccio Nuovo is the Augustus of Prima Porta, a statue of the Emperor Augustus (hands added later) found in 1863 in the country villa of his wife Livia. This famous prototype of Roman imperial statues stands over 2m/6¹/₂ ft tall and dates from 19 B.C.; it was designed to stand in a niche and is therefore carved to be viewed from the front only. Like the deities, Augustus is depicted barefooted with Eros – the child of the goddess Venus as progenitrix of the Roman ruler – riding on a dolphin. Unique is his relief-decorated breastplate, the lower part of which portrays Mother Earth with her children. Above and to the sides are Apollo (left) and Diana (right), tutelary deities of Augustus. The centre of the muscle-like armour is decorated with a scene showing a bearded panther handing back to a Roman general in 20 B.C. the legionary eagle captured at the battle near Carrhae in 53 B.C. The figure to the left of centre represents a mourning Germania above which the sun god is driving his chariot up to the heavens with the goddess of the dawn fleeing before him. The noble countenance and imperious bearing of Augustus make him appear a worthy ruler of the world. Later statues of Roman emperors in armour are all modelled on this one.

Braccio Nuovo

★★Augusto di Prima Porta

Also worthy of note are the impressive statue of the politician Demosthenes, the personification of the god of the Nile with 16 children representing its estuaries (a 1st c. A.D. Roman copy, discovered in 1513); the statue of Titus wearing a toga (ruled 79–81) and the Athena Giustiniani (copy of that by Praxiteles, 4th c. B.C.).

The Doryphorus ("Spear Carrier"), a copy of the Greek, has been used as a pattern by many generations of sculptors right up to the Neo-Classical era in the 18th/19th c. It is well-proportioned, simple and balanced with one standing and one free leg clearly reflecting thythmic movement yet at the same time suggesting a figure at rest.

★Museo Gregoriano Etrusco

The Etruscan Museum, founded by Pope Gregory XVI (1831–46), contains in its 18 rooms works of art and everyday objects which throw light on the life of the Etruscans and their idea of the afterlife. The collection also includes Greek and Roman works. Particulary notable items include the rich grave goods from the Regolini-Galassi tomb at Cerveteri (7th c. B.C.), the large bronze statue of Mars by Todi (4th c. B.C.), the Stele del Palestrita from Attica (5th c. B.C.) and the marble head of Athena (fragment of the frieze from the Parthenon, 5th c. B.C.).

Vase collection
The Vase Collection contains numerous valuable items.
In the Sala della Meridiana Etruscan and Greek vases predominate, with the magnificent Caretan Hydras, including one particularly richly decorated hydra with fine contrasts of light and shade and showing Hercules slaying the giant Alkyones while he slept. In the Sala Astarita there is an impressive large late Corinthian bowl with a painted scene showing Odysseus and Menelaos being despatched to rescue the kidnapped Helena. In cabinet F of the Hermicyclus (emiciclo) can be seen a masterpiece of Attic silhouette decoration on vases, the amphora, signed by Exekias and dating from ca. 525 B.C., showing Achilles and Ajax playing dice on one side and Leda and King Tyndareos on the other, Of equal importance is the Achilles amphora (middle of the 5th c. B.C.) in the Upper Hemicyclus; it portrays the bareheaded warrior in short armour and chiton (long woollen garment) in red against a black background. No less interesting is the Attic dish (early 4th c. B.C.) with a fine-lined picture on the inside of Triptolemos who, seated in a carriage drawn by serpents, is bringing a gift of ears of corn to the people.

Sala della Biga
Near the entrance to the Sala delle Biga stand two Discus Throwers, copies of works by Myron and Polyklet (5th c. B.C.) and a carriage and pair ("Biga", 1788) by Antonio Franzoni.

★Museo Gregoriano Profano

The Museum of Secular Art was also founded by Pope Gregory XVI (1831–46). Until 1963 it was housed, together with the Museo Pio Cristiano and Museo Epigrafico Cristiano, in the Lateran Palace. It now occupies a modern museum building adjoining the Pinacoteca which was built during the reigns of Popes John XXIII (1958–63) and Paul VI (1963–78). The works of ancient sculpture in this excellently arranged museum were mostly found in the territories of the Papal States. The collection includes Roman copies of Greek sculpture and originals of Roman Imperial sculpture – statues, reliefs, funerary monuments and sarcophagi, together with works of political and religious content.

First section
Greek originals, including a fragment of a horse's head from the west gable of the Parthenon, and a head of Athena, probably from a large Greek cult picture of about 460 B.C..

2nd section
Roman copies and re-workings of Greek originals, including Sophocles (found in 1839 in Terracina; carved ca. 340 B.C., a copy of a Greek bronze original of the 5th c. B.C.); Niobide Chiaramonti (4th. c. B.C.) – a daughter of Niobe, wife of King Amphion of Thebes, who boasted that Leto had been responsible for her many children, whereupon his offspring Apollo and Artemis killed the fourteen Niobe chil-

dren; a fragment of the head of Athena (the original by Myron of Eleutherai of ca. 450 B.C. stands on the Acropolis in Athens) and a torso of Marsia from Castel Gondolfo.

Roman sculptures from the 1st and 2nd c. A.D., mainly portraits of the Late Republican and Early Imperial periods, including colossal seated figures of Emperors Tiberius (A.D. 14–37) and Claudius (A.D. 41–54), a charming portrait of Livia, consort of the Emperor Augustus and the two large relief friezes showing the arrival of Emperor Vespasian in Rome in the year 70 and the departure of Emperor Domitian in A.D. 96. | 3rd section

A gallery of sarcophagi, assembled by subject-matter, including works linked to the Adonis and Orest myth, bacchanalian, hunting and agricultural scenes and sporting contests. | 4th section

Roman sculpture of the 2nd/3rd c., including a Mithras group and an altar with twelve tablets illustrating the labours of Hercules. | 5th section

★Biblioteca Apostolica Vaticana

Judging by the vaue of its contents, the Vatican Library is the richest in the world. Sixtus IV officially opened it on 15 June 1474. Although there had been previous book collections of some importance – including the libraries of Boniface VIII, Clemence V or Gregory XIII – details of their composition are sketchy in the extreme. With the Papal Bull of 1475, however, the extensive manuscript collections of the Papal palace found a permanent home. Since then the Vatican library has been systematically built up and now contains, in addition to books printed since the end of the 15th c., some 25,000 medieval handwritten books, 7000 incunabula and more than 100,000 manuscripts. In the library hall, 70m/230ft long and built by Domenico Fontana, are cases displaying some of its greatest treasures – Biblical codices, illuminated Gospel books, finely printed books, valuable parchments and ancient papyri and scrolls. With over one million printed works covering all spheres of learning the library also possesses one of the major collections of secondary literature in Rome. Over 2000 newspapers are kept, underlining the importance attached to current research. Since 1995 the library's stocks have been put on computer so that in future they will be available on the Internet for study purposes.

Museo Sacro

At the end of the long range housing the Vatican Library will be found the Museum of Sacred Art, containing material found during the excavation of catacombs and early Christian churches in Rome. Pope Pius XI (1922–39) showed a particular interest in the smaller works of Christian art. Particular mention must be made of a gold crucifix decorated with enamel inlay (seven scenes from the life of Jesus) using the cloisonné technique, with five panels painted by Pope Paschalis (817–24); a silver reliquary (11th c.) made for the bust of St Praxedis and an ebony cover made for a Book of the Gospels (ca. 800). In a side room is the "Aldobrandini Wedding" (Nozze Aldobrandine), an antique fresco from the augustinian period which was found about 1604/5 on the Esquiline Hill and was owned by Cardinal Petro Aldobrandeschi. It portrays a wedding ceremony: the bride in a white dress is seated on a bed, beside her is Venus and before her a companion pouring oil; to the left near a bowl of water is the bride's mother, to the right at the end of the bed is Hymenaeus as the person giving the bride away and dressed in Dionysian robes. Also of interest are the Late Republican frescoes (ca. 40 B.C.) with scenes from the Odyssey.

★Appartamento Borgia

The Borgia Pope Alexander VI (1492–1503; see Prominent Figures in Roman History) had a private residence built for himself and his family within the Vatican Palace, and commissioned Pinturicchio to decorate it with wall and ceiling paintings. Between 1492 and 1495 the painter and his assistants and pupils painted a series of scenes combining Renaissance, humanist and ancient themes with Christian subjects. The Sala delle Sibille is adorned with portrayals of prophets and sibyls, the Sala del Credo shows the Creed, with prophets and Apostles, the Sale delle Arti Liberali contains allegories of the seven liberal arts – dialectics, rhetoric, grammar, geometry, arithmetic, music and astronomy. Sacred legends of St Sebastian, St Susanna, St Barbara, St Catharine and of the recluses Antony and Paul are in the Sala dei Santi, while the Sala dei Misteri della fede houses scenes from the life of Jesus and the Virgin as well as a portrait of Pope Borgia. The Papal portaits formerly in the sixth room have not survived; the stucco ceiling with astronomical portrayals dates from the pontificate of Leo X.

★★Stanze di Raffaello

These rooms above the Appartamento Borgia, built by Pope Nicholas V, contain a magnificent series of frescoes by Raphael, who was commissioned by the art-loving Pope Julius II in 1508 to repaint the rooms. Raphael, in rediscovering the traditions of historical painting, established a trend in art which was to be followed in subsequent centuries. As a classicist he adhered to strict compositional symmetry in the frescoes. The characters are positioned, according to their roles in the story, around a perspectival and pictorial focal point, usually in

"Parnassus" by Raphael in the Stanze della Signatura

the centre of the picture. The Stanza della Segnatura and the Stanza di Eliodoro are both by Raphael's own hand: the Stanza dell'Incendio di Borgo was executed by his pupils under his supervision; the Stanza di Constantino was painted after Raphael's death by Guilio Romano and Gian Francesco Penni.

The ceiling fresco symbolically portraying the Holy Trinity was the work of Perugino, Raphael's teacher; the four historical scenes were painted between 1514 and 1517 by pupils of Raphael; Leo IV was responsible for miraculously extinguishing the burning of the Borgo (the district around St Peter's) in 847 when it threatened the church itself; the coronation of Charlemagne by Leo III in St Peter's on Christmas day 800; Leo IV'S naval victory over the Saracens off Ostia in 849 after they had landed at the mouth of the Tiber: and Leo III's oath before Charlemagne and the assembled clergy in 795 when he denied the false accusations levelled against him by the nephews of Hadrian I. All the paintings commemorating his predecessors of the same name were commissioned by Pope Leo X (1513–21).

Sala dell'Incendio di Borgo

The frescoes in this room (the meeting place of an ecclesiastical tribunal), painted by Raphael in 1508–11, represent the supreme achievement of Renaissance painting. They depict the culture of the period in all its richness and splendour. The four ceiling bosses with allegorical figures representing Theology, Justice, Philosophy and Poetry symbolise the four basic themes of the room. The Disputa del Sacramento stands for theology, the School of Athens for philosophy, Parnassus for poetry, and the three scenes depicting the cardinal virtues and the introduction of civil and canon law represent justice. The whole composition of the vaulted ceiling expresses the Neo-Platonic thoughts of the High Renaissance, namely that humanism and Christianity should become as one.

Sala della Segnatura

The Disputa del Sacramento, a theological disputation on the doctrine of transubstantiation, depicts the world of religious faith. In the lower zone around the altar four Fathers of the Church are assembled, and approaching them are groups of popes, bishops, teachers, theologians and believers, including Pope Innocent III, Bonaventura and Dante; above them, under God the Father, are Christ with the Virgin and John the Baptist, attended by apostles and prophets.

The Scuola d'Atene (School of Athens), set in monumental Renaissance architecture, represents the field of the natural sciences – attainable without divine revelation – and depicts representatives of philosophy (the two central figures are the older Plato and the younger Aristoteles, symbolising natural and moral philosophy; to their left Socrates is in discussion with Alcibiades), architecture (Bramante), history (Xenophon). and mathematics (Pythagoras, crouching, front left, Euclid, bending over a slate tablet; Heraclitus leaning on a block of marble; Ptolemaeus, wearing a crown, on the right edge of the picture, Diogenes lying on the stairs), together with Raphael himself (second from the extreme right).

Above one window is an associated scene depicting Parnassus, with Apollo playing a violin and attended by nine Muses, the blind Homer and other ancient poets and writers, including Virgil, Dante, Petrach, Sappho, Ariosto, Boccaccio, Ovid, Catullus and Horace. Above the others are a scene depicting the glorification of canon and civil law and allegorical representations of the virtues of Prudence and Temperance.

The paintings by Raphael in the Room of Heliodorus (1512–14) show still greater expressive power and a livelier sense of movement than those in the Sala della Segnatura. They depict four scenes: Leo the Great repulsing Attila (with ancient Rome in the background), the Mass of Bolsena (in which in 1263 an unbelieving Bohemian priest

Sala d' Eliodoro

who had broken his journey in Rome was convinced of the truth of the doctrine of transubstantiation), the Expulsion of Heliodorus from the Temple (from a Bible story whereby Heliodorus, while stealing from the Temple of Jerusalem, is discovered by three angels and expelled), and the Liberation of St Peter from Prison, Raphael's first depiction of a night scene, with effective use of light and contrast. As in the "Mass of Bolsena", the dungeon scene consists of three events which flow into each other without disrupting the unity of the picture.

Sala di
Constantino

The paintings in the Room of Constantine date almost exclusively from the reign of Clement VII (1520–24), after Raphael's death. On the long wall is a fine fresco of Constantine's victory over Maxentius at Milvian Bridge, with the scene depicting Constantine's vision of the Cross shortly before the battle when he received a sign that he would be victorious. Other scenes include Constantine's baptism in the Lateran baptistry, and the "Presentation of Constantine", showing the emperor in the midst of a great crowd of people bestowing upon the pope the power to rule over Rome as the centre of Christendom. These later paintings are all the work of Raphael's pupils Giulio Romano and Gian Francesco Penni.

★Cappela
di Niccolï V

Near the Stanze di Raffaello lies the small Nicholas V's Chapel, decorated by Fra Beato Angelico with two frescoes on the life and martyrdom of SS. Stephen and Lawrence (1447–49). These formed a model for those in the churches of St Stephen in Jerusalem and St Lawrence in Rome.

★Galleria
delle Carte
Geografiche

The Map Gallery, 120m/395ft long, contains maps of all the different parts of Italy, often with views of cities and countryside (1580–83). The maps, originating from the studio of Antonio Dantes, contain valuable cartographical detail and were designed to be used as decoration in a palace.

Galleria dei
Candelabri e
degli Arazzi

Designed in the late 18th c. and fitted out in the late 19th c., the Gallery of Candelabras and Tapestries houses a large number of small statues and few notable larger ones. Particularly important are the beautiful ancient marble candelabras with triangular bases decorated in relief, a plant-like stem and a bowl for the flame. On the window wall hangs a series of seven tapestries (17th c.) showing scenes from the life of Pope Urban VIII, while on the opposite wall hang ten tapestries produced in Brussels in the 16th c. to designs from the Raphael school, with events from the life of Jesus.

★★Cappella Sistina

History

The Sistine Chapel, built in the Vatican Palace between 1473 and 1484 on the instructions of Pope Sixtus IV, replaces a capella magna (palace chapel, 13th c.) dating from the time of Nicholas III. It is a plain rectangular hall 13.2m/43ft high; its length of 40.93m/134ft and width of 13.71m/45ft are the same as those of the Temple of Solomon. The division of the chapel into presbytery and nave is achieved by the varying geometric design of the coloured marble floor and by a marble balustrade designed by Mino da Fiesole and Andrea Bregno. The chapel is the Pope's domestic chapel and is also used for services and special occasions. After the death of a Pope the conclave to elect his successor is held here.

From 1980 to 1994 the Sistine Chapel, the pinnacle of Renaissance painting, was extensively restored. Layers of candle-soot, dust, varnish, oil and grease as well as overpainting were removed from the Michelango frescoes and damage was repaired, and now once again the remarkable luminous colours can be admired.

The "Creation of Adam": part of Michelangelo's masterpiece depicting the Creation as described in Genesis

Frescoes on side walls

The side walls are covered with large frescoes painted for Sixtus IV (1481–83) by the most celebrated painters of the day – Perugino, Botticelli, Rosselli, Pinturicchio, Signorelli and Ghirlandaio – depicting Biblical scenes against a background of the Umbrian and Tuscan scenery familiar to the artists. These late 15th c. paintings already reflect the discovery of man as an individual and his importance in the historical process, and with consummate artistic skill depict him acting within an architectural and landscape setting, thus preparing the way for the further development of this trend by Michelangelo.

Left wall

The left-hand wall shows scenes from the life of Moses, liberator of the Jewish people from their captivity in Egypt; the circumcision of Moses; Moses with the shepherds and the burning bush; the crossing of the Red Sea; Moses receiving the tablets of the law on Mount Sinai; the destruction of the company of Korah, with the Arch of Constantine in the background, dramatically portrayed by Botticelli; and the death of Moses.

Right wall

The right-hand wall depicts events in the life of Christ, the Liberator of Mankind from Sin – His baptism in the Jordan; the Cleansing of the Lepers and the Temptations of Christ (a magnificent work by Botticelli); the Calling of Peter and Andrew, by Ghirlandaio; the Sermon on the Mount, by Rosselli; Christ giving the Keys to Peter (Perugino's masterpiece); and the Last Supper by Cosimo Rosselli and Pietro di Cosimo.

Ceiling paintings

The frescoes on the ceiling were painted by Michelangelo in the reign of the great Pope and Renaissance prince Julius II, most of them being his own unaided work. They were painted between the autumn of 1508 and August 1510 and, after a pause, completed in October 1512. Michelangelo's idea was an ambitious one, never attempted on such a scale before; no less than to depict the Creation as it is described in Genesis. It is interesting that, in contrast to the chronological order, he began with the Flood and not with the Creation of Light.

The central part of the ceiling (from the front) depicts God separating light from darkness; creating heavenly bodies and plants;

separating land and sea; creating Adam and then Eve; the Fall; Noah's thanksgiving; the Flood; Noah's drunkenness. In the lower ranges of the vaulting are colossal figures of the prophets and sybils who conveyed God's message to the Jews and the Gentiles. The Creation of Adam reflects in a special way, by means of exchanged glances and hand gestures, the artistic strength and intensity of Michelangelo through which he succeeded in portraying mankind's principal longing, to be inspired with the very breath of God. The way he depicts God more in an active role and Adam as a semi-passive figure, parallel to and almost mirrored in one another, is extremely effective.

Painting on altar wall

Michelangelo began work on the large fresco on the altar wall almost 22 years later (1534), in the reign of Pope Paul III, when he was 59. As a counterpart to the depiction of the Creation on the ceiling, on this wall he painted the final scene in the story of the world, the Last Judgement, showing Christ returning as the Judge to summon the righteous to paradise and to consign the damned to hell. The theme in all its details is based on the scriptural account. With its dramatic presentation of his subject, which Michelangelo sees as a judgement on the life of the individual human being, this ranks as one of the greatest achievements of European painting. In the Last Judgement Christ is depicted as a powerful youthful god standing on a cloud, surrounded by the Virgin, the Apostles and other saints. The righteous (to the left) rising up into heaven, and the damned (on the right) tumbling into hell form a powerful and upward and downward movement which determines the eternal fate of mankind, while below the dead are seen rising from their graves. In the middle are angels blowing their trumpets to summon all men to judgement, and up above other angels carry in triumph the instruments of the Passion.

The 391 figures are represented with athletic forms, and many of them have readily recognisable attributes (Peter with his key, Sebastian with his arrows, Lawrence with his gridiron, Bartholomew with his flayed skin, which bears a portrait of Michelangelo himself, and Catherine with her wheel).

Museo Pio Cristiano

This museum, founded by Pope Pius IX (1846–78) and extended by Pius XI (1922–39), contains material which until 1963 was housed in the Lateran Palace (see Palazzo Laterano); it includes early Christian antiquities, mainly sarcophagi and grave inscriptions. Most notable, although heavily restored, is the statue of the Good Shepherd, a clean-shaven youth with long hair carrying a lamb on his shoulders; it is one of the rare full length statues in early Christian art. In ancient times the pastoral concept, in the form of oblatory gifts, for example, was already well known. In later Christian times it took on a new dimension in portraying Christ as the Good Shepherd seeking lost souls. Among the sarcophagi, the "Dogmatic Sarcophagus" (4th c.) with the locket of a married couple and two painted friezes are of special interest; the friezes show scenes from the Old Testament (including the Creation and the Fall, Daniel in the Lion's Den) and the New Testament (Adoration of the Magi, the Miracle of the Bread and Wine, the Healing of the Blind, Betrayal and Imprisonment of Peter).

Museo Missionario Etnologico

Objects brought back to Rome from the various mission fields of the Church were originally (from 1927 onwards) displayed in the Lateran palace (see Palazzo Laterano). Pope Pius XI directed that they should be brought together in a systematic arrangement, and in 1973 all material of interest to scholars as well as to the general public was transferred to the Museo Missionario Etnologico; among the exhibits are statues from Colombia, Polynesia, China, Mexico, New Guinea and Africa.

Museo Storico

The Vatican's Coach and Weapons Museum is housed in a room furnished in 1963/4 on instructions from Pope Paul VI under the Giardino Quadrato (Square Gardens), near the Pinacoteca. On display are the carriages of Popes and cardinals (including that of Leo XII), a number of old cars (including Pius XIII's black Landauer) and uniforms and weapons of the Papal Guard.

Collezione d'Arte Religiosa Moderna

Pope Paul VI was interested in modern religious art and made available 55 rooms in the Vatican for the display of works of art presented to or acquired by the Popes. The collection contains more than 800 works by artists of many different countries, including Rodin, Barlach, Matisse, Modigliani, Kokoschka, Dali, Munch, de Viaminck, Feiniger, Ernst, Beckmann, Nolde, Le Corbusier, Kadinsky, de Chirico, Marini, Manzó, Rouault, Hartung and Sutherland.

★Palazzi Vaticani

Some impression of the size of the Vatican Palace, which lies imme-   History
diately to the right of St Peter's Square and St Peter's itself, can be gained by starting from the fountain on the left-hand side of St Peter's Square, from which the huge bulk of the main range of buildings can be seen rearing up above the square, and then continuing along to the right outside the walls to the entrance to the Vatican Museums.

There would no doubt have been some form of lodging for the Bishop of Rome near Old St Peter's (then well outside the city) as early as the 6th c., but initially the Popes resided in the Palazzo Laterano. The first Pope to consider the Vatican as a residence was Nicholas III (1277–80), and this alternative seemed all the more attractive when the Popes returned from exile in Avignon in 1377 and found the Lateran Palace in a state of dilapidation. From 1450 onwards successive Popes embellished and enlarged the Vatican, enlisting the best architects in Rome. The most notable contributions were made by Nicholas V, Sixtus IV (Sistine Chapel), Alexander VI (Appartamento Borgia), Julius II (Cortile del Belvedere, Loggias in the Cortile di San Domasol), Paul III (Cappella Paolina, with frescoes by Michelangelo), Pius V and Sixtus V (the present private apartments, reception rooms and library).

The total area covered by buildings, excluding the gardens, is 55,000sq.m/13$\frac{1}{2}$ acres, of which 25,000sq.m/6 acres are accounted for by courtyards. The total number of rooms and chapels is 1400. Surely no other palace in the world can compare with the Vatican in historical and artistic importance. In addition to the Pope's own residential apartments and offices the palace houses a number of ecclesiastical bodies as well as the Vatican Museums. The main entrance is the bronze door at the end of the right-hand colonnade which leads into the Corridorio del Bernini and, at the far end of this, Berni's Scala Regia.

Habemus Papam

The faithful gathered in St Peter's Square waited expectantly for the white smoke from the burning ballot papers to issue forth from the Cappella Sistina where the conclave has on these occasions met behind closed doors since the 16th c.; this would be the sign that a new pope had been elected. And then, on this memorable 16 October 1978, the senior cardinal appeared on the balcony of St Peter's Church to give the traditional message announcing the successful election of a new pope: "Habemus Papam Carolum Wojtyla qui sibi nomen imposuit Joannem Paulum II" (we have elected a pope, Karol Wojtyla, who has taken the name of John Paul II). The rules

Pope John Paul II

governing the election of a new pope which still pertain today were first laid down by a Roman synod in 1059; they stated that on the death of a pope the cardinals – who at that time numbered 50 – had to elect a successor. After numerous debates as to how this should be done, it was decided at the Council of Rome in 1179 that a two-thirds majority of the Sacred College of Cardinals should suffice. The first recorded conclave, the election of the pope in a sealed room, was in 1241 when Pope Coelestin IV was elected. In 1274 a strict conclave procedure was finally laid down and this has essentially been perpetuated to this day. In 1586 Sixtus V increased the number of members of the Sacred College to 70. Paul VI in 1975 limited the number of cardinals under 80 years of age entitled to vote to 120; today they elect the new Pope with a majority of two-thirds plus one – in an emergency a simple majority plus one could suffice. With but one exception in the 16th c. (Pope Hadrian VI, 1522–23), the conclave of the cardinals during the last 600 years has always resulted in the election of an Italian Pope, until Pope Karol Wojtyla was chosen in 1978.

The title of pope, derived from *papa* (father), was restricted during the 5th c. to the bishop of Rome and since the 11th c. was borne solely by him. The form of address "Holy Father" or "Your Holiness" relates to the holiness of the office which surrounds the living pope but does not protect the dead whose personal holiness must be shown through miracles. The canonical and political position of the pope is indicated by his current official title – Bishop of Rome, Representative of Jesus Christ, Successor to the

Apostolic Princes, Summus Pontifex of all the Churches, Patriarch of the Christian West, Primate of Italy, Archbishop and Metropolitan of the Ecclesiastical Province of Rome, Sovereign of the Vatican State, Servant of the Servants of God.

The history of the papacy from Peter to John Paul II shows that the office has been held by some 270 incumbents, each contributing through his own personality to the 1950-year-old institution. While the early Christian popes were all revered as saints, the anti-papists of the Great Schism of 1378–1415 when rival popes had seats in Rome, Pisa and Avignon soon fell into disrepute, as did the Renaissance popes following the succession of the corrupt Alexander VI. Only in one individual case, that of Coelestin V, has a pope resigned after only five months in 1294. Nevertheless he was canonized as a morally pure and humble hermit. As a result of the way they were revered by their contemporaries, history has bestowed the title of "Great" on two popes – Leo I and Gregory I. During his pontificate from 440 to 461 Pope Leo I, a scion of a noble Roman family with good contacts at court and a self-confident head of the church with sole powers of imprisonment and pardon as passed down from St Peter, greatly influenced the history of the church and – during a difficult period of mass migration of the peoples and religious controversy – succeeded in increasing both the power and reputation of the bishopric of Rome.

During the period in office of Gregory I (590–604), who came from a well-to-do Roman family but was of a monastic disposition, the papal mission came into being. Among others, he sent the missionary St Augustine to England, where he succeeded in converting Ethelbert, king of Kent, to Christianity and founded the archbishopric of Canterbury. His inner enlightenment

and numerous writings elevated him, along with SS Ambrose, Hieronymus and Augustine of Hippo, to the ranks of the fathers of the church. From a papal point of view, at least, Leo III (795–816) played a part in the renewal of the Western Empire when, on Christmas Day 800, he crowned Charlemagne Holy Roman Emperor in St Peter's in Rome. No less important was the protection afforded to the papacy by Charlemagne during the riots in Rome; he also promoted the growth of the papal state. The 11th c. has gone down in history as a period of ecclesiastical reform, especially by Gregory VII (1073–85), who presented the case for papal world rule in his "Dictatus Papae". By no means squeamish in his methods, he intervened in 1076 in the dispute regarding the excommunication by the German bishops of King Henry IV, and in 1077 the king was pardoned after making a penitential pilgrimage to Canossa. Gregory's fanatical sense of mission, however, soon proved to be his downfall and he died in exile in Salerno, after Henry VI had been crowned Holy Roman Emperor by an antipope. The investiture struggle was finally settled at the Concordat of Worms in 1122 under Calixtus II. The policy adopted by Gregory VII to promote an all-powerful papal church was pursued further by Innocent III (1198–1216), a highly educated theologian and lawyer. When he was invested he preached as follows: "I am set at the head of the House of God, therefore my position overrules all others. I have been told by the prophet: I will place you above peoples and kingdoms. The apostle has said to me: I will give you the key to the Kingdom of Heaven. This servant who is set over the whole house is the representative of Christ on Earth . . . he has been placed between God and Man, smaller than God but greater than Man." He involved himself vehemently in politics, doubled the size of the Papal State and arranged for the young Frederick II to be made the future Holy

▶

Roman Emperor. In the Crusades he was less successful, for instead of Jerusalem the crusading army captured and plundered Constantinople. Self-confidence was again demonstrated by the imperious pope, however, at the opening of the fourth Lateran Council in 1215 before a backcloth of over 1200 assembled bishops, abbots and prelates who were taking important decisions on canon law. The very peak of papal world dominance was reached under Boniface VIII (1203–1303), who was guaranteed a place in hell as a result of his quest for earthly goods by his contemporary Dante Alighieri. The envoy of the King of Aragon reported thus about Boniface: "The new pope concerns himself with only three things: to live long, to make money and to enrich his family . . ." For financial reasons he declared that the year 1300 was to be the first Holy Year and celebrated this with a grand jubilee which was guaranteed to be repeated every 50 or 25 years in return for great piety and good money. Politically, the pope clashed with King Philip IV of France over the latter's attempts to tax the clergy to finance his wars. Boniface issued his famous bull "Unam Sanctam" which begins with the words; "We are driven by faith to acknowledge and obliged to emphasise that there is but one holy catholic and apostolic church", ending with the sentence: "Now we declare, state, emphasise and proclaim: to achieve salvation it is absolutely imperative for every human being to bow down before the Pope of Rome".

When Boniface died following an assassination attempt in 1303 the papacy subsequently came under French dominance and moved to Savignon. It was 1417 before Pope Martin V, who was then elected at the Council of Constance following the settlement of the 1378 schism in the church, finally moved back to Rome and made the city into the papal residence. Among the Renaissance popes Alexander VI (1492–1503) from the Spanish House of Borgia was a

The conclave leaving after choosing a pope at the Council of Constance in 1417 (15th c. book illustration)

person of impassioned violence, cold intelligence and absolutely unscrupulous in all he did. Pope Julius II (1503–13), who ordered the painting of the Sistine Chapel by Michelangelo, made a name for himself as a great patron of the arts.

Leo X (1513–21) and Clement VII (1523–34) of the Medici lineage enjoyed the glitter of papal office and increased the family wealth but could not prevent the schism nor the catastrophic plundering of Rome in 1527, and they totally underestimated the power and dynamism of the Reformation. It was Pope Pius V (1566–72), a former member of the Dominican order and later canonised, who determined to carry out the decisions of the Council of Trent (1545–63) to reform the Catholic church with ascetic strictness and inquisitorial mercilessness. Sixtus V (1585–90) was equally driven by reforming zeal; he restricted the number of cardinals to 70, imposed limitations on the bishops' visits to Rome and strengthened the centralised power of the church. He tapped new sources of income by selling high posts to the highest bidders and imposing taxes and duty. He then used the money to finance bridges, roads, palaces and church buildings in Rome. The popes of the 17th and 18th c. varied in their official conduct between absolutism and enlightenment, improved the appearance of Rome with numerous buildings, but countered the growing secularisation of many spheres of life with little in the way of spiritual regeneration. When, on Ascension day 1846, Jacob Burckhardt (1818–97) from Basle watched the procession of Pope Gregory XVI (1831–46) he wrote in verse: ". . . the golden throne rises slowly upwards,/peacock fans waft over it,/and thereon sits the son of St Peter/. . . all kneel, bells ring;/ the old man stands up straight,/ stretches out his brittle arms – /ah, you are no longer part of this world!"

His successor Pius IX (1846–78) began as a genial pope embracing liberal ideals, but after the 1848 Revolution he became a reactionary and opposed the unification of Italy. But even he could not prevent Italian troops from taking the Vatican City and Rome on 20 September 1870. As a "prisoner" he sought refuge in the Vatican, although in 1871 the Italian government declared the person of the pope to be sovereign and inviolate, allowed him to use the palaces of the Vatican, the Lateran and Castel Gandolfo, and paid him a pension of three million gold marks per annum. The religious decisions made during his pontificate proved more difficult than the political ones. In 1854 the teaching of the "Immaculate Conception of the Virgin Mary" was declared dogma. Ten years later the pope officially turned his face against the "principal errors of our time" as he called them, including rationalism and naturalism. After more than three hundred years Pius IX convened the 20th Ecumenical and First Vatican

Council in Rome in 1869, which ended in 1870 with the promulgation of the dogmas of universal papal episcopacy and papal infallibility. The succeeding popes Leo XIII (1878–1903) and the later canonized Pius X (1903–14) tried to combat the overwhelming influences of the modern world on the Catholic church. Under Pius XI (1922–39) a gradual change took place, and in 1929 the so-called Lateran Concordat was signed between the Papal See and Italy's fascist government in an attempt to resolve the conflict between the two. This three-part agreement guaranteed the sovereignty of the Papal See with the Vatican City and a number of extra-territorial regions as sovereign territory, with the pope as head of state. In addition, the Roman Catholic faith was confirmed as the state religion of Italy; this was rescinded in 1984. The largely uncritical approach adopted by the papacy against totalitarian regimes was also demonstrated by the failure of Pius XII to take a stand against the Nazi terror.

A cautious policy of openness within and outside the Catholic church began under John XXIII (1958–63). With the convening of the 21st Ecumenical and Second Vatican Council (1962–65) he introduced new measures involving the teaching and life of the Catholic church and its more open approach towards other Christian and non-Christian religions. In spite of broad agreement within the Catholic church, loud criticism was subsequently forthcoming seeking a return to traditional ways, but it was outweighed by those demanding urgent and far-reaching reforms in keeping with the times. However, with the new emphasis placed on papal authority and centralisation in Rome since 1978 under Pope Paul II, the realisation of the aims of the Second Vatican Council appears to many Christians to be in doubt. Any hope of ecumenical unity among all Christians will probably come about only if the office of pope again takes precedence and he is regarded and accepted as being pre-eminent and serving all churches.

Giardini Vaticani

The Vatican Gardens, behind St Peter's and the Vatican Palace, occupy a large part of the area of Vatican City. In the gardens stand a variety of buildings serving particular purposes, churches and offices, towers and fountains designed by Jan van Xanten, the extended Casina di Pio IV with the Accademia delle Scienze (seat of the Pontifical Academy of Sciences), the Palazzo del Governatorato, the Studio del Mosaico and a coffee-house. The north end of the gardens is bounded by the Leonine Walls, the railway station, the Radio Vaticano transmitter and the Vatican Museums.

Guided tours
Mar.–Oct.
Mon. Tue.,
Thur.–Sat.
10am
(Booking at
Uffizio
Informazioni,
Piazza San Pietro)

A minor sensation was caused in 1994 when the first nunnery in the Vatican, initially housing just seven cloistered nuns, was opened in the former Papal Guard building behind St Peter's. The nuns, who are strictly cut off from the outside world, will be changed every five years. Pope John Paul expressed the wish that, by founding this convent, "he could thank the Virgin Mother for saving his life following the assassination attempt in 1981".

Mater Ecclesiae

★★Piazza San Pietro

St Peter's Square, in front of St Peter's Church, was laid out by Bernini between 1656 and 1667 to provide a setting in which the faithful from all over the world could gather; the square he created – perhaps the most famous square in the world – has maintained its fascination right down to our own day. It is in two parts – a large ellipse measuring 340×240m/372×263yds and a smaller trapezoid area, the Piazza Retta, from which a broad flight of steps, flanked by statues of the Apostles Peter and Paul, leads up to the church. The oval is enclosed at each end by semicircular colonnades formed by 284 columns and 88 pillars of travertine in four rows. Around the balustrade on the roof of the colonnades are set 140 statues of saints. On either side of the oval stand fountains 14m/45ft high with large granite basins, the one on the right erected in 1613 by Maderno, that on the left in 1677, probably by Carlo Fontana. Two discs set into the paving mark the focal points of the ellipse (Centri del Colonnato). From these points the four lines of columns in the colonnade look like just one.

Underground station
Ottaviano
(line A)

Buses
23, 49, 51, 64, 81,
907, 990, 991

Trams
19, 30

In the centre of the square, towards which the square slopes gently down, stands an Egyptian obelisk 25.5m/87ft high. It was brought from Heliopolis to Rome by Caligula in A.D. 39 and set up in his circus (later known as the Circus of Nero). Throughout the Middle Ages this obelisk remained in its original position – the only one in Rome to do so – until Pope Sixtus V directed in 1586 that it should be moved here. Domenico Fontana was charged with the very difficult task of transporting the huge mass of stone weighing 322 tonnes to its new site. The operation took four months (from April 30th until September 10th) and involved the employment of 900 workmen, 140 horses and 44 winches. It is said that at one point the ropes were on the point of breaking under the strain when one of the workmen, disregarding the Pope's strict order that there should be absolute silence, shouted "Pour water on them", and thus saved the situation. The story goes that the Pope then granted him and his family the privilege of supplying the palm branches used in the Palm Sunday service, a practice which his descendants have maintained until the present day.

◄ *St Peter's Square, the most famous open space in the world, draws dense crowds of people every day*

★★San Pietro in Vaticano

Opening times
Daily 7am–6pm
(7pm in summer)
Dome: daily
8am–4pm
(6pm in summer)

The most famous church in Christendom is St Peter's, dedicated to the Apostle who is believed to have been the first Bishop of Rome, and whose successor each Pope, as supreme head of the Roman Catholic Church, feels himself to be. The history of St Peter's reflects that of the Papacy. Until the early 1990s St Peter's was the largest Christian church in the world, until an even larger copy was built in Yamoussoukro on the Ivory Coast of Africa.

History

The original church of St Peter was built in A.D. 326, thanks to the patronage of the Emperor Constantine. It must have been evident even then that the site, on the slopes of the Vatican hill, was a difficult one to build on, involving considerable differences of level which had to be allowed for in the foundations; and in addition it was well outside the city. That this inconvenient site was nevertheless selected suggests – with some archaeological evidence in support –that it was honoured in the long memory of Rome as the site of the Apostle's tomb, for Peter was traditionally believed to have been martyred in 64 or 67 during the reign of Nero in the Imperial gardens on the Vatican hill. We know from medieval descriptions that Old St Peter's – a five-aisled basilica of the classical type – was frequently restored and richly embellished, but after the Popes' return from exile in Avignon and the western schism (when there were a number of Popes at the same time) it was in an advanced stage of dilapidation. Pope Nicholas V accordingly resolved in 1452 to erect an entirely new church and to seek the help of all Christendom in building it (one source of income for this purpose being the sale of indulgences, which provoked Martin Luther to his protest). Construction began in 1506 and was pushed ahead with all speed, but the completion and embellishment of the church involved every Pope from Julius II (1503–13) to Pius VII (1775–99). A number of architects were engaged. The first plan was prepared by Bramante, who suggested a triple-aisled centralised building with a ground plan in the Greek cross style. He was followed by Giuliano da Sangallo together with Fra Giocondo and Raphael; the latter discarded Bramante's plan in favour of a triple-aisled basilica with side chapels and a transept. Baldassare Peruzzi favoured Bramante's plan while Antonio da Sangallo preferred Raphael's design. Michelangelo finally took over in 1547 at the age of 72; he decided on a simplified version of Bramante's plan. He was responsible in particular for the design of the dome, the drum of which was completed by the time he died in 1564. Other architects were Vignola, Ligorio, della Porta, Fontana and Maderno; the latter, at Paul V's request, extended the original centralised building towards the square by the addition of a nave.

Façade

In addition to calling for the lengthening of the church towards the square, Paul V desired that St Peter's should be linked with the Palazzo Apostolico (Vatican Palace), and for the sake of symmetry this involved a corresponding extension on the other side, giving the façade a total length of 114.7m/376ft. The height (45.5m/149ft) could not be increased, however, since this would have hidden still more of Michelangelo's dome. Maderna sought to palliate these unfortunate proportions by an elaborately articulated pattern of columns and pillars, doorways, balconies and windows. From the central balcony on the façade the senior member of the college of cardinals proclaims the name of a new Pope elected by the conclave; from this balcony, too, the Pope pronounces his "urbi et orbi" blessing on certain festivals, and beatifications and canonisations are announced. On the top of the façade are statues, 5.7m/19ft high, of Christ flanked by John the Baptist and the Apostles (except Peter). The two clocks above the bell-towers were added by Giuseppe Valadier in the 19th c.

The portico (71m/233ft wide, 13.5m/44ft deep and 20m/66ft high), is
entered through five doorways with bronze grilles. On the outside are
two equestrian statues – Charlemagne to the left, Constantine (by
Bernini) to the right. Above the main doorway can be seen fragments
of a mosaic by Giotto from Old St Peter's, the "Navicella" (the Apostles' ship in the storm). The double bronze doors, also from Old St
Peter's, were the work of the Florentine sculptor Filarete (1433–45);

Portico

San Pietro in Vaticano

50 m

1 Main entrance
2 Porta Santa
3 Michelangelo's "Pietà"
4 Monument to Christina of
   Sweden
5 St Sebastian's Chapel
6 Monument to Margravine
   Mathilda of Tuscany
7 Chapel of the Sacrament
8 Gregorian Chapel
9 Altar of St Jerome
10 Statue of St Peter
11 Entrance to Vatican Sacred
   Grotto
12 Exit from Grotto
13 Altar of Archangel Michael
14 Altar of St Peter (restoring
   Tabitha to life)
15 Tomb of Pope Urban VIII
16 Cathedra Petri (by Bernini)
17 Tomb of Pope Paul III

18 Chapel of the Column
19 Altar of St Peter (healing
   the lame man)
20 Tomb of Pope Alexander VII
21 Statue of St Veronica
22 Statue of St Helena
23 Statue of St Andrew
24 Altar of the Cruxifixion
   of St Peter
25 Tomb of Pope Pius VIII
26 Altar of Pope Gregory
   the Great
27 Clementine Chapel
28 Monument to Pope Pius VII

29 Choir Chapel
30 Tomb of Pope Innocent VIII
31 Tomb of Pope Pius X
32 Memorial relief to
   Pope John XXIII
33 Chapel of the Presentation
34 Memorial statue to
   Pope Benedict XV
35 Monument to Maria
   Sobieska and
   Stuart Monument
36 Baptistery
37 Sacristy
38 Canons' Sacristy

they depict Christ and the Virgin, the Apostles Peter and Paul and their martyrdom, and other historical scenes. To the left is the "Door of Death", a modern work by Giacomo Manzó, while the Porta Santa, to the right, is kept closed except in Holy Years.

The huge dimensions of the interior produce an overwhelming effect. The church is 185m/610ft long, rises to a height of 46m/150ft in the nave and 119m/390ft in the dome, covers an area of 15,160sq.m/ 18130sq.yds and can accommodate a congregation of some 60,000. In the floor of the nave, for purposes of comparison, are marked the lengths (measured from the apse) of other great churches. In spite of its enormous size, however, the simple architectural plan (in the form of a Latin cross, with the nave longer than the transepts) and the great dome which crowns it allow the church to be seen and appreciated as a whole.

Going round the church

The following features are worth particular note when going round the church: a few yards from the main doorway a red porphyry disc in the floor marks the spot on which Charlemagne was crowned Emperor of Rome in Old St Peter's by Pope Leo III on Christmas Day in the year 800.

★★Pietà by Michelangelo

In the Capella della Pietà (on the right of the north aisle) can be seen Michelangelo's famous "Pietà" (1498–1500), since 1972 protected by a reinforced glass screen. Michelangelo was just 24 years old when he sculpted it as a memorial to Cardinal Jean de Bilhères de la Groslaye. It depicts a youthful Virgin holding in her arms the body of Christ just taken down from the Cross. A ribbon on her breast is inscribed with the sculptor's name. The facial expressions and the consummate skill of the carving reveal Michelangelo as a great artist even at this early age.

Michelangelo's "Pietà"

St Peter's throne, by Bernini

On the adjoining pier a monument commemorates Queen Christina of Sweden, who abdicated as queen and became a Roman Catholic.

Just beyond this lies St Sebastian's Chapel, with a fine mosaic above the altar (after a painting by Domenichino) depicting the saint's martyrdom. Most of the paintings in the church have been replaced by mosaics; the originals are in the Vatican Museums (Musei Vaticani).

By the near pier will be found the mausoleum (designed by Bernini) of Countess Matilda of Tuscany, who played an important part in the conflict between the Emperor and the Pope in the 11th c.

Next comes the richly decorated Chapel of the Sacrament, to which both Bernini (the tabernacle) and Borromini (the bronze grille) contributed. The chapel was built for Pope Urban VIII of the Barberini family; hence the bees from the Barberini coat-of-arms which feature in the decoration.

In the passage to the right lies the tomb of Pope Gregory XIII, reformer of the calendar (1572–85), with the heraldic dragon of the Buoncompagni family to which he belonged.

The right transept was the meeting-place of the First Vatican Council (1869–70), attended by 650 bishops. The Second Vatican Council (1962–65) when the number of bishops had risen to over 3000, was held in the nave. In the passage beyond the transept is the monument of Clement XIII, a youthful work by Canova (1788–92).

★★Crossing and dome

Four massive pentagonal piers with a diameter of 24m/79ft and a circumference of 71m/233ft support the dome, designed by Michelangelo as the culminating point of the church, over the tomb of St Peter. The dome, set over a drum with 16 windows, has a diameter of 42.3m/139ft (slightly less than the dome of the Pantheon, 43.2m/142ft). It consists of an inner dome and an outer protective shell, with enough space between the two for a person to climb up to the roof (see below). Above the dome is the lantern, giving a total interior height of 137.5m/451ft. In niches in the piers stand figures of St Veronica with her napkin, St Helena with the True Cross, St Longinus with his lance and St Andrew with his saltire cross, and in the loggias above relics of the Passion are displayed on special festivals. Around the dome stretches a frieze with the Latin text (in letters 2m/61/2ft high) of the text from St Matthew's Gospel on which the Pope's claim to the headship of the church is based: "Tu es Petrus . . ." ("Thou art Peter, and upon this rock I will build my church . . . And I will give unto thee the keys of the Kingdom of Heaven.")

Ascent to the roof of St Peter's

The roof of St Peter's can be reached on foot via a gallery in the inside of the dome and then a flight of very narrow, steep steps (330!) to the crown of the lantern. The visitor has a choice between the staircase ascent (142 steps) and a lift (entrance outside near the Gregorian Chapel; fee). From the roof of the basilica and from the lantern there is a wonderful view across St Peter's square to the city. At the same time Michelangelo's dome and the details of its architectural construction can be seen at close quarters.

★★Papal altar

Under the dome, immediately above St Peter's tomb, stands the Papal altar, with a 29m/95ft high bronze baldacchino (canopy) created by Bernini when he was just 25 years old (1624–33) for Pope Urban VIII, using bronze from the portico of the Pantheon. With its twisted columns and fantastic superstructure this is a masterpiece of Baroque sculpture. In front of the altar, on a lower level, is the Confessio, lit permanently by 95 gilded oil lamps, beyond which lies the tomb of St Peter. Against the pier with the figure of Longinus will be seen a bronze statue of St Peter enthroned, the right foot of which has been worn smooth by the touches and kisses of the faithful. It was created by Arnolfo di Cambio in the 13th c., modelled on an ancient sculpture of a philosopher which can be seen in the Sacre Grotte Vaticane.

★Statue of St Peter

Statue of St Peter, in bronze

Apse

The Cathedra Petri (1657–66) in the apse, a bronze throne made by Bernini for Alexander VII, shows the same Baroque sense of movement as the baldacchino. Figures of the four Doctors of the Church (Ambrose and Augustine representing the Roman church and Athanasius and John Chrysotom the Greek church) support a throne, St Peter's Bishop's Chair, on the back of which two Cupids bear the Papal emblem "Key and Tiara". Before this chair became St Peter's throne it was used as such by Charles the Bald (11th c.).

Above the throne is an alabaster window framed in gilded stucco and with the symbolic dove of the Holy Ghost.

Flanking the Cathedra Petra lie the tombs of Popes Urban VIII Barberini (on the right; by Bernini, 1628–44) and Paul III Farnese (on the left; by Guglielmo della Porta, 1549–75).

In the left-hand aisle are the tombs of other famous Popes by leading artists of their day:

In the passage at the front, the monument of Alexander VII (carved under the direction of Bernini, 1672–78).

Diagonally across from the huge sacristy built in 1776–84 in the reign of Pius VI, the monument of Pius VII (by Thorvaldsen, 1823). This is the only work in the church by a Protestant sculptor, and this gave rise to protests at the time it was commissioned.

In front of the Choir Chapel (opposite the Chapel of the Sacrament), is a mosaic copy of Raphael's "Transfiguration".

In front of the Cappella della Presentazione, the tomb of Innocent VIII (by Pollaiolo, 1498), on which the Pope is represented twice (enthroned and recumbent). This is the only monument from Old St Peter's which was transferred to the new church. Opposite is a statue of Pius X.

In the Cappella della Presentazione is a bronze relief of Pope John XXIII (1958–63); to the right) as well as a statue of Benedict XV (1914–22; to the left)

The entrance to the "Vatican Grottoes" (crypt) is at the St Longinus pillar. This spacious undercroft was created when prior to 1546 Antonio da Sangallo raised the floor by 3.20m/10^1/$_2$ft to protect the church from damp. The tombs of earlier Popes were transferred here from the Old St Peter's, and many later Popes have also been buried here, including the last four, namely, Pius XII, who between 1940 and 1957 ordered extensive excavations to be undertaken under St Peter's, as a result of which the old cemetery was discovered (see below), John XXIII, Paul VI and John Paul I.

★**Sacre Grotte Vaticane**

Opening times
daily 9am–5pm

With special permission (applications in writing to the Reveranda Fabrica di San Pietro near the Arco delle Campane) it is also possible to see the excavations (scavi) under St Peter's. Here the archaeologists have brought to light the old cemetery on the Vatican Hill – including what is believed to be the tomb of St Peter himself – and the foundations of the original Constantine basilica.

Excavations

★Via Appia Antica   F/G 9/10

Outside the Porta San Sebastiano in the Aurelian Walls (see Mura Aureliane) lies the Via Appia Antica, one of the oldest and most important of the Roman consular highways. It was built about 300 B.C. by the censor Appius Claudius Caecus to link Rome with Capua, and was extended to Brindisi about 190 B.C. The road is now metalled for almost its entire length. From the port of Brindisi communications were established across the Mediterranean with the eastern territories of the Empire. Just outside Rome, running parallel with the road, can be seen the ruins of the aqueducts which supplied the city with water. On either side of the road are the remains of tombs belonging to the aristocratic families of Rome – built outside the city since burials were not permitted within its walls. The ruins of these tombs and memorial stones (see below, Catacombe di San Callisto and Tomba di Cecilia Metella; see also entry for San Sebastiano) combine with the pines and cypresses of the Roman Campagna to give the Via Appia Antica its characteristic and picturesque aspect.

Buses
118, 218, 613

Pedestrian zone
On Sundays
and holidays
the first 15km
between the
Roman Forum
and the ring
road is closed
to vehicles

Legend has it that the Apostle Peter, fearing martyrdom, decided to flee Rome after he was freed from prison. On the Via Appia he met a traveller and asked him, "Sir, whither goest thou? (Domine, quo vadis?), whereupon the traveller replied "I am come to be crucified a second time" (Venio iterum crucifigi!). Peter, then realising that Christ had spoken to him, returned to Rome.

In memory of this tale – which also formed the basis of the novel "Quo Vadis?" by Henryk Sienkiewicz – a little church known as Domine Quo Vadis (actually Santa Maria in Palmis) was erected in the 9th c., and rebuilt in the 17th c. Inside, at the entrance in the centre, can be seen a copy of the footprint of Christ. On the left there is a bust (1977) by Bogudslav Langman in memory of the author Sienkiewicz.

Domine Quo
Vadis

The Catacombs of Calixtus (Via Appia Antica 110) were described by Pope John XXIII as "the most eminent and most famous in Rome". These subterranean tombs on the Via Appia Antica extend to four storeys, cover an area of 300×400m/330×440yds and form a tortuous network of funeral chambers and passages cut into the soft volcanic

★**Catacombe di San Callisto**

Via Appia Antica

Via Appia Antica: a short stretch with ancient paving

Opening times
Mon., Tue., Thur.–
Sun.
8.30am–noon and
2.30–5pm
(5.30pm in
summer)

rock. Some 20km/12½ miles of these passages have been explored
and the number of graves is estimated at 170,000.

In the catacombs six sacramental chapels from the period between
A.D. 290 and 310 with pagan Roman and early Christian paintings are
open to visitors. Thirty-five steps lead down to the "Crypt of the Popes"
where most of the papal martyrs of the 3rd c. are buried, as can be seen
from the Greek inscriptions for Urban I, Pontius, Anteros, Fabianus,
Lucius, Sixtus II and Eutychianus. To the left near the papal chapel lies
the chamber of St Cecilia with 8th c. wall-paintings; her grave is now to
be found in the church of Santa Cecilia in Trastevere (see entry). Mention should also be made of the burial chambers of Pope Eusebius (309–
311), the Lucina Crypt with 2nd c. wall-paintings (fish symbolising the
Eucharist) and the grave of Pope Cornelius (251–253).

San Sebastiano

See entry

**★Tomba di
Cecilia Metella**

Visible from afar, the tomb of Cecilia Metella and her husband
Crassus is one of Rome's best known memorials. It lies just before the
third milestone along the Via Appia Antica.

Opening times
Tue.–Sat.
9am–4pm
(6pm in summer)
Mon., Sun.
9am–1pm

This cylindrical building, 11m/36 high, 20m/65ft in diameter and clad
in avertine rock, was erected for the Metelli family in the 1st c. B.C.
Cecilia was the daughter of general Qunitus Metellus Cretius (con-
queror of Crete), her husband Crassus was the son of Crassus who,
together with Caesar and Pompey, formed the first Triumvirate.
Cecilia's sarcophagus can today be seen in the courtyard of the Palazzo
Farnese (see entry). In 1302 the Caetani incorporated the Metella tomb
into the fort that had been built back in the 11th c. and added battlements. The fort, which at one time extended to both sides of the Via
Appia, protected the strategically important south entrance to the city.

A columbarium is a communal burial chamber with niches for the reception of cinerary urns. It gets its name from its similarity to a dovecote or pigeon-house (colomba being Latin for a dove or pigeon). A particularly well-preserved example can be found on the Via di Porta San Sebastiano near the Sepolcro degli Scipioni between the Via Appia and the Via Latina; it is that of Pomponius Hylas and his wife. Vitalinis Pomponius Hylas was a liberated slave who became prosperous during the time of the Emperors Augustus and Tiberius.

Colombario di Pomponio Hylas

Opening times
Tue.–Sat.
10am–5pm
(6pm in summer),
Sun. 9am–noon

Via Condotti

See Piazza di Spagna

★ Via Veneto (Via Vittorio Veneto)   E 5

This famous boulevard, which sweeps down in two large curves from the Porta Pinciana to the Piazza Barberini, has attracted tourists from all over the world ever since it was built in the early years of this century. In the 1950s its name was synonomous with the famous "dolce vita" then enjoyed by the "in-people" in Rome. Liz Taylor, Richard Burton, Ava Gardner, Vittorio Gassmann, Marcello Mastroianni and Anita Eckberg have all sipped a cappuccino in the Café de Paris; actors, directors, roués and minor film stars waited to be photographed by the paparazzi for some magazine or other, possibly leading to some form of scandal – they were called paparazzi, incidentally, because the most successful of all was named Paparazzo. People saw and were seen, and more or less felt a part of this great

Underground station
Barberini (line A)

Buses
52, 53, 56, 58,
90b, 95, 490, 492,
495

Cocktail time in Harry's Bar

wide world which seemed so enticingly sinful compared to the holy city of Rome.

The legend of the 1950s looks set to be revived. In 1993 the upper section of the street between Porta Pinciana and Via Ludovisi was declared a pedestrian zone in order to entice back – by means of chic street cafés and traditional bars like the "Doney" and "Harry's Bar", elegant boutiques and luxury hotels such as the Excelsior and the Eden – the streams of passers-by who earlier had made the Via Veneto into a boulevard of the first order.

Fountain of Bees

The beginning of the Via Veneto is marked by the Fountain of Bees, unveiled in 1644, Bernini chose to adorn it with the insects appearing on the coat-of-arms of his patron, Pope Urban VIII of the Barberini family.

Santa Maria della Concezione

A few yards along the street, on the right-hand side (No. 27), stands the church of the Capuchins, with a single central aisle. It was commissioned by Cardinal Antonio Barberini, a Capuchin monk and brother of the Pope, and built at the beginning of the 17th c. by Antonio Casoni. The Cardinal's memorial in front of the altar bears the Latin inscription "Hic iacet pulvis, cinis et nihil" ("here lies dust, ashes and nothing"). The altarpieces, Guido Reni's "Archangel Michael battles with Satan" (to the right in the first chapel) and Domenichino's "Francis and the Angels" (third chapel) are particularly impressive.

★Cimitero dei Cappuccini

The most unusual feature of the church is the macabre cemetery in five chapels, where the skulls and bones of some 4000 Capuchin monks have been arranged to form an intricate Baroque decoration.

★Villa Borghese   D/E 4/5

Underground stations
Flaminio and Piazza di Spagna (line A)

Buses
3, 52, 53, 490, 495, 910

Trams
19, 19b, 30, 225

The great families of Papal Rome had their palaces in the city and their villas in the country, which might be just outside the city or further afield, sometimes as far away as the Alban Hills. It is always necessary in Rome, therefore, to distinguish between the *palazzo* and the *villa* associated with a particular family name.

The Borghese family, which produced Pope Paul V (1605–21), several cardinals and other important figures, had this villa built in an area of vineyards on the outskirts of Rome for Cardinal Scipione Caffarelli Borghese in 1613–16. The villa is complete with extensive grounds, laid out with artificial lakes and garden pavilions, which now combine with the Pincio Gardens (see entry) to form one of the largest parks in Rome.

Park

Prince Marc'Antonio Borghese had considerable alterations carried out by an architect of German origin, Christoph Unterberger. Notable features of the gardens are the central artificial lake, with an Aesculapian temple on its peninsula (1786; a copy by Asprucci of a Greek temple); temples to Diana (1789) and to Faustina (1792); the museum of the Italian sculptor Pietro Canonica (1869–1959); a race-track (galoppatoio) and the Piazza di Siena, on which the international riding and jumping competition of the same name is held every year. Also, in summer, the famous open-air opera is performed on the Piazza di Siena; until 1994 it was housed in the Terme di Caracalla (see entry).

Monuments

There are several monuments, including one to Byron, a 1959 copy of the original by Thorvaldsen, to Goethe (1902–04) on the Viale San Paolo del Brasile and to Victor Hugo (1905), both by Gustav Eberlein.

The extensive parkland also accommodates the collection of the

Galleria Nazionale d'Arte Moderna and the Museo Nazionale Etrusco di Villa Giulia (see entries).

There is also a small zoological garden built in 1911 and modelled on the Hamburg zoo. Planning permission has been obtained to convert it into a biopark, with larger enclosures reflecting the animals' natural habitats as closely as possible. In the longer term there will be little in the way of exotic fauna, but at present visitors can enjoy seeing flamingos, monkeys and elephants. Admission is free for children and senior citizens (open: daily 8am–6.15pm/5pm in winter).

Giardino Zoologico

★★Museo e Galleria Borghese

At the east end of the gardens can be found the Casino Borghese, erected by the young Dutchman Jan van Santen (later known as Giovanni Vasanzio) in 1613–15. It now houses the collection of antiquities and paintings assembled by Cardinal Scipione Borghese, a nephew of Camillo Borghese, who later became Pope Paul V.

Opening times
Tue.–Sat. 9am–5pm, Sun. 9am–1pm (entrance on Piazzale Brasilie)

After fourteen years of restoration work the two-storey building, with twin rectangular towers, was again open to the public in 1997. The ground floor has a loggia of five arcades covered with a large open terrace.

The art-loving Cardinal Scipione Borghese, a great collector of antiquities, also commissioned work from contemporary artists; Bernini, for example, received his first commission from him. The Cardinal's collection was then housed in the Casino and formed the basis of the Borghese Museum as it is today. Borghese's successors were also interested in art and they extended and improved the museum and the villa. Under Marcantonio IV (1730–80), in particular, extensive restoration work was carried and the gardens re-designed. Unfortunately, during the Napoleonic period Prince Camillo Borghese, husband of Pauline Bonaparte, was compelled by his brother-in-law Napoleon to sell a large part of the antique collection to the Louvre in Paris. At the beginning of the 20th c. the collection of pictures was formed into the Borghese Gallery.

The five fragments of a mosaic pavement from Torrenuova near Tusculum, contained in the richly decorated entrance hall, date from the 3rd c. and show gladiator contests and hunting scenes. The Baroque ceiling frescoes, by Mariano Rossi, represent "Camillus after the parley with Brennus, Commander of the Gallic Army" and "Allegory of Glory".

Entrance hall

Outstanding works of sculpture in the museum include Canova'a figure of "Venus at Rest" (1805), probably a portrait of Pauline Borghese, sister of Napoleon; "David with his Sling" (1623–24), commissioned by Scipione Borghese from Bernini, who gave it his own features; "Apollo and Daphne", a masterpiece by the young Bernini, depicting the transformation of Daphne into a laurel-bush to save her from pursuit by Apollo; "Rape of Prosperina by Pluto", also by Bernini (1621–22) and a fine example of his technical skill; "The Sleeping Hermaphrodite" (Roman copy of a Greek original in the Louvre); "Aeneas, Anchises and Ascanius", probably also by Bernini (1619); and Bernini's uncompleted group "Truth revealed by Time" (ca. 1642).

Sculptures

The picture collection includes works by Raphael, including "Male Portrait" (1502), the "Entombment" (1507) commissioned by Atalanta Baglioni for the family chapel in Perugia, in memory of his son Grifone who was killed in the fighting around Perugia in 1500; "Virgin with Child and John as a Boy", by Andrea del Sarto (ca. 1517),

Picture gallery

The "Entombment" by Raphael: a memorial to Grifone Baglioni

the "Crucifixion with SS Hieronymus and Christopher", by Pin-turicchio (1470–80), a "Virgin with Child" by Perugino, founder of the Umbrian Renaissance, executed in delicate pastel shades. The German Renaissance is represented by "Venus and Cupid with the Honeycomb" (1527) by Lukas Cranach the Elder, while Sodoma's "Pietà" (ca. 1540) shows the influence of Leonardo da Vinci. "Sybil" and "Diana the Huntress" were commissioned from Domenichino by Cardinal Scipione Borghese. An important early self-portrait by Carvaggio is "Boy with a Basket of Fruit" (ca. 1594); other works by the same artist include "St Hieronymus the Scribe" (ca. 1605) and "Madonna dei Palafrenieri" (1605/6), intended as an altar-piece for the Palafrenieri brotherhood. The transition from early Renaissance to Mannerism is reflected in Corregio's "Danae" (post-1530); Titian's "Heavenly and Earthly Love" (ca. 1516) is one of the artist's early works; "Male Portrait" by Antonello da Messina was probably painted during his sojourn in Venice in 1475–76. The "Lamentation of Christ" (1601) is by Rubens, while Bellini's sensitively painted "Virgin with Child" dates from ca. 1508. "John the Baptist Preaching" (ca. 1562) by the Mannerist artist Paolo Veronese includes a number of figures in Oriental dress, a common sight in Venice at that time.

★Villa Doria Pamphili   A/B 7/8

Location
Via Aurelia
Antica

Buses
31, 41, 75, 982

To the west of Gianicolo Hill lie the extensive grounds of the Villa Doria Pamphili, the largest municipal park (9sq.km/3½sq. miles) in Rome, with broad areas of lawn and clumps of pine trees offering welcome shade. The villa was built in 1644–52 by Alessandro Algardi for Prince Camillo Pamphili, a nephew of Pope Innocent X. On a terrace alongside the Via Aurelia Antica stands the Casino dei Quattri Venti (country house of the four winds), decorated with statues and reliefs.

★★Villa Farnesina   C 6

The Villa Farnesina, which now belongs to the State and houses the National Print Cabinet (Gabinetto Nazionale delle Stampa; viewing by appointment only), was built in the 16th c. with all the lavishness and splendour of the period.

The Renaissance palace, surrounded by parkland, was designed and constructed by Baldassare Peruzzi between 1508 and 1522 for the banker Agostino Chigi, known as "il magnifico" because of his glittering parties. It was decorated by famous artists including Raphael, Giulio Romano, Sebastiano del Piombo, Peruzzi himself and Sodoma. Here popes, cardinals, princes, diplomats, artists and men of letters were entertained in princely fashion. Illustrious guests were given silver dishes bearing their own coat-of-arms, which they threw into the nearby Tiber after the banquet (though a net spread in the river enabled them to be recovered afterwards). After the banquets party games were sometimes held in the gardens and mock challenges issued – feigned duels, for example. The palace was acquired by the Farnese family in 1580, and later it went to the Bourbons of Naples.

On the walls and ceiling of the garden loggia are scenes from the myth of Cupid and Psyche (after Apuleius), painted by Raphael and his pupils Giulio Romano and Francesco Penni (1517); in the fashion of the period they depict Greco-Roman ideals combined with Christian themes. The figures in the spandrels are by Raphael himself.

Location
Lungotevere della Farnesina

Buses
23, 28, 65

Opening times
Mon.–Sat. 9am–1pm
Closed in Aug.
Entrance Via della Lungara

Garden loggia

One of the magnificent frescoes which decorate the Villa Farnesina

199

Villa Giulia

Sale di Galatea

In the Sale di Galatea, besides lunette frescoes by Sebastiano del Piombo (scenes from Ovid's Metamorphosis) and Baldassare Peruzzi's "Starry Sky", can be seen Raphael's magnificent fresco "Triumph of the Nymph Galatea" (1511), who was pursued by the one-eyed Cyclopes Polyphemus, The assumption that Imperia, the beloved of Chigi, was portrayed in this painting is not verified.

Salone delle Prospettiva

Also of interest in the Salone delle Prospettiva (Hall of Perspective) on the upper storey are the *trompe-l'oil* paintings by Baldassare Peruzzi. These were painted at the beginning of the 16th century and provide a view of squares in ancient Rome with the colonnades appearing to open out to the viewer.

Works of Sodoma

Sodoma's masterpiece in the bedroom of Agostino Chigi is "The Marriage of Alexander the Great and Roxana" (daughter of the Persian King Darius), painted in 1511–12. The painting shows the bedchamber with the Macedonian commander presenting his bride with the crown, symbolising the victory of love; Hymen and little Cupids with love's arrows helping to disrobe Roxanne emphasise the erotic nature of the situation. Sodoma also painted "Alexander's Pardon of the Persian Family Darius".

Villa Giulia

See Museo Nazionale Etrusco di Villa Giulia

Villa Madama   A/B 2/3

Location
Via di Villa Madama

Buses
28, 32, 90, 391

On the slopes of Monte Mario, on the side looking towards the city, stands the Villa Madama, now used by the Italian government for receptions and conferences. The villa was designed by Raphael for Cardinal Giulio de'Medici, later Pope Clement VII, and subsequently altered by Antonio da Sangallo the Younger. It passed into the hands of "Madama" Margareta, daughter of the Emperor Charles V, who married Alessandro de'Medici as her first husband and Ottavio Farnese as her second, and in 1735 the property passed to the Bourbons of Naples. The villa fits harmoniously into its natural setting and offers a magnificent view of the city.

Villa Medici   D 5

Location
Viale della Trinità dei Monti

Underground station
Piazza di Spagna (line A)

To the north of the Trinità dei Monti church, a few paces from the Piazza di Spagna (see entry), is the Villa Medici (visits by arrangement with the French Academy). It is a late Renaissance mansion with a severe main façade and a richly articulated garden front to the rear, facing the Pincio (see entry). The villa was built in 1544 by Annibale Lippi for Cardinal Ricci da Montepulciano. It later passed to the Medici and then the Grand Dukes of Tuscany, and was finally occupied in Napoleonic times by the French Academy (established by Richelieu in Paris in 1666), a foundation still existing for French artists here in Rome. From 1630–33 Galileo was imprisoned in the villa on the order of the Inquisition.

Villa Torlonia   G 4

The Villa Torlonia park (area 13ha/32½ acres), with the Neo-Classical Palazzo Torlonia (early 19th c.), formerly the property of the Torlonia family, was the private residence of Mussolini during the Fascist period. Today the park belongs to the city of Rome and is open to visitors; the building itself, however, is closed to the public.

Location
Via Nomentana

Buses
36, 37, 60, 62, 63, 136, 137

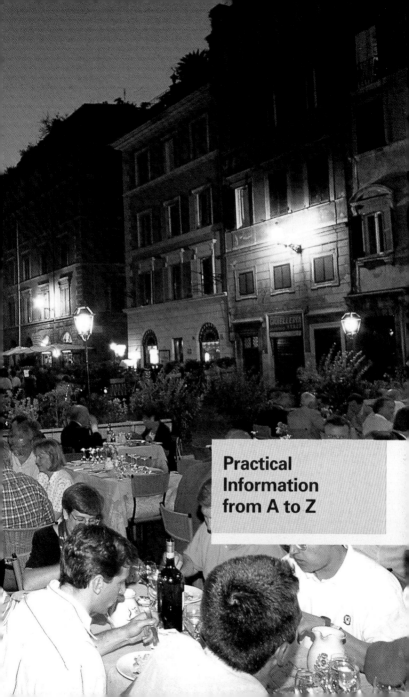

**Practical
Information
from A to Z**

Practical Information

Airlines

Alitalia
Via Leonida Bissolati 20; tel. 6 56 21, 6 56 41, 6 56 42
Aeroporto Leonardo da Vinci; tel. 6 56 31, 65 63 32 79, 6 56 43

British Airways
Via Leonida Bissolati 54; First Floor tel. 48 54 80 or toll free in Italy
1478 1266

TWA
Via Barberini 59–67; tel. 47 212

Canadian Airlines International
Via Carlo Venziani 58, Palazzina C, First Floor, tel. 659 1300, 655 7117

Cathay Pacific
Via Barberini 3; tel 4 82 07 03

Antiques

In the narrow streets behind the Piazza Navona are the workshops of craftsmen highly skilled in the restoration of antique furniture and pictures no matter how badly damaged they may be. Visitors will find numerous little shops all competing fiercely with one another, selling antique furniture, silver, jewellery, dolls, pictures, lamps, lace covers and much else besides. Twice a year, in the second half of May and the second half of October, "antiquarian weeks" are held in the Via dei Coronari. Rome's art market is concentrated in Via del Babuino and Via

Alitalia operates to and from Rome's Leonardo da Vinci airport

Giulia. Dozens more galleries and antique dealers are located in the area between Via Nazionale and Via Cavour. Restored country furniture can be found in Via dei Cappellari behind the Campo dei Fiori. A flea market is held on Sunday mornings at the Porta Portese in Trastevere.

Aldo di Castro, Via del Babuino 71, tel. 6 79 49 00 (17th–19th c. European engravings, including works by Pinelli, Vasi and Rossini)
Antichita' Davide Sestieri, Via Margutta 57, tel. 3 20 75 90 (18th and 19th c. Italian and Chinese porcelain)
Antique Armoury, Via del Babuino 161, tel. 3 61 41 58 (antique furniture, old uniforms, coins and prints)
Enrico Camponi, Via della Stellata 32, tel. 6 86 52 49 (Murano glass)
Luciano Coen, Via Margutta 63, tel. 3 20 12 64 (16th–18th c. French and Flemish tapestries, oriental carpets)
Nicoletta Lebole Art Gallery, Via del Babuino 38, tel. 6 78 39 02 (Art deco)

Antique dealers

Antiquariato all'aperto all'EUR; antique market by the artificial lake in the EUR district, first opened in 1995. Information: tel. 5 83 67 84
GAL. PA. DA., Via Ugo Ojetti 380e (antiques wholesaler situated in the north-east of the city)
M. Fortuna, Via Nomentana 1141, Grande Roccardo Annuale (antiques wholesaler)

Antique markets

Christie's, Piazza Navona 114, tel. 6 87 27 87
Finarte, Via Margutta 54, tel. 3 20 76 37

Auction houses

Banks

See Currency

Bicycle, moped and Vespa rental

1 Bike Rome, at the top end of the Via Veneto, on the lower level of the Villa Borghese car park. tel, 322 5240
Largo Lombardi, Via del Corso, abreast the Via Condotti
Romabike, at the entrance to the Metropolitana station on the Piazza di Spagna

Pedal cycles

St Peter Moto Rent, Via di Porta Castello 43, tel. 6 87 57 14
Scoot-a-long, Via Cavour 302, tel. 6 78 02 06

Moped and Vespa hire

Camping sites

Camping Tiber, km 1.4 on the Via Tiberina, tel & fax 33 61 23 14; 5ha/12-acre site on the banks of the Tiber
Capitol, Via di Castelfusano 195 (4km/2^1/$_2$ miles), tel. 5 657344, fax 5652143, 33ha/81 acres
Fabulous, km 18 on the Via C. Colombo, tel. and fax 5 25 93 54
Flaminio, Via Flaminia Nuova 821 (4km/2^1/$_2$ miles), tel. 3 33 2604 fax 3 33 06 53; 8ha/20 acres
Happy Camping, Via Prato della Corte 1915, tel. 33 62 64 01, fax 33 61 38 00; 4ha/10 acres
Roma Camping, Via Aurelia 831 (8.2km/5miles), tel. 6 6418147; 3ha/7^1/$_2$ acres
Seven Hills, Via Cassia 1216 (18km/11 miles), tel. 30 31 08 26, fax 30 31 00 39; 5ha/12 acres

Car rental

Avis	Piazza Esquilino 1/c, tel. 4 70 12 16 Aeroporto Leonardo da Vinci, tel. 60 15 79 or 65 01 15 31
Thrifty-Italy by car	Via Ludovisi 60, tel. 482 0966
Europcar	Piazza Vivona 3, tel. 5 91 38 75 Via Lombardia 7, tel. 4 87 12 74/4 81 71 62 Aeroporto Leonardo da Vinci, tel. 61 45 64
Hertz	Montemario Hilton, Via Cadiolo 101, tel. 353 43758 Aeroporto Leonardo da Vinci, tel. 65 01 15 53
Bicycle, moped and Vespa hire	See entry

Chemists (Farmacie)

Opening times	Generally Mon.–Fri. 9am–1pm and 4–8pm.
International pharmacies	Open day and night: Via Cavour 2, tel. 488 0019 Piazza Barberini 49, tel. 46 29 96, 4 75 54 56, 4 82 54 56
Useful phrases	Please could I have *Mi puï dare* ... a thermometer *un termometro* ... a sticking plaster *un cerotto* ... a medicine for ... *una medicina per ...* ... stomach pains *mal di pancia* ... diarrhoea *diarrea* ... a temperature *febbre* ... flu *influenza* ... a sore throat *mal di gola* ... a cough *tosse* ... a headache *mal di testa* ... sunburn *scottatura solare* ... constipation *costipazione* ... toothache *mal di denti*

Currency

Currency	The unit of currency is the *lira* (plural *lire*). There are banknotes of 1000, 2000, 10,000, 50,000 and 100,000 lire and coins in denominations of 50, 100, 200 and 500 lire. On 1 January 1999 the euro became the official currency of Italy, and the Italian lira notes and coins continue to be a legal tender during a transitional period. Euro bank notes and coins are likely to be introduced by 1 January 2002.
Movement of currency	There are no restrictions on the import of Italian and foreign currency into Italy. The export of currency is restricted to a maximum of 20 million lire, except where substantial sums have been declared on entry (using form Modulo V2).
Changing money	You should take enough lire with you to cover any immediate needs

(such as motorway tolls). Money changing facilities are found at frontiers, in larger hotels and at railway stations in addition to banks and bureaux de change. The bureaux de change in travel agencies are not recommended on account of their administrative charge. Bank machines (see below) offer the most convenient way of obtaining lire. All receipts of exchange – and other transactions – should be retained, failure to do so rendering the visitor liable to a possible fine.

Eurocheques can be cashed up to a value of 300,000 lire, subject to a charge of about £1 for each cheque.

Eurocheques

Banks, the larger hotels, better class restaurants, car rental companies and many shops accept most types of international credit cards. Visa cards are particularly widely accepted, also American Express, Eurocard and Diners Club. Loss of a credit card should be reported immediately (make a note of the number to call before leaving home).

Credit cards

Banks are open Mon.–Fri. 8.30am–1.15pm; afternoon opening hours vary but are generally ca. 2.30–3.30pm. On the eve of public holidays (prefestivi) banks close at 11.20am.

Banks

Bank machines (bancomat) for use with Eurocheque and credit cards (look for the appropriate sign) are found everywhere in Rome. The maximum withdrawal using a Eurocheque card is 300,000 lire. The limit for credit cards is higher (depending on the individual holder).

Bank machines

Customs regulations

Citizens of countries in the European Union are no longer subject to import restrictions on personal effects and articles for their own use. The limits on "duty free" goods remain: 200 cigarettes or 100 cigarillos or 50 cigars or 300 grammes tobacco; 3 litres of wine and 1 litre spirits over 22° Gay-Lussac (38.8° proof) or 2 litres fortified or sparkling wine up to 22° proof; 50 grammes perfume and 0.25 litres of toilet water.

Videos, CB radios, car telephones and fuel in cans must be declared. The import of weapons, including imitations, and large hunting knives is prohibited.

Some of the concessions enjoyed by citizens of EU countries also apply to visitors from elsewhere, including the United States and Canada.

There are no restrictions on personal effects, etc. taken out of Italy. Additionally, no export duty is payable on items purchased in Italy up to a value of 500 US dollars. The export of antiques and objets d'art requires a permit issued by the Chamber of Art.

It is advisable when taking large amounts of currency into Italy to complete a declaration on entry (see Currency).

Note

Electricity

The current is 220 volts AC. In most circumstances an adapter will be required, the only exception being appliances fitted with the standard narrow pin type of European plug.

Embassies

United Kingdom	Via XX Settembre 80A; tel. 4 82 54 41 or 482 5551
United States of America	Via Vittorio Veneto 119A; tel. 4 67 41
Canada	Via G. Bastia de Rossi 27; tel. 44 59 81

Emergency services

Ambulance and police emergency	Tel. 1 13 (polizia soccorso pubblico)
Police	Tel. 1 12 (carabinieri)
Fire brigade	Tel. 1 15 (vigili del fuoco)
Breakdown service	Tel. 1 16 (soccorso stradale ACI)
Medical help	See entry

Events

Note	Day-to-day information about events can be found in daily newspapers and in the weekly magazines "Città Aperta", "Romac'è" and "Roma – Giorno & Notte".
January	Mid December to January 6th: Christmas Market in the Piazza Navona. January 6th: Epiphany (children's fair in the Piazza Navona). Alta Moda Italiana (Spring and Summer fashions) Roma Ufficio (Office Equipment Trade Fair, continuing into February).
February	Martedì Grasso (Shrove Tuesday and weeks leading up to it): costume and mask street processions.
March	March 9th: Santa Francesca Romana – blessing of motor vehicles at the Colosseum. March 19th: San Giuseppe (St Joseph); *zeppole* (cream choux) sold and consumed in large quantities. Spring Festival in the Piazza di Spagna (continuing into April)
March/April	Maundy Thursday: Washing of the Feet, San Giovanni in Laterano (Papal Mass). Holy Week: services conducted by the Pope on Palm Sunday, Maundy Thursday, Good Friday and Easter Saturday. Good Friday: Stations of the Cross in the Colosseum in the presence of the Pope. Easter Day: Papal blessing "Urbi et Orbi" ("the City and the World) from the balcony of St Peter's.
April	Second half of April: azaleas in the Piazza di Spagna
May	Second half of May: antiques fair in the Via dei Coronari. Rose show in the Valle Murcia rose garden on the Aventine.

Fiera di Roma: exhibition of products from all over Italy, along the Via Cristoforo Colombo (until June).

June 23rd–24th Midsummer Night (fireworks).
Estate Romana ("Roman Summer"): mostly open-air concerts, theatre and exhibitions throughout the summer, continuing until October.
Tévere Expo: exhibition on the banks of the Tiber of products from all regions of Italy (until July).

June

Festa dei Noiantri: popular festival in Trastevere (fireworks, sucking pig roasted and consumed in the street).
Season of opera in the Villa Borghese.
Season of concerts, Accademia di Santa Cecilia.
Roma musica (until September)
Season of theatre, Ostia Antica.
Alta Moda Italiana (Autumn and Winter fashions).

July

August 5th: Festa della Madonna della Neve (Festival of Our Lady of the Snow) marked by celebrations in the church of Santa Maria Maggiore.
Concert season continues (Accademia di Santa Cecilia).
Theatre season continues (Ostia Antica).
Open-air pop concerts and song recitals.

August

Children's fashion show.
Tévere Expo Internazionale: international trade fair on the banks of the Tiber.
Antiques fair (continuing until October).

September

MOA: furniture and interior design show.
Antiques fair in the Via dei Coronari.

October

December 8th: Immacolata Concezione (Immaculate Conception), with religious ceremony in the Piazza Navona.
December 15th: Christmas Market in the Piazza Navona (until 6 January).
December 24th: Solemn Mass in St Peter's.
December 25th: Solemn Christmas Mass in St Peter's followed by the Pope's annual Christmas Address from the balcony of St Peter's.
Nativity scenes in churches and in the Piazza di Spagna.
Exhibition Natale Oggi ("Christmas Today").

December

Excursions

Bookings for excursions in and around Rome can be made at most travel agents. Visitors who prefer to make their own way will find most of the sights easily accessible by public transport (see A to Z, Ostia, Tivoli) or more easily accessible still by car (see A to Z, Ceverteri, Colli Albani).

Of those excursions best made by car, one of the most rewarding is to Palestrina, the old Praeneste, 38km/24 miles south-east of Rome. It is reached via motorway A2, taking the Zagarolo exit, or on Strada Statale N6. The huge complex of the former Roman shrine of Fortuna Primigenia (1st and 2nd c. B.C.), in which part of the town is built, is well worth seeing. Numerous finds from the shrine and from graves in the surrounding areas are exhibited in the Museo Nazionale Archeologico Prenestino (open: daily 9am–sunset) located in the Palazzo Colonna Barberini on the uppermost terrace of the shrine.

Palestrina

Food and drink

Tarquinia

About 100km/62 miles north-west of Rome lie remains of the Etruscan city of Tarquinia. They are reached via motorway A12 in the direction of Fiumicino, turning off to Civitavecchia where the motorway ends and then driving along the Via Aurelia (SS N1). Preserved in the necropolis are the most beautifully decorated graves of the Etruscan culture. Due to deterioration of the paintings in the burial chambers, caused in no small measure by the large number of tourists, only eight chambers are opened to the public (four at a time, alternate days). Finds from the graves are displayed in the Museo Nazionale Tarquiniense (open: Tues.–Sun. 9am–2pm and, in summer, 4–7pm also).

Monte Circeo/
San Felice

From a scenic point of view there is a delightful excursion to the coastal town of San Felice, 90km/56 miles south-east of Rome. Leaving Rome in the direction of Lido di Ostia, turn south-eastwards along the coast road and drive via Anzio, Nettuno and Saubadia to San Felice. About 5km/3 miles before San Felice rises Monte Circeo. Here, according to legend, stood the palace of the sorceress Circe who turned the companions of Odysseus into swine.

From San Felice in clear weather it is possible to see as far as Ischia, Capri, Vesuvius and the Ponza Islands.

Food and Drink

Meals

Most Italians do not eat breakfast. For many in the morning it is "un caffè e via" (a strong coffee and get going). Sitting down to a substantial breakfast is considered an unusual habit, even if it is only cereal and toast. Nevertheless most hotels now serve the kind of breakfast (colazione) familiar to many north Europeans, consisting of rolls, butter and jam. Italians usually content themselves with a quick caffè or cappuccino in a bar, occasionally with some sort of pastry. Taking their lead, why not forgo breakfast in the hotel, which is likely to be uninspiring and relatively expensive and start the day with a roll in the rather more interesting surroundings of a bar. The kinds of coffee the Italians drink every day are in any case generally superior to the blends served up to tourists in hotels.

Lunch (pranzo) is usually eaten early, at about 12.30 or 1pm; dinner on the other hand is rarely to be had before 8pm. In Italy lunch and supper always consist of a first course (primo) of risotto, pasta or soup followed by a second (secondo) of meat or fish. So visitors from abroad professing to be satisfied with just a plate of spaghetti are likely to have difficulty making themselves understood. The very hungry might order a hot or cold starter (antipasto), and the secondo can always be followed by a pudding, a piece of cake say, or an ice-cream (gelato) or soft ice.

Roman cuisine

Roman cuisine lays little store by extravagance or sophistication. Instead it retains its regional character, distinguished by the use of good, unadulterated ingredients and careful preparation according to simple traditional recipes. If a restaurant advertises itself at the door or in its bill of fare as offering "cucina romana", you can expect the dishes to have been prepared according to Roman recipes. Visitors should certainly not miss the chance of trying these particular Roman specialities.

Soups

Zuppa: chicken broth with vegetables, meat dumplings, rice or pasta.

Starters

Broccoli romani: broccoli steamed in white wine.

Cannelloni: pasta squares stuffed with meat, spinach, egg and cheese.
Carciofi alla guidà: artichokes baked in an earthenware pot.
Carciofi alla romana: artichokes seasoned with peppermint and stuffed with anchovies.
Fettucine: ribbon noodles with a sauce of butter, eggs, anchovies and cheese.
Gnocchi alla romana: semolina dumplings.
Gnocchi di polenta: maize flour pasta, either grilled or breaded and fried in fat.
Lumache: snails in tomato sauce, seasoned with ginger.
Panzarottini: small packets of pasta with cheese and butter, finished off with eggs, anchovies, etc.
Suppli di riso: croquettes of rice and egg with meat ragout.

Anguilla: eels stewed in white wine.   Fish dishes
Calamari fritti: fried rings of squid.
Orate ai ferri: grilled redfish.

Anitra: stuffed duck with calves' feet.   Poultry
Cappone: capon with bread stuffing, seasoned with cheese.
Pollo: chicken in tomato sauce with white wine.

Abbacchio: lamb in white wine.   Meat dishes
Polenta: maize flour polenta slices with lamb stew.
Salsa romana: a brown sweet and sour sauce with raisins and chestnut and lentil purée (served with game).
Saltimbocca: slices of veal and ham seasoned with sage, steamed in butter and doused in marsala.
Testarelle di abbacchio: lambs' heads fried in oil and flavoured with rosemary.
Trippa: tripe in tomato sauce with white wine.

It goes without saying that wines from all over Italy are available in **Drinks**
Rome. As regards wines from the Rome area itself, the best known are those of the Castelli Romani, often called Frascati after the chief place of production; from here come strong white wines with a flowery bouquet. Other locations renowned for wine growing are those clustered around the Lago Albano, such as Grottaferrata, Marino, Genzano, Velletri (for red wine also), and in the Colli Lanuvini and Colli Albani. Table wine is often served in carafes holding a litre, half litre or quarter litre ("un litro", "mezzo litro", "un quarto") as well as by the glass ("un bicchiere"). Alternatives to wine with a meal are beer or mineral water.

As everywhere in Italy, people finish their meal with a caffè espresso.   Caffè and
Foreign visitors to Rome often prefer a cappuccino, a strong caffè with   cappuccino
a lot of hot milk crowned with the familiar milky froth. In the early morning nothing tastes better than a cappuccino. But take note: if you want to avoid being branded instantly as a tourist, never order a cappuccino after lunch. Italians only drink coffee with milk early in the day. In Rome there are more than five thousand bars, in which the central feature is the espresso machine. Furnishings are minimal, seats are few, and customers stand at the bar, the choice of coffee being what matters most to the citizen of Rome. Espresso is simply called "caffè" in Rome and is served "doppio" (double), "corretto" (corrected) with grappa, cognac or bitters, or even "ristretto" (stretched) shortened and strong. Cappuccino comes in still more varieties, which can be drunk light or dark ("chiaro" or "scuro"), at various temperatures and with as much froth as desired. A plain coffee with milk is a "caffelatte" "(stained with a dash of milk.).

Food and drink

Grappa   The right thing to end a rich meal with is a grappa. It must be strong, dry and have a pleasantly fruity bouquet. The best varieties come from the South Tyrol, Trentino, Friuli, Veneto and Piedmont.

Restaurants   See entry

Menu

English	Italian
Menu	Listino
Wine list	Lista dei vini
Meat soup	Brodo
Thick vegetable soup	Minèstrone
Starters	Antipasti
Meat course	Piatti di carne
Roast	Arrosto
Veal	Vitello
Rabbit	Coniglio
Lamb	Agnello
Pork	Maiale
Escalope	Scaloppina
Wiener schnitzel	Costoletta alla milanese
Liver	Fegato
Kidneys	Rognoni
Poultry	Volatili
Duck	Anatra
Goose	Oca
Chicken	Pollo
Wild boar	Cinghiale
Sausage	Salsiccia
Ham	Prosciutto
Fish	Pesce
Fried fish	Fritto di pesce
Boiled	Bollito
Seafood	Frutti di mare
Trout	Trota
Prawns	Granchi
Pike	Luccio
Crab	Gambero
Salmon	Salmone
Spiny lobster	Aragosta
Mussels	Cozze
Venus molluscs	Vongole
Sole	Sogliola
Tuna	Tonno
Squid	Calamare
Vegetables	Verdure, legumi
Aubergines	Melanzane
Cauliflower	Cavolfiore
Beans (white)	Fagioli
Beans (green)	Fagiolini
Peas	Piselli
Potatoes	Patate
Paprika	Peperoni
Mushrooms	Funghi
Mixed salad	Insalata mista
Spinach	Spinaci
Tomatoes	Pomodori

Noodles	Pasta
Rice	Riso
Dumplings	Gnocchi
(made from potato dough)	
Pudding	Dessert, dolce
Ice-cream	Gelato
Ice-cream with fruit	Gelato con frutta
Ice-cream with candied fruit	Cassata
Fruit salad	Macedonia
Cheese	Formaggio
Whipped cream	Panna montana
Zabaglione	Zabaglione
Fruit	Frutta
Apple	Mela
Banana	Banana
Cherry	Ciliege
Grape	Uva
Orange	Arancia
Peach	Pesca
Pear	Pera
Plum	Prugne
Strawberry	Fràgole
Watermelon	Cocómero
Drinks	Bevande, bibite
Beer	Birra
Espresso coffee	Caffè
Freshly squeezed orange	Spremuta d'arancia
Fruit juice	Succo di frutta
Lemonade	Aranciata
Milk	Latte
Mineral water	Acqua minerale
Cream	Crema
Tea	Tè
Water	Acqua
Wine	Vino
White wine	Vino bianco
Red wine	Vino rosso
Dry	Secco
Sweet	Amabile
Bread	Pane
White bread	Pane bianco
Roll	Panino
Biscuits	Biscotti
Cake	Torta
Macaroons	Amaretti
Butter	Burro
Jam	Marmellata
Honey	Miele
Salt	Sale
Pepper	Pepe
Sugar	Zùcchero
Vinegar	Aceto
Oil (olive-)	Olio (d'oliva)
A soft-boiled egg	Un uovo alla coque
Omelette	Frittata, omeletta
Scrambled egg	Uovo strapazzato
Fried egg	Uovo al tegame

Galleries

Galleria Borghese
See A to Z, Villa Borghese

Galleria Colonna
See A to Z, Galleria Colonna

Galleria Doria Pamphili
See A to Z, Palazzo Doria Pamphili

Galleria Nazionale d'Arte Antica
See A to Z, Palazzo Barberini
See A to Z, Palazzo Corsini

Galleria Nazionale d'Arte Moderna
See A to Z, Galleria Nazionale d'Arte Moderna

Galleria dell Accademia di San Luca
Piazza dell'Accademia di San Luca 77
Open: Mon., Wed., Fri., and last Sun. in the month 10am–1pm
(Paintings by Raphael, da Bassano, Rubens, etc.)

Galleria dell'Oca
Via dell'Oca 41
Open: Mon.–Sat. 10am–1pm, 4–8pm
(20th c. abstract paintings)

Galleria Spada
See A to Z, Palazzo Spada

Getting to Rome

By car

Roads to Rome

It is a long drive from northern Europe to Rome. Motorists are therefore advised to make use as far as possible of motorways (see Motoring) and main trunk roads.

There is a wide choice of routes from the English Channel to Rome,
depending on individual preference and time available – through
France over one of the Alpine passes into Italy; down to the south
coast of France and then on the coastal motorway into Italy; via
France or Germany, Switzerland and one of the Alpine passes or
tunnels. The journey can be shortened by using one of the motorail
services from stations in north-west Europe.

Frontier
crossing-points

The following frontier crossing-points remain open throughout the
year, weather permitting;

Swiss-Italian frontier:
Great St Bernard (Tunnel): Lausanne–Aosta–Turin road (the road over
the pass is usually closed from November to June).
Simplon Tunnel: Brig–Iselle–Milan road
Chiasso: Lugano–Como–Milan road
Castasegna/Chiavennna (Maloja Pass): St Moritz–Milan road

Austrian-Italian frontier:
Brenner: Innsbruck–Bolzano road
Reschen Pass: Landeck–Merano–Bolzano
Winnbach (Prato alla Drave): Lienz–Bolzano or Venice road
Tarvisio: Villach–Udine–Venice road

See Travel Documents

Documents
required

See Motoring

Driving in Italy

By bus

There are numerous package coach tours, either going direct to Rome or including Rome in a longer itinerary. Information can be obtained from any travel agent.

There are also regular coach services between Britain and other north European countries and Rome. Euroways run a regular service from London to Rome via Milan (information from Euroways Express Coaches Ltd., 52 Grosvenor Gardens, London W1; tel. (0171) 837 6543, or from a travel agent).

By rail

The fastest route from London to Rome takes about 26 hours (via Calais), leaving London Victoria. Alternatives are to travel via Paris or Brussels, from where there are convenient through trains.

Trans-European trains terminating in Rome arrive at the city's main railway station, the Stazione Termini (information: tel. 47 75; lost property tel. 47 30–6682).

Stations
Stazione Termini

Most trains travelling on to southern Italy arrive at Stazione Tiburtina (information: tel. 4 95 66 26).
There are taxi, bus and Metro services from both stations.

Stazione
Tiburtina

The Italian state railways offer worthwhile discounts for international rail travellers, for example for small groups, senior citizens (carta res) and young people (Eurotrain Twen Tickets: Inter Rail; BIJ). Euro Domino tickets (Euro Domino Junior for young people under 26) allow the holder unlimited travel in Italy on 3, 5 or 10 days of choice, as well as a 25% reduction on the fare from home to the Italian frontier.

Reductions

By air

There are daily scheduled flights from London to Rome and weekly flights from Manchester.

Airports

All scheduled and most charter flights land at the international Leonardo da Vinci Airport, (more usually known by its colloquial name of Fiumicino) situated about 28km/17$^{1}/_{2}$ miles outside Rome, not far from the port of Fiumicino. Trains runs every 20 minutes between the airport and Roma Tiburtina, Tuscolana and Ostiense, and there are half-hourly (or hourly) services to the Stazione Termini. A taxi to the city centre takes about 45 minutes (much longer in the rush-hour). Information: tel. 6 52 94 76.

Aeroporto
Leonardo da
Vinci

Ciampino Airport in south-east Rome is primarily a military airfield but is also used by charter flights (and by the Pope when travelling). COTRAL buses operate a shuttle service every 30 minutes between the airport and Anagnina Metro station (Line A). Information: tel. 79 49 41.

The Urbe city airport is for light aircraft and helicopters only.

See entry

Airlines

Golf

General	The great variety of courses in or near Rome make it an ideal destination for anyone wanting to combine cultural pursuits with golf.
Circolo del Golf di Roma	Acquasanta, Via dell'Acquasanta 3, Via Appia Nuova 716a, 1–00178 Roma tel. 7 80 34 07, fax 78 34 62 19 18-hole course founded in 1903; 5.6km/6000yds, par 71.
Circolo del Golf Fioranello	Viale del Falcognana 61, 100040 Santa Maria delle Mole, Roma tel. 7 13 80 598, fax 7 13 82 12 18-hole course laid out in 1979; 5.4km/5900yds, par 70.
Torvaianica Golf Club	Via Enna 30, 1–00040 Marina di Ardea, Roma tel. 9 13 32 50, fax 9 13 35 92 9-hole course opened in 1989; 4.4km/4800yds, par 62.
L'Eucalyptus Circolo Golf Aprilia	Via Cogna 3/5, 1–04011 Aprilia, Latina tel. 92 62 52, fax 8 44 33 14 18-hole course opened in 1988; 6.4km/7000yds, par 72.
Golf Club Nettuno	Via della Campana 18, 1–00048 Nettuno, Roma tel. 9 81 94 19, fax 98 94 19 18-hole course laid out in 1989; 6.3km/6900yds, par 72.
Sheraton Golf Hotel/Golf Club Parco de'Medici	Viale Parco de'Medici 20/22, 1–00148 Roma Hotel: tel. 65 97 78, fax 65 97 77 42 Golf: tel. 6 55 34 77m fax 6 55 33 44 Close to the banks of the Tiber in the EUR district, just 10km/6 miles from the historic centre of Rome, stands the luxurious Sheraton Golf Hotel, with 179 guest rooms, 14 suites, 56 apartments and a splendid and extensive (70ha/173 acre) park. It was here in the 15th c. that Pope Leo X made sport with his cardinals and noblemen, since 1989 however these acres have been enjoyed by devotees of golf. The Golf Club Parco de'Medici boasts an excellent 18-hole course (6.2km/6800yds, par 72) and a 9-hole course (2.4km/2600yds, par 34) soon to be extended to a full 18 holes.

Help for people with disabilities

Getting to Rome	Information regarding fares and facilities for people with disabilities travelling by rail, coach or air is available from most travel agents.

Hotels

Categories	The official Italian classification divides hotels into five categories ranging from luxury hotels (5 stars) to hotels/pensions with modest facilities (1 star). However in the following list hotels are divided into four categories on the basis of price. Category III represents hotels in the lower price range (double room from 140 lire; ★★), Category II the middle price range (double room from 180,000 lire; ★★★), and Category I the upper price range (double room from 270,000 lire; ★★★★). Luxury hotels (double room from 350,000–400,000 lire; ★★★★ and ★★★★★) make up a fourth category, usually denoted by an L. Accommodation prices vary according to the season, sometimes doubling at peak periods; "r" means room, "SP" swimming pool.

Since accommodation is in heavy demand throughout the year in Rome, but especially so during the peak season, the main religious festivals, and trade fairs, it is essential to book well in advance. Reservations can be made direct or through travel agents and operators such as Airtours, Italiatour, etc.

Reservations

Hotels in Rome

Aldrovandi Palace, Via U. Aldrovandi 15, tel. 3 22 39 93, fax 3 22 14 35, 137 r, SP (turn-of-the-century palazzo with 18th c. furnishings; enchanting garden with swimming pool)

Cavalieri Hilton, Via Cadlolo 101, tel. 34 50 91, fax 3509 2241, 359 r, SP (luxury hotel on the Monte Mario; fine view from the terrace and lovely grounds)

Eden, see Baedeker Special page 218

Excelsior, Via Vittorio Veneto 125, tel. 47081, fax. 4826205, 282 r, 45 apartments. (prestigious, long-established hotel of considerable style)

Le Grand Hotel, Via V. Emanuele Orlando 3, tel. 47091, fax 4 74 73 07, 168 r (visitors of state are often accommodated in this elegant hotel; the Art deco-style entrance hall alone is overwhelming, not to mention the luxurious top-class restaurant)

Hassler, see Baedeker Special page 218

Lord Byron, Via G. de Notaris 5, tel. 3 22 04 04, fax 3 22 04 05, 28 r (extremely stylish hotel with an excellent restaurant)

Parco dei Principi, Via G. Frescobaldi 5, tel. 85 44 21, fax 8 84 51 04, 165 r, SP (enchanting small garden with swimming pool)

Majestic, see Baedeker Special page 218

Minerva, see Baedeker Special page 218

Luxury hotels
★★★★★L

Furnished with expensive antiques and with a sea view,
La Posta Vecchia was the former residence of John Paul Getty

Roman Dreams

Just the location of the luxurious **Hassler**, one of the best hotels in the world, is unique – a few paces from the Spanish Steps and the celebrated Valentino fashion house. The five-star hotel opened by Alberto Hassler in 1885 has become the traditional rendezvous for the rich and famous when in Rome. In the visitors book, alongside names such as Kennedy and Elizabeth Taylor, are those of many of Europe's royalty. In the evening diners in the panoramic restaurant enjoy an unforgettable view of the Eternal City (Piazza Trinità dei Monti 6, 1–00187 Roma, tel. 6 79 26 51 or 699 340, fax 6 78 99 91; 100 rooms; double rooms from 620,000 lire).

The five-star **Eden Hotel**, which reopened in 1994 following extensive restoration, has also been among the foremost addresses in Rome for over 100 years. Its rooms afford splendid views of the Eternal City, the first-class restaurant on the fifth floor providing a panorama which extends from the Villa Borghese over the Old Town and Vatican to the Piazza Venezia (Via Ludovisi 49, 1–00187 Roma, tel. 4 74 35 51, fax 4 82 15 84; 92 rooms;11 apartments; double rooms from 550,000 lire).

Everything about the **Majestic**, a five star hotel in the Via Veneto, is presented to the highest standards. The comfortable rooms are furnished with antiques, and 18th c. frescoes by Domenico Bruschi adorn the Verdi Room. The elegant terrace restaurant serves incomparable fish dishes. (Via Vittorio Veneto 50, tel. 48 68 41; fax. 4 88 09 84; 83 rooms; double rooms from 550,000 lire).

Only a few minutes walk from the Pantheon, the five-star Holiday Inn Crown Plaza **Minerva**, another luxury hotel, occupies a superb 17th c. building. The rich and famous have been staying here since 1889, among the most prominent of present day guests being Luciano Pavarotti and Madonna. The excellent La Cesta restaurant offers a varied cuisine, and the outlook from the panorama terrace leaves a lasting impression (Piazza della Minerva 69, 1–00186 Roma, tel. 6994 1888, fax 6 79 41 65; 118 rooms and 3 apartments; double rooms from 500,000 lire).

In the heart of the Old Town, not far from the Piazza Navona, stands the four-star **Hotel Raphaël**, its façade virtually hidden beneath tendrils of green ivy. The fairy-tale exterior is matched by the care lavished on the interior, tastefully furnished with antiques. The restaurant has few rivals when it comes to creative cooking (Largo Febo 2, 1–00186 Roma, tel. 65 08 81or 682831, fax 6 87 89 93; 90 rooms; double rooms from 300,000 lire).

The newly-opened four-star **Hotel Mecenate** takes its name from Caius Maecenas, great patron of the arts who, in the 1st c. B.C., here on the Esquiline, one of the city's seven hills, gathered about him famous men of the day such as Horace, Virgil and Propertius. The hotel, situated directly opposite Santa Maria Maggiore, makes a fitting tribute to its famous name-sake, a feel for beauty, enchanting rooms and superlative service leaving nothing to be desired (Via Carlo Alberto 3, 1–00185 Roma, tel. 44 70 20 24, fax 4 46 13 54; 62 rooms; double rooms from 400,000 lire).

Only a stone's throw from the Spanish Steps, in the elegant shopping street Bocca di Leone, stands the **D'Inghilterra**. Opened in 1850 this historic hotel is today – appropriately – part of the Charming group. A luxury hotel in the four-star category it has exceptionally stylish rooms. Franz Liszt, Felix Mendelssohn and Ernest

Pure romance: an enchanting bedroom in the four-star Mecenate Hotel

Hemingway are numbered among its distinguished former guests (Via Bocca di Leone 14, 1–00187 Roma, tel. 6 99 81, fax 69 92 22 43; 95 rooms,10 apartments; double rooms from 400,000 lire).

The four-star **Atlante Star** is famous in particular for its magical view from the roof terrace across to the dome of St Peter's. Equally unrivalled is the exquisite cuisine enjoyed in Les Etoiles, the elegant roof garden restaurant (Via Vitellschi 34, 1–00193 Rome, tel. 6 89 34 34 or 687 3233, fax 6 87 23 00; 61 rooms; double rooms from 270,000 lire).

Next to the Porta Pia the **Turner**, a three-star hotel, is named after the wonderfully gifted English painter whose feeling for atmosphere has evidently been an influence through-out. Guest rooms, comfortably furnished with antiques, have moiré-covered walls (Via Nomentana 27–29, 1–00161 Roma, tel. 44 25 00 77, fax 44 25 01 65; 37 rooms; double rooms from 180,000 lire).

Situated right next to the sea barely 40km/25 miles west of Rome Airport is **La Posta Vecchia**, former residence of John Paul Getty. This 17th c. villa, originally the guest-house of the neighbouring castle, is now an oasis of perfect luxury, with a swimming pool and private helicopter pad. All seventeen rooms of the five-star hotel are furnished with expensive antiques including Flemish Gobelin tapestries and furniture once belonging to Maria de'Medici. The hotel's own museum on the lower floor documents the first building to stand on the site, a 1st c. Roman patrician villa which the philanthropic Getty had carefully excavated. An aperitif on the terrace looking out to sea makes a delightful prelude to a meal in the exquisite restaurant (1–00055 Palo Laziale, tel. 9 94 95 01, fax 9 94 95 07; double rooms from 640,000 lire).

Hotels

★★★★L   Sheraton Golf Hotel, see Golf
Imperiale, Via Vittorio Veneto 24, tel. and fax 4 82 63 51, 85 r (tastefully renovated in 1994; excellent restaurant, facilities for underwater massage)
L'Inghilterra, see Baedeker Special page 218
Mecenate, see Baedeker Special page 218
Regina Baglioni, Via Vittorio Veneto 72, tel. 47 68 51, fax 48 54 83, 130 r (renovated 1994; superb suites with dream views on the seventh floor)

Category I
★★★★   Aris Garden, Via Aristofane 101, tel. 6 06 24 43, fax 6 05 29 68, SP (modern, meticulously maintained hotel in a green setting between EUR and the airport; fitness centre, tennis courts and swimming pool)
Eliseo, Via di Porta Pinciana 30, tel. 4 87 04 56, fax 4 81 96 29, 51 r (hotel with an emphasis on comfort; piano bar and restaurant)
Forum, Via Tor dei Conti 25–39, tel 6 79 24 46, fax 6 78 64 79, 81 r (elegant, long-established hotel; specially recommended: brunch on the roof terrace looking out towards the Forum Romanum)
Raphael, see Baedeker Special page 218

Category II
★★★   Atlante Star, see Baedeker Special page 219
Gregoriana, Via Gregoriana 18, tel. 6 79 42 69, fax 6 78 42 58, 19 r (15th c. palazzo in the heart of the city)
Laurentia, Largo degli Osci 63, tel. 4 45 02 18, fax 4 45 38 21, 40 r
Santa Chiara, Via Santa Chiara 21, tel. 687 2979, fax 6 87 31 44, 93 r (centrally situated between the Pantheon and the Piazza della Minerva)
Turner, see Baedeker Special page 219

Panoramic view from the Atlante Star Hotel

A prestigious luxury hotel – the Excelsior

Valle, Via Cavour 134, tel. 4 81 57 36, fax 4 88 58 37, 33 r (lovingly maintained hotel near the Stazione Termini)

Campo dei Fiori, Via del Biscione 6, tel. 68 80 68 65, fax. 687 6003 (small, but prettily furnished rooms)

Category III
★★

Igea, Via Principe Amedeo 97, tel. 4 46 69 13, fax 4 46 69 11, 42 r (well maintained accommodation)

Prati, Via Crescenzio 89, tel. 6 53 11 11, 23 r (attractive, friendly pension close to the Vatican)

Insurance

Although not a legal requirement for citizens of EU countries, it is nevertheless advisable to carry an international certificate of insurance ("green card"). It is also important to have fully comprehensive insurance including cover against legal costs. Be sure to take out additional short-term insurance if not already covered. Italian insurance companies tend to be slow in settling claims.

Car insurance

UK visitors to Italy, like citizens of any EU country, qualify for the same medical care as Italians, conditional upon having obtained a certificate of entitlement (Form E111) prior to departure. Treatment by doctors or hospitals belonging to the state health insurance scheme (Unità Sanitaria Locale, U.S.L.) is provided in accordance with the regulations current in Italy. The address of the appropriate U.S.L. service can be obtained from hotels, the town hall or tourist offices. The U.S.L. will exchange Form E111, if correctly completed and signed, for a book of health insurance certificates. These will be accepted in lieu of payment by doctors on the scheme. Generally speaking you will be required to pay part of the cost of treatment and of any medication prescribed (keep all receipts).

Medical insurance

In view of the risk of theft it is essential to have adequate insurance against loss of, and damage to, baggage.

Baggage insurance

Language

English is spoken in the major hotels in Rome. The municipal police wear a badge on the left arm to indicate which foreign language(s) they speak.

Note

The emphasis is usually placed on the second to last syllable of the word or is indicated by an accent on the last vowel (perchè, città), or on the third to last syllable (chilòmetro, sènepa). Accents: é or ó are closed sounds: è or ò are open sounds. Diphthongs are split, e.g. "causa" becomes "ka-usa"; there are no "silent" e's in Italian, but "h" is silent.

Pronunciation

C or cc in front of e or i	"tsch"	Pronunciation table
G or gg in front of e or i	"dsch"	
C and g/ch and gh in front of other vowels	"k" and "g"	
Gn and gl between vowels	"ny" and "ly"	
Qu	"kw"	
S at the beginnings of a word, in front of a vowel is a soft "ss" sound;		
S in front of consonants and between vowels is a harder sound.		
Sc in front of e and i	"sch"	
Z	"ds"	

Language

<table>
<tr><td>Cardinal
numbers</td><td>

0 zero
1 uno, una, un, un'
2 due
3 tre
4 quattro
5 chinque
6 sei
7 sette
8 otto
9 nove
10 dieci
11 undici
12 dodici
13 tredici
14 quattordici
15 quindici
16 sedici
17 diciasette
18 diciotto

</td><td>

19 diciannove
20 venti
21 ventuno
22 ventidue
30 trenta
31 trentuna
40 quaranto
50 cinquanta
60 sessanto
70 settanta
80 ottanta
90 novanta
100 cento
101 cento uno
153 centociquantatre
200 duecento
1000 mile
5000 cinque mila
1 mil un milione

</td></tr>
</table>

<table>
<tr><td>Ordinal numbers</td><td>

1 primo (prima)
2 secondo
3 terzo
4 quarto
5 quinto
6 sesto
$^1/_2$ un mezzo (mezza)
$^1/_4$ un quarto
$^1/_{10}$ un decimo

</td><td>

7 settimo
8 ottavo
9 nono
10 decimo
20 ventesimo/vigesimo
100 centesimo

</td></tr>
</table>

Useful phrases		
	Good morning, good day	Buon giorno!
	Good evening	Buona sera!
	Goodbye	Arrivederci!
	Yes, no	Si, no!
	Excuse me	Scusi!
	Please	Per favore!
	Don't mention it/you are welcome	Prego!
	Thank you (very much)	(Molte) grazie!
	If you will allow me	Con permesso!
	Do you speak English?	Parla inglese?
	A little, not much	Un poco, non molto
	I don't understand	Non capisco
	What is that in Italian?	Come si dice in italiano?
	What is the name of this church?	Come si chiama questa chiesa?
	The cathedral	Il duomo
	The square	La piazza
	The palace	Il palazzo
	The theatre	Il teatro
	Where is street X?	Dov'è la via X?
	Where is the road (motorway)?	Dov'è la strada (l'autostrada)?
	Where to ...?	Dov'è per ...?
	Left, right	A sinistra, a destra
	Straight on	Sempre diritto
	Above, below	Sopra, sotto
	When is it open?	Quando è aperto?
	How far?	Quando è distance?
	Today	Oggi
	Yesterday	Ieri
	The day before yesterday	L'altro ieri
	Tomorrow	Domani
	Is there a vacant room?	Ci sono camere libere?

I would like ... — Vorrei avere ...
A room with bath — Una camera con bagno
A room with shower — Una camera con doccia
Full board — Con pensione completa
How much does it cost? — Qual'è il prezzo
— Quanto costa?

Inclusive? — Tutto compreso?
That is too dear! — E troppo caro!
Waiter the bill! — Cameriere, il conto!
Where is the ... — Dove si trovono i ...
  toilet? — gabinetti?
— (il servizi, la ritirata)
Wake me up — Può svegliarmi
  at six — alle sei!
Where is there a ... — Dove sta ...
  doctor? — un médico?
  dentist? — un dentista?

Address	Indirizzo	At the post office
Letter	Lettera	
Post Box	Buca delle lettere	
Stamps	Francobolli	
Postman	Postino	
Express post	Espresso	
Registered post	Raccomandata	
Air mail	Posta aerea	
Postcard	Cartolina	
Poste restane	Fermo posta	
Telephone	Telefono	
Telegram	Telegramma	

Departure	Partenza	Travelling
Departure (at airport)	Partenza, Decollo	
Arrival	Arrivo	
Stop-over	Sosta	
Station	Stazione	
Platform	Marciapiede	
Ticket	Biglietto	
Timetable	Orario	
Fare	Brezzo del biglietto, Tariffa	
Flight	Volo	
Airport	Aeroporto	
Aeroplane	Aeroplano	
Luggage	Bagagli	
Porter	Portabagagli, facchino	
Track	Binario	
Stop, station	Fermata	
Non-smoking	Vietato fumare	
Smoking	Fumatori	
Conductor	Conduttore	
Ticket office	Sportello	
To change (trains, etc.)	Cambiare treno	
Waiting room	Salla d'aspetto	
Train driver	Capotreno	

Monday	Lunedi	Days of the week
Tuesday	Martedi	
Wednesday	Mercoledi	
Thursday	Giovedi	
Friday	Venerdi	
Saturday	Sabato	
Sunday	Domenica	

	Day	Giorno
	Weekday	Giorno feriale
	Public holiday	Giorno festivo
	Week	Settimana
Holidays	New Year	Capo d'anno
	Easter	Pasqua
	Whitsuntide	Pentecoste
	Christmas	Natale
Months of the Year	January	Gennaio
	February	Febbraio
	March	Marzo
	April	Aprile
	May	Maggio
	June	Guigno
	July	Luglio
	August	Agosto
	September	Settembre
	October	Ottobre
	November	Novembre
	December	Dicembre
	Month	Mese
Road Signs	Road works, resurfacing	Lavori stradali, Acciottolato
	Stop!	Alt!
	Caution!	Attenzione (attenti)
	Beware of trains	al treno
	mine works/blasting	alle mine
	falling rocks	Caduta sassi (c. massi)
	Diversion	Deviazione
	No stopping	Divieto di sosta
	Crossroad	Incrocio
	Road works	Lavori in corso
	Level crossing	Passaggio a livello
	Reduce Speed!	Rallentare
	Closed	Sbarrato
	No-entry	Senso Proibito
	One-way street	Senso unico
	Dangerous bend	Svolta pericolosa
	Keep to the right!	Tenere la destra
	No through road	Transito interrotto
	Drove slowly!	Veicolo al passo
	Maximum speed 15km p.h.!	Velocità non superiore ¡15km/h!
	No access for heavy vehicles	Vietato (proibito) il transito per tutti i veicoli pesanti

Libraries

Rome has a large number of libraries, including many foreign ones, housing valuable collections of old manuscripts and rare books as well as modern books and periodicals. The few listed below are among the most important:

Alessandra Universitaria, Città Universitaria, tel. 4 95 68 20
Open: Mon.–Fri. 8.30am–10pm, Sat. 8.30am–7.30pm

Archivo di Stato di Roma, Corso Rinascimento 40, tel. 6 54 38 23
Open: Mon.–Sat. 8.30am–1.30pm

Archivo Storico Capitolino, Piazza della Chiesa Nuova 18, tel. 6 54 26 62
Open: Mon.–Sat. 9am–1pm

Biblioteca Angelica, Piazza Sant' Agostino 8, tel. 65 58 74
Open: Tue., Thur., Sat. 8.30am–1.30pm; Mon., Wed., Fri. 8.30am–7.30pm (in the summer months until 1.30pm)

Biblioteca dell'Istituto Nazionale d'Archeologia e Storia dell'Arte
Piazza Venezia 8, tel. 6 78 11 67
Open: Mon.–Fri. 9am–8pm; Sat. 9am–1pm

Biblioteca Hertziana, Via Gregoriana 28, tel. 6 79 73 52
Open: Mon.–Fri. 9am–1pm, 4–7pm (special permission required)

Lost property offices (Servizi oggetti rinvenuti)

Municipal transport ATAC
Via Volturno 65; open: Mon.–Sat. 10am–noon

Municipal lost property office
Via Nicola Bettoni 1; open: Mon.–Sat. 9am–noon. tel. 5816040

Medical help

Ambulance and emergency no. (throughout Italy): 1 13.

Emergency

The Guardia Medica notturna e festiva provides on-call medical services throughout the night (8pm–8am) and on public holidays. In addition to hospitals

Medical services

(ospedali), the White Cross (Croce Bianca), Green Cross (Croce Verde) and Red Cross Italiana (Croce Rosso Italiana) render first aid (pronto soccorso). Addresses will be found on the first page of the telephone book ("Aventielenco"). Dentists are listed in the telephone book under "Medici dentisti".

First aid

Red Cross (Croce Rossa): tel. 51 00
Medical emergency service (home visits): Pronto Soccorso a domicilio, tel. 4 75 67 41–4

San Camillo, Circonvalazione Gianicolense 87, tel. 5 87 01
San Giovanni, Via Amba Aradam, tel. 7 70 51
Santo Spirito, Lungotevere in Sassia (near the Vatican), tel. 65 09 01
San Giacomo, Via Canova 29 (corner of Via del Corso), tel. 67 26 or 36261
San Filippo, Via Martinotti 20, tel. 3 30 61
San Eugenio, Viale Umanesimo (EUR), tel. 59 04 (day), 5 01 75 71 (night)
Sant'Agostino, Lido di Ostia, tel. 5 69 22 10, 5 61 55 41
Policlinico Umberto 1., Viale del Policlinico 1, (Città Universitaria), tel. 4 99 71, 49 23 41
Policlinico A. Gemelli, Largo Gemelli 8, tel. 3 30 51

Hospitals with emergency facilities

Motoring

Detoxification centres (Centri antiveleni)	Policlinico Umberto 1., tel. 49 06 63 Policlinico A. Gemelli, tel. 33 56 56
Children's clinic	Ospedale del Bambin Gesù, Piazza Sant'Onofrio 4, tel. 6 51 91
Medical insurance	See Insurance

Motoring

A car would not be everyone's choice as a means of getting about in Rome. Local practice is to drive fast and with what might seem a certain degree of recklessness. In fact this is more a matter of flexibility in response to the city's traffic. Drivers – at least those who know where they're going – willingly give way, and skilful manoeuvring and an alertness to others are often more important than any traffic signs. The general traffic regulations applying in Rome are the internationally agreed ones. The following are some of the more important road signs:

Deviazione	Diversion
Senso unico	One-way street
Sbarrato	Closed
Rallentare	Drive slowly
Tenere la destra	Keep to the right
Tutti direzioni	All directions
Zona di silenzio	No hooting
Zona tutelata INIZIO	Start of no parking zone

Parking

Parts of central Rome are out of bounds to private cars or anyone without a special permit – apart, that is, for hotel access. Parking places are in short supply everywhere. For security reasons cars should only be left in manned car parks or underground car parks with surveillance. Though street parking is haphazard, no-parking signs should be strictly observed; offending cars are liable to be towed away. Avoid parking on spaces reserved for buses or taxis (look out for the yellow sign) or where the kerb has black and yellow markings.

Speed limits

Within built-up areas the speed limit is 50 km.p.h./30 m.p.h.; outside built-up areas the limit on ordinary roads is 90 km.p.h./56 m.p.h.

On motorways the speed limit for cars under 1100 cc and motorcycles up to 349 cc is 110 km.p.h./68 m.p.h.; for cars of 1100 cc or over and motorcycles of 350 cc or over it is 130 km.p.h./81 m.p.h.

Motor cars with trailers may not exceed 100 km.p.h./62 m.p.h. on motorways and 80 km.p.h./50 m.p.h. on ordinary roads.

Priority

Traffic on main roads has priority where signposted, the priority sign being a square with a corner pointing downwards, either white with a red border or yellow with a black and white border. Elsewhere, including on roundabouts, traffic coming from the right has priority. On narrow roads ascending traffic has priority. Vehicles on rails (trams, etc.) always have priority.

Motorways

Tolls are payable on Italian motorways (*autostrade*). The tickets/receipts for each section should be retained for surrender when leaving the motorway. Payment can be made either in cash or with a Viacard obtainable from automobile clubs (see below), at frontier crossing-points, major motorway approach roads, tobacco shops and filling stations.

On motorways tows may be undertaken only by authorised Italian recovery vehicles.

Motorcyclists must be 21 or over if riding machines of 350 cc or more. Motorcycles of less than 150 cc are not allowed on motorways, nor are motorcycles with sidecars, irrespective of cubic capacity.

Motorcycles

On well-lit roads sidelights only may be used; dipped headlights are compulsory in tunnels.

Lighting

The wearing of seat belts is compulsory for anyone over fourteen years. Children up to four years old must by law travel in a child seat.

Seat belts
Child seats

Petrol coupons have been discontinued for the time being. Carrying reserve fuel in cans is prohibited, as is filling cans at petrol stations. Unleaded petrol (benzina senza piombo or benzina verde; 95 octane), Super (97 octane) and diesel (gasolino) are all widely available. Currently the price of petrol in Italy is above the European average.

Fuel

While motorway filling stations remain open 24 hours a day, those on other roads and in towns are generally closed between noon and 1.30pm and from 10pm to 7am. Drivers, beware! Even in Rome many filling stations close at weekends. Automatic petrol pumps accept notes of 10,000 lire upwards.

Credit cards are rarely accepted, except at motorway filling stations.

Automobile Club d'Italia (ACI), Via Marsala 8, tel. 4 99 81
Automobile Club di Roma (ACR), Via Cristoforo Colombo 261, tel. 51 06
Touring Club Italiano (TCI), Via Ovidio 7/A, tel. 38 86 02, 38 86 58

Automobile Clubs

AIC (Automobile Club d'Italia): tel. 1 16

Breakdown assistance

AIC (Automobile Club d'Italia): tel. 42 12

Traffic reports

See entry

Emergency services

If your car is a write-off you should inform Italian customs immediately; otherwise you may be required to pay full import duty on the vehicle.

Total write-offs

Museums

Since museum opening times tend to change frequently, those given here cannot be guaranteed correct. To avoid disappointment visitors are advised to check before setting out for a particular museum.

Note

Antiquarium Romano
Viale del Parco del Celio 22
Open: Tue.–Sat. 10am–4pm, Sun. 10am–1pm
Closed since 1939, a small section of the Antiquarium reopened in 1994; it houses ancient sculptures and grave artifacts.

Museums

Cineteca Nazionale
Via Tuscolana 1524
Open: Mon.–Fri. 9am–4pm
Cinecittà (Cinema City) film museum

Galleries: See entry

Musei e Gallerie del Vaticano
See A to Z, Vatican – Musei Vaticani

Museums

Museo Archeologico Ostiense
See A to Z, Ostia Antica

Museo Astronomico e Copernicano
Viale del Parco Mellini 84
Open: Wed., Sat. 9.30am–noon (closed all of August)
Museum of Astronomy

Museo Barracco: see A to Z, Museo Barracco

Museo Borghese: see A to Z, Villa Borghese

Museo Capitolino: see A to Z, Campidoglio

Museo Centrale del Risorgimento: see A to Z, Monumento Nazionale
a Vittorio Emanuele II.

Museo delle Cere
Piazza SS Apostoli 67
Open: daily 9am–8pm
Waxworks

Museo Civico di Zoologia
Viale Giardino Zoologico 22
Open: daily 9am–1pm, 2.30–6pm
Zoological museum

Museo della Civiltà Romana: see A to Z, EUR.

Museo Criminologico
Via del Gonfalone 29
Open: Tue., Wed., Fri., Sat. 9am–1pm, Tue., Thur. 2.30–6.30pm

Museo Ebraico: see A to Z, Sinagoga

Museo dell'Energia Elettrica
Piazza Elio Rufino 287
Open: daily 9am–1pm, 4–8pm
Electricity museum

Museo del Folclore e dei Poeti Romaneschi
in the former monastery of Sant'Egidio, Piazza Sant'Egidio 1/b
(Trastevere)
Open: Tue.–Sat. 9am–1.30pm, Tue., Thur. also 5–7.30pm, Sun. daily
9am–12.30pm
Museum of Roman folklore and poetry; sculptures, sketches of
Roman life and memorabilia of the Roman poets

Museo di Goethe
Via del Corso
Re-opened in 1997 the museum recreates Goethe's Roman home
(1786) in the residence of his friend Tischbein

Museo di Keats e Shelley
Piazza di Spagna 26
Open: Mon.–Fri. 9am–1pm, 3–6pm
Situated at the foot of the Spanish Steps where Keats died in 1821;
dedicated to the English poets Keats, Shelley and Lord Byron.

Museo dell'Alto Medioevo
Viale Lincoln 3 (EUR)
(in the Palazzo delle Scienze)
Open: Mon.–Sat. 9am–2pm, Sun. 9am–1pm
Art and culture of late antiquity and the high Middle Ages.

Museo delle Mura: see A to Z, Mura Aureliane

Museo Napoleonico
Piazza di Ponte Umberto 1
Open: Mon.–Sat. 9am–7pm, Sun. 9am–1.30pm.
Memorabilia of Napoleon (who was never in Rome!) and his sisters
Caroline and Paolina.

Museo delle Navi
Via Alessandro Guidoni 37, Fiumicino
Open: daily 9am–1pm, Wed., Thur. also 2–6pm
Maritime museum

Museo Nazionale d'Arte Orientale
Palazzo Brancaccio, Via Merulana 248
By guided tour only: Mon., Wed.–Fri. 9am–2pm, Tues., Thurs. 9am–
7pm, Sun. 9am–1pm.
Italy's national museum of oriental art is housed in the Palazzo
Brancaccio, designed in the second half of the 19th c. by Luca
Carimini. Fourteen rooms are devoted to the cultures of the Near and
Far East from prehistoric times to the present day. Among the most
interesting of the many exhibits are objets d'art from various parts of
Asia, in particular the finds from Italian excavations in Iran and Pales-
tine. There are valuable porcelains and superb silks from Japan,
China and Korea and gold jewellery, bronzes, vases, costumes and
paintings from Afganistan, Pakistan, Iraq, India, Nepal and Tibet.

Museo Nazionale delle Arti e Tradizioni Popolari
Piazza Marconi 10 (EUR)
Open: Mon.–Sat. 9am–2pm, Sun. 9am–1pm
The museum has ten sections on Italian folk art, illustrating through
flags, costumes, musical instruments and models, the customs in the
different regions of Italy.

Museo Nazionale di Castel Sant'Angelo
See A to Z, Castel Sant'Angelo

Museo Nazionale Etrusco di Villa Giulia
See A to Z, Museo Nazionale di Villa Giulia

Museo Nazionale delle Paste Alimentari
See A to Z, Museo Nazionale delle Paste Alimentari

Museo Nazionale Preistorico Etnografico Luigi Pigorini
Piazza Guglielmo Marconi 14 (EUR)
Open: Mon.–Sat. 9am–1.30pm, Sun. 9am–1pm (closed the 1st and 3rd
Monday of each month)
Museum of prehistory and ethnography

Museo Nazionale Romano o delle Terme
See A to Z, Museo Nazionale Romano

Museo Nazionale degli Strumenti Musicali
Piazza Santa Croce in Gerusalemme 9/a
Open: Mon.–Sat. 9am–2pm
Some 3000 exhibits from all over the world illustrating the history of music from antiquity to the end of the 18th c.; they include the celebrated Barberini harp (17th c.).

Museo Numismatico della Zecca Italiana
Istituto Poligrafico, Via XX Settembre 94
Open: Mon.–Fri. 9am–1pm (closed Sat., Sun.)
Museum of the Italian state mint, with a comprehensive collection of coins dating from the 15th c. onward and an impressive treasury.

Museo Palatino and Loggia Mattei
Piazza Santa Maria Nova 53
Open: Mon.–Fri. 9am–5pm
Re-opened in 1998 in the former aquarium
Finds from the Palatine from the founding of Rome to the 3rd c. A.D.

Museo di Palazzo Venezia
See A to Z, Piazza Venezia

Museo delle Poste e Telecommunicazioni
Viale Europa 190 (EUR)
Open: Mon.–Sat. 9am–1pm
Post and telecommunications museum

Museo del Presepio
Via Tor de'Conti 31/a, Chiesa dei SS Quirico e Guidetta
Open: Wed., Sat. 6–8pm
Crib museum

Museo di Roma
See A to Z, Museo di Roma

Museo Storico dei Bersaglieri
Piazzale di Porta Pia
Open: Tues. and Thurs. 9am–1pm
Historical museum of the Bersaglieri; military history including documents from the War of Liberation, from the African campaign and from the First World War.

Museo Storico dei Carabinieri
Via Crescenzio 92
Open: Tue.–Sun. 9am–12.30pm
Documents and memorabilia illustrating the history of the Carabinieri

Museo Torlonia
See A to Z, Museo Torlonia

Palazzo Altemps
Piazza Sant'Apollinare 44
Open: Tue.–Sun. 10am–6pm
Since the end of 1997 ancient marble treasures from the Ludovisi, Mattei and Altemps collection have been displayed in 33 rooms

Palazzo delle Esposizioni
Via Nazionale 194
Open: Mon., Wed.–Sun. 10am–9pm
The architect Pio Piacentini produced the design for the building in 1882. Today excellent temporary exhibitions, films, theatrical performances and concerts are put on here.

Music

In Rome, as elsewhere in Italy, the opera has no fixed repertoire. As many as a dozen different productions are put on one after the other in the course of the season (November to May), each being given six to eight performances. In addition to those in the opera house, in summer there are also open-air performances in the Piazza di Siena in the spacious grounds of the Villa Borghese (which replaced the Terme di Caracalla as the venue in 1994). The opera's second home, the Brancaccio Theatre, has its own ballet ensemble, which mainly stages modern works. Dance shows and musicals can be seen at the Teatro Olimpico.

Opera/Ballet

Teatro dell'Opera, Piazza Beniamino Gigli 8
Tickets: Piazza Beniamino Giglo 8 and Via Firenze 72
Tel. 48 16 01, 4 88 17 55

Teatro Brancaccio, Via Merulana 224
Tickets: as Teatro dell'Opera

Teatro Olimpico, Piazza Gentile da Fabriano 17
Tickets: tel. 3 23 48 90

Concerts are given throughout the year in Rome's concert halls and churches. Details are published in the daily papers, in the weekly magazines "Romac'è" and "Roma – Giorno & Notte", and in the English-language brochure "Where • Rome" which appears monthly.

Concerts

Accademia Filarmonica Romana
in the Teatro Olimpico, Piazza Gentile da Fabriano 17
Tel. 3 23 48 90
Rome's oldest music academy, established in 1821; among illustrious former members were Rossini, Donizetti, Paganini and Verdi.

Concert halls

Accademia Nazionale di Santa Cecilia
in the 'Auditorio Pio' auditorium of the same name at Via della Conciliazione 4, tel. 68 80 10 44
N.B. This academy frequently changes its 'home'

Instituzione Universitaria dei Concerti
Auditorio di San Leone Magno, Via Bolzano 38
Aula Magna, Piazzale Aldo Moro 5
Tickets: Lungotevere Flaminio 50, tel. 3 61 00 51 or 361 0052

Auditorio del Foro Italico
Piazza Lauro di Bosis 28, tel. 36 87 81

Oratorio del Gonfalone
Via del Gonfalone 32/a, tel./fax 6 87 59 52
Mainly chamber music.

Palasport
Piazzale dello Sport, tel. 59 24 04 or 59 25 205
Venue for major rock and pop concerts as well as sports events.

Concerts are also often held in Rome's theatres (see Theatres).

Nightlife

As elsewhere in Europe it is late-ish in the evening before Rome's nightlife really gets going and it is hardly worth heading for a discothèque before midnight. In summer people meet together out of doors in one of the numerous cafés and bistros in Rome's delightful, lively squares. Here they while away the hours in idle enjoyment until late into the night.

Bars, night clubs and discothèques
(just a few of the many)

Alibi, Via Monte Testaccio 39 (strident discothèque)
Alien, Via Velletri 13/19 (superior disco with doorman)
Alpheus, Via del Commercio 36 (jazz, blues, rock and cabaret)
Bar della Pace, Via della Pace 4–7 (popular with artists)
Big Mama, Vicolo di San Francesco a Ripa 18 (best live blues and rock)
Black Out, Via Saturnia 18 (hip hop)
Café de Paris, Via Vittorio Veneto 90 (the stars of the film "La dolce vita" used to meet here)
Caffè Caruso, Via di Monte Testaccio 36 (bar with Latin-American music)
Gilda, Via Mario dei Fiori 97 (disco favoured by theatre and TV celebrities)
Harry's Bar, Via Vittorio Veneto 150 (unrivalled for cocktails)
Horus Club, Corso Sempione 21 (night club on two floors; jazz, acid and techno-pop)
La Cabala, Via dei Soldati 25 (exclusive piano bar)
Paladium, Piazza B. Romano 8 (the biggest venue for rock, soul, hip hop and acid-jazz; features international artists)
Saint Louis Music City, Via del Cardello 13 (the finest jazz)
Yes Brasil, Via San Francesco a Ripa 103 (long established night club; live Brazilian music and shows)

Opening times

Shops

With no official opening times, shops are free to keep their own hours. Generally speaking, Sundays and public holidays excepted, you can expect to find them open 9am–1pm and 4–8pm.

Chemists

See entry

Banks

See Currency

Museums

See entry

Post offices

See Postal services

Parks and open spaces

Gianicolo: see A to Z, Gianicolo
Villa Ada: extensive park on the Via Salaria north of the city centre
Villa Borghese and Giardino Zoologico: see A to Z, Villa Borghese
Villa Celimontana: between the Colosseum and the Terme di Caracalla
Villa Corsini (botanical garden), Largo Cristina di Svezia 24
(open: Mon.–Fri. 9am–3pm, Sat. 9am–1pm)
Villa Doria Pamphili: see A to Z, Villa Doria Pamphili
Villa Glori: small park in the bend of the Tiber north of the city centre

Villa Sciarra: picturesque park in Trastevere with the 18th c. "Teatro delle Stagioni"
Villa Torlonia: see A to Z, Villa Torlonia

Police (Polizia)

Questura, Office for foreign tourists, Via San Vitale 15, tel. 46 861	Police HQ
Polizia Stradale, Via Portuense 185; tel. 5 57 79 05. (Accidents)	Traffic police
Vigili Urbani, Via della Consolazione 4; tel. 6 76 91.	Municipal police
Viale Romana 45; tel. 8 09 81 (H.Q.); tel. 1 12 (emergency)	Carabinieri
Tel. 1 13	Accident

Postal services

Post offices provide postal and post office banking services only; they have no facilities for making telephone calls (see Telephone). Main post offices are generally open Mon.–Fri. 8.25am–6pm, Sat. 8.25am–1.30pm, (Aug. Mon.–Fri. 8.25am–2pm, Sat. 8.25am–1.30pm), branch offices from 8.10am to 1.25pm. All PO's close two hours earlier on the last day of the month.

Post offices

Letter boxes in Italy are red, those in Vatican City blue.

Letter boxes

Postage stamps (francobolli) can be bought at tobacconists displaying a "T" sign over the entrance as well as from post offices.

Stamps

By phone: tel. 1 86

Telegrams

Public holidays

1 January	New Year (Capo d'anno)
6 January	Epiphany
	Easter Monday
25 April	Liberation Day
1 May	Labour Day
2 June	Proclamation of the Republic
29June	Patron Saint's day, Rome only, (St. Peter & St. Paul)
15 August	Ferragosta; Assumption
1 November	All Saints (Ognissanti)
8 December	Immaculate Conception
25 and 26 December	Christmas

Radio

Information on overseas broadcasts can be obtained from BBC External Services, P.O. Box 76, Bush House, London WC2B 4PH.

Programmes in English

Rail services

Ferrovie dello Stato (FS)	The Italian railway system has a total length of 16,000km/10,000 miles. Most of it is run by the Italian State Railways (Ferrovie dello Stato, FS), Central Office, Via Marsala 53, tel. 47 03 01.

Information about rail services can be obtained from the Italian State Tourist Office (see Tourist Information) or from the Italian State Railways offices abroad: |
| United Kingdom | 50 Conduit Street, London W1; tel. (0171) 434 3844 |
| United States of America | 765 Route 83, Suite 105, Chicago, Ill.
5670 Wilshire Boulevard, Los Angeles, Cal.
668 Fifth Avenue, New York, NY. |
| Canada | 2055 Peel Street, Suite 102, Montreal
111 Richmond Street West, Suite 419, Toronto |
| In Italy | Stazione Termini, Rome, tel. 47 75; and in towns throughout the country. |
| Tickets | Various special tickets are available, e.g. the Italy Railcard which allows the holder unlimited travel over the whole network within a specified period of availability.
A network booklet carries a reduction of 10% and allows up to 3000km travel on all ordinary FS trains; surcharges are payable on special trains. Accompanied children up to five years of age not occupying a seat may travel free of charge; children up to the age of thirteen pay half fare. The Inter-Rail tickets (for young people up to the age of 26), the Rail-Europe-Family tickets (for families of at least three), and the Rail-Europe-Senior tickets (with a Senior Citizen card) entitle the holders to fare reductions. |

Railway stations

Stazione Termini	Rome's main station: international services and services to all parts of Italy. Information: tel. 47 75 or 1478 88 088 in Italy
Lost property: tel. 4730 6682
Stazione Tiburtina	Trains to north and south Italy, motorail
Tel. 4 95 66 26 or 1478 88 088 in Italy.
Stazione Trastevere	Trains to Genoa and Pisa
Stazione Roma-Nord	Trains to Viterbo
Stazione Prenestina	Trains to Pescara
Stazione Tuscolana	Trains to Grosseto and Viterbo
Stazione San Pietro	Local services
Stazione Porta San Paolo	Trains to Viterbo and Ostia Lido

Restaurants

In Rome, as everywhere in Italy, people enjoy eating and as a consequence eat very well. There is everything you could want, from gourmet temples accorded the highest accolades, to simple osterias serving good, wholesome Roman food, or friendly bistros offering just a light morsel, to legendary fish restaurants serving superbly prepared seafood. Since Rome's restaurants are nearly always busy, it is advisable to book early.

For hungry customers who have to watch their purses, there is nothing better than a visit to a pizzeria. Here the waiter does not look askance at customers who have a pizza and a beer and then ask for the bill. The comfortable, modestly-priced osteria where three or four wholesome dishes are prepared by grandma in the kitchen, and a jug of honest, full-bodied wine stands on the table, is sadly disappearing. Too often nowadays visitors find themselves in some prettified restaurant masquerading as an osteria. But a couple of hours spent in a genuine osteria yields a far more vivid impression of Roman life than any number of visits to expensive ristoranti. Trattorias offer fast and good service too – a primo, a secondo, a bottle of wine, a caffè and "il conto per favore" (the bill, please).

Pizzeria, Osteria, Trattoria

The food in a ristorante is usually more lavish and ambitious. White tablecloths, sophisticated atmosphere, excellent selection of wines and carefully prepared dishes. Here customers can and should be more demanding, since they should expect good value for their money. Sometimes diners will be offered a combination of different primi (misto di primi). Since now nearly all restaurants call themselves a ristorante, it is virtually impossible to differentiate between them in the traditional way.

Ristoranti

Enoteche offer a good choice of well-known wines, which can be tasted as well as purchased (see Shopping and Souvenirs). They also serve a bite to eat. Sometimes a restaurant which prides itself on its wines will also refer to itself as an enoteca.

Enoteche

Restaurants in Rome

Category I: over 50,000 lire
Category II: around 40,000 lire
Category III: around 30,000 lire

Categories

These price categories are for à la carte meals and are intended as no more than rough guides. If fine wines or expensive specialities are ordered the bill can of course be higher.

★Agate e Romeo, Via Carlo Alberto 45, tel. 446615; I; closed Sun and August (very tastefully furnished; try the fish menu; a different Italian wine is served with every course; simply fabulous)

★Da Agustarello a Testaccio, Via G. Branca 98–100, tel. 5 74 65 85; II; closed Sun. (typical Roman cuisine, substantial, good and good value)

Al 34, Via Mario de'Fiori 34, tel. 6 79 50 91; I; closed Mon and August. (rustic elegance; first class Latium cooking at reasonable prices)

★Alberto Ciarla, Piazza San Cosimato, tel. 5 81 86 68: I; Open for dinner only, closed every lunch (Rome's best known fish restaurant; extremely well run, with first class service; try the mixed starters "del pescatore", perch fillets cooked with herbs; excellent wine list)

An evening at the Alberto Ciarla Restaurant is a delight for lovers of fish dishes

Alfredo a Via Gabi, Via Gabi 36, tel. 77 2067 92; II; closed Tue. (informal atmosphere; Roman dishes ranging from classic minestrone to tripe with mint and sheep's cheese)

Antico Falcone, Via Trionfale 60, tel. 39743385 or 39736404; II; closed Tue. (long-established trattoria; try the braised air-dried fish with onions)

★L'Antiquario, Piazzetta San Simone 26/27, tel. 6 87 96 94; I; closed Sun. (smart restaurant with the finest haute cuisine)

Il Bacaro, Via degli Spagnoli 27, tel. 6 86 41 10; II; closed Sun. (tiny cellar restaurant with a pleasant atmosphere; perfect risotto and irresistible amaretto ice-cream)

★Le Bistroquet, Via B. Sacconi 55, tel. 3 22 02 18; I; closed Sun and lunch all week, open evenings only. (without doubt the best Roman oyster bar; in the style of a Paris bistro)

★Camponeschi, Piazza Farnese 50, tel. 6 87 49 27; I; closed Sun. (stylish ambience with Louis XV chairs and Venetian stucco)

★Il Convivio, Via dell'Orso 44, tel. 6 86 94 32; I; closed Sun. (very imaginative cooking; not far from the Piazza Navona)

★Cul de Sac 2, Vicolo dell'Atleta 21, tel. 5 81 33 24; I; closed Mon. (enchanting restaurant in Trastevere; traditional dishes in an original setting)

★Eden: panorama restaurant in the Hotel Eden, see Baedeker Special page 218

★Les Etoiles: roof-garden restaurant in the Atlante Star Hotel, see Baedeker Special page 219

Da Felice, Via Mastro Giorgio 29, tel. 5 74 68 00; III; closed Sun. (simple trattoria serving helpings as tasty as they are substantial)

★Galeassi, Piazza Santa Maria in Trastevere 3, tel. 5 80 37 75; II; closed Mon. (immensely comfortable and with perfect service; excellent fish dishes)

La Gensola, Piazza della Gensola 15, tel. 5 81 63 12; I; closed Sun. and lunchtime Sat. (delicious Sicilian specialities)

★George's, Via Marche 7, tel. 4208 4575; I; closed Sun and August. (elegant, with a delightful garden; haute cuisine and fantastic wine list)

Da Gino, Vicolo Rosini 4, tel. 687 34 34; III; closed Sun. (plain cooking, like Mama's, at reasonable prices)

★Gudi, Vicolo dell'Atleta 21, tel. 5 81 33 24; I; closed Mon. (charming restaurant in Trastevere with reliable food creatively produced.

Lilli, Via Tor di Nona 26, tel. 6 86 19 16; III; closed Sun. (cosy trattoria; creative Roman cuisine)

Da Marcello, Via dei Campani 12, tel. 4 46 33 11; III; closed Sat. evenings and Sun. (favourite of students and regulars from the colourful San Lorenzo quarter; good, reasonably priced dishes from Roman recipes; small but distinguished wine list)

Da Moschino, Piazza Benedetto Brin 5, tel. 5 13 94 73; II; closed Sun. (friendly osteria in the Roman style serving excellent food)

★Relais La Piscine, Via Mangili 6,(part of Aldrovandi Palace Hotel) tel. 3 21 61 26; I; closed Sun. evenings (extremely elegant and with first-class cuisine)

Mekong, Corso V. Emanuele 333, tel. 6 86 16 84; II; closed Tue. (friendly Chinese restaurant serving light food) — Foreign cuisine

Mitsukoshi, Via Torino 34, tel. 4 81 78 51; I; closed Sun. (delectable dishes from the Land of the Rising Sun; perfect Japanese sushi)

★Suria Mahal, Piazza Trilussa 50, tel. 5 89 45 54; II; closed Sun. (traditional Indian dishes; small but good wine list; enchanting garden)

Thien Kim, Via Giulia 201, tel. 68 30 78 32; II; closed Sun. (delightful Chinese restaurant, refined cooking)

★Antico Caffè Greco, Via Condotti 86 (former 18th c. literary café, haunt of Casanova, Baudelaire, Goethe, Franz Liszt, Mendelssohn, Wagner and Nietzsche, to name but a few) — Cafés

Babington, Piazza di Spagna 23 (elegant British tearoom)

★Canova, Piazza del Popolo 16 (meeting place of artists; seemingly inexhaustible selection of tramezzini and dolce)

Casino Valadier, Pincio (the splendid view over Rome has a price)

Dagnino, Galleria Esedra, Via V E Orlando 75, tel. 481 8660. An authentic 1950s *pasticceria,* famous for Sicilian specialities and fine ice cream

Doney Gran Caffè, Via Veneto 145 (recently reopened, it was once *the* place for the dolce vita generation of the 60s)

★Giolitti, Via Uffici del Vicario 40 (fantastic ices served in a turn-of-the-century setting)

Gran Caffè Pasticceria Berardo, Piazza Colonna 200 (19th c.-style coffee house)

Grand Cafè Aragno, corner of Via delle Convertile/Via del Corso (cafè and pasticceria; huge variety of sweet and exceptionally tasty delicacies)

Pepy's Bar, Piazza Barberini (American bar; unrivalled selection of mouth-watering tramezzini)

★Rosati, Piazza del Popolo 5 (old established artists' café)

Sant'Eustachio, Piazza Sant'Eustachio 82, tel. 686 1309. A claimant to the finest coffee in the city, with tables outside

★Tazza d'Oro, Via degli Orfani 84–86, by the Pantheon (its famous coffee can be purchased as well as drunk)

Tre Scalini, Piazza Navona 28–32 (the tartufo is a must – sheer temptation in chocolate)

The Antico Caffè Greco in the elegant Via Condotti has had many famous customers

Shopping

Fashion capital	Rome is one of the fashion capitals of the world. What greater holiday pleasure on a sunny afternoon than an hour or two spent sampling the busy shopping streets of the Eternal City. Whether it be silk or leather, elegant or eccentric, footwear or jewellery, every possible taste is catered for in the shops between the Piazza di Spagna and Via del Corso, in Via Frattina and Via Condotti. One thing is common to all these establishments however; if you intend to buy rather than just window shop, you will need deep pockets. And do not forget to glance into the city's many delicatessen, where every imaginable Italian delicacy can be found.
Antiques	see entry
Books	Economy Book Center (English language books), Via Torino 136 Libreria Modernissima, Via della Mercede 43 Rappaport (Antiquarian books), Via Sistina 23
Childrens wear	Babies, Via Paolo Emilio (everything for little ones) Nicol Caramel, Via di Ripetta 261 (large selection for the mother-to-be) Prenata, Via della Croce 48 (colourful practical children's things)
Clerical outfitters	Euroclero, Via Sant'Uffizio 31 (the cleric's entire wardrobe can be bought here) Massimiliano Gammarelli, Via dei Cestari (even the Pope has his robes made here)

Ai Monasteri, Piazza delle Cinque Lune (sweet Roman specialities in a vintage setting)

Annibale, Via Ripetta 236 (Art Nouveau butcher's shop; the best veal and beef in Rome)

Antica Norcineria Viola, Campo dei Fiori 43c (more than 60 varieties of pork sausage)

Il Forno, Campo dei Fiori 22 (Rome's oldest bakery; inimitable nut loaf)

Fratelli Fabbi, Via della Croce 27 (typical Roman salumeria selling aromatic ham and much-acclaimed mozzarella)

Pasta all'Uovo, Via della Croce 8 (third generation pasta makers – more than 40 varieties to be precise)

Franco Rossi, Piazza della Rotonda 4 (probably sells the best culatello ham in Italy, and wonderful ricotta.)

Delicatessen

Coin, Piazzale Appio 7 (beautiful bed linen and small items of furniture)

La Rinascente, Piazza Colonna and Piazza Fiume (stylish clothes and a comprehensive parfumerie)

Standa, Via del Corso 379, Viale Trastevere 62, and elsewhere (affordable fashion)

Upim, Via Nazionale, Piazza Santa Maria Maggiore, and elsewhere (reasonably priced range)

Department Stores/ Supermarkets

Eldo, Via del Corso 263

Leone Limentani, Via del Portico d'Ottavia 47/48

Espresso and pasta machines

Fashion clothes, shoes and handbags are found on sale all over the city in great variety and all price categories. The capital's most expensive shopping street is the elegant Via Condotti. Here, as in adjacent streets around the Piazza di Spagna, are branches of all the well-known Italian and international fashion houses. The boutiques in the Via del Corso, in the alleyways around the Campo dei Fiori, in the Via Frattina and the Via della Croce, offer favourable prices for the younger buyer. There are second-hand shops in the Via del Governo Vecchio beyond Piazza Navona.

Fashions

Giorgio Armani Emporio, Via del Babuino 140, Via Condotti 77

Renato Balestra, Via Sistina 36

Laura Biagiotta, Via Borgognona 43–44 (extravagant fashion; don't miss the perfume called "Roma")

Escada, Piazza di Spagna 78 (fashion for the confident woman)

Fendi, several shops, including Via Borgognona 36–40 and Via Fontanella Borghese 57 (exclusive fashion and leather goods)

Gianfranco Ferre, Via Borgognona 42/b (designer clothing)

Guccio Gucci, Via Condotti 8 (luxurious dresses and accessories)

Krizia, Piazza di Spagna 77b

Pino Lanzetti, Via Condotti 61

La Mendola di Albertina, Piazza Trinità dei Monti 15 (unusual designer clothes)

Milla Schon, Via Condotti 64–65

Trussardi, Via Condotti 49

Ungaro, Via Bocca di Leone 24

Valentino, unquestionably the most famous of Rome's fashion designers: branches at Via Condotti 13 (men), Via Bocca di Leone 15–19 (women), Via del Babuino 61 (young fashions) and Via Gregoriana 24

Gianni Versace, fabulous creations: Via Bocca di Leone 26 (women), Via Borgognona 29 (men)

Haute couture/ Designer clothes

Annabella, Via del Tritone 47 (vast selection)
Fendi, Via Borgognona 39 (Rome's most exclusive furrier)

Furs

Borsalino, Via IV Novembre 157b (nostalgia-evoking hats with the gangster look have been made here since the 1930s; gave its name to the cult film "Borsalino" with Jean-Paul Belmondo and Alain Delon)

Hats

Rome's jewellery shops are every bit as numerous as its fashion and leather shops. So only a few can be mentioned here:
Bedetti, Piazza San Silvestro 9/12 (famous clock-maker since 1882)
Buccellati Federico, Via Condotti 31 (celebrated Florentine family of jewellers)
Bugia, Via Frattina 66 (unusual fashion jewellery)
Bulgari, Via Condotti 10 (what Cartier is to France and Tiffany is to the USA, so Bulgari is to Italy; only the finest, and wickedly expensive)
Gold Point, Via Barberini 91 (reasonably priced gold jewellery)
Massoni, Largo Carlo Goldoni 48 (known for quality since 1796)
La Stelletta, Via della Stelletta 4 (costume jewellery)

Jewellery

Artigianato del Cuoio, Via Belsiana 19 (large selection of leather clothes at fair prices)
Dominique Cetera, Via Liguria 36a
Fellini, Via del Corso, Via Buonarroti 36, and elsewhere (lovely belts)
Fendi, Via Borgognona 36–40 (irresistible bags)
Antinio Pelleterie, Via Ferruccio 34a (leather clothes)
Louis Vuitton, Via Condotti 15 (manufacturer of exquisite luggage for more than a century)

Leather goods

Brighenti, Via Frattina 7 (for over 100 years one of the best lingerie shops)
Intimo 3, Via Due Macelli 67 and Via Campo Marzio 45 (everything from bodies to boxer shorts at reasonable prices)
La Perla, Via Condotti 78/79 (tantalising lingerie)

Lingerie

Rome has nearly 140 provision, flower and junk markets.
Campo dei Fiori; colourful provision and flower market with an enchanting backdrop. Open daily Mon.–Sat., Closed Sundays.
Mercati Generali; wholesale provision market in the Via Ostiense; open to the public daily from 10am
Piazza Testaccio; colourful provision market open every morning
Piazza Vittorio Emanuele; large provision market each morning; every sort of spice and unusual Asian and African ingredients
Porta Portese (Trastevere); large flee market every Sunday morning
Via Sannio (behind the church of San Giovanni in Laterano, near the Coin department store); clothes market every morning except Sundays
Via Trionfale; large flower market every Tuesday morning
Via Francesco Crispi 96; junk market every first Saturday and Sunday in the month (except July, August and September)

Markets

Vertecchi, Via della Croce 70 (fine writing materials)

Paper

Beltrami, Via Condotti 19 (long established house)
Campanile, Via Condotti 58 (top quality Neapolitan shoe designers)
Le Cuir, Via della Stazione Vecchia 23, Lido di Ostia (shoes by Fendi, Versace, Prada and Dolce e Gabbana)
Fragiacomo, Via Condotti 35 (lovely range)
Pollini, Via Frattina 22–24 (chic and classic cut)

Shoes

◀ *High fashion at La Mendola di Albertina*

Colourful fruit and vegetable markets are part of the Roman scene

Salvatore Ferragamo, Via Condotti 73–74 (elegant ladies' shoes and bags)

Bruno Magli, Via del Gambero and elsewhere (timeless elegance)

In addition to those mentioned, there are shoe shops on almost every corner and in almost every shopping street, where attractive and reasonably priced shoes can be bought

Wine
(Enoteche)

All the establishments listed serve wine as well as selling it. People often arrange to meet friends there for an aperitif before a meal. Enoteche usually close between 8 and 9pm, but some stay open until midnight.

Wine merchants

Enoteca Buccone, Via Ripetta 19–20 (has dealt since 1895 in wines and champagne from such famous names as Antinori and Fattoria dei Barbi)

Enoteca al Parlamento, Via dei Prefetti 15 (in addition to unusual Roman wines Gianfranco Achilli also offers an unrivalled selection of spirits including 400 varieties of whisky alone)

Vineria, Campo dei Fiori/corner of Vicolo di Gallo (where the younger generation meet; open until midnight)

Sightseeing tours

City tours

The easiest way to find out about city and day tours is to enquire at the Rome Tourist Office (EPT, see Tourist Information) or a travel agent. Among organisations offering multi-language tours are American Express (Piazza di Spagna 38, tel. 67641) and CIT (Compagnia Italiano Turismo, Piazza della Repubblica 68, tel. 4746533).

The municipal transport authority A.T.A.C. also run a bus tour of the city (Bus No. 110). Taking approximately two to three hours, it leaves from the A.T.A.C Information Office on the Piazza dei Cinquecento, opposite the Stazione Termini.

A.T.A.C

For the equivalent of about 35 pence sterling you can enjoy an informal "tour" aboard tram no. 30 on its delightful route from the Viale delle Belle Arti, past the park of the Villa Borghese, to the suburb of Ostiense.

Tram No. 30

Trolley bus no. 119 makes what is to all intents and purposes a mini tour of the city's historic centre.

Bus No. 119

See Introduction Section, Circular Walks

On foot

A ride in one of these old-fashioned vehicles, affectionately known locally as *botticelle* (little barrels), is particularly recommended for tours of the city's parks (e.g. the Villa Borghese) and historic centre around the Pantheon. The cabs take up to five people and can be engaged for any period of time from half an hour up to the whole day. The price should always be agreed with the driver before setting out. Horse-drawn cabs are stationed at Piazza San Pietro, Colosseum, Piazza Venezia, Piazza di Spagna, near the Fontana di Trevi, at Via Vittorio Veneto, the Villa Borghese and Piazza Navona.

Carrozzelle (horse-drawn cabs)

For those preferring individually tailored tours, authorised guides can be hired through the Rome Tourist Office (EPT; see Tourist Information) or the Sindicato Nazionale Guide Turistiche (C.I.S.L.), Rampa Mignanelli 12, tel. 6 78 98 42.

Authorised guides

Horse-drawn carriages waiting in the Piazza San Pietro to take visitors for a nostalgic ride around the city

Sport

Art history tours	Guided art history tours can be arranged through the following:

Soprintendenza Comunale ai Musei e Monumenti
Piazza Caffaeli 3, tel. 67 10 30 69

Sport

What is on offer

Football (Calcio)	Anyone wondering what it must have been like to be among the spectators on the terraces of the Colosseum or Circus Maximus, could hardly do better than join the crowd at one or other of Rome's two top football clubs: Lazio and AS Roma. Home matches are played in the Stadio Olimpico. Kick-off is Sunday afternoon except during the summer break in July and August. The tifosi, (i.e. the fans) are of all ages and both sexes.
Golf	See entry
Horse riding	The main event of the year is the international equestrian show in May with riding and show-jumping competitions. The venue is the pine-encircled Piazza di Siena in the spacious park of the Villa Borghese (see A to Z, Villa Borghese). Flat and hurdle racing takes place at the Ippodromo Capannelle (Via Appia Nuova 1255, km 12).
Swimming	For a capital city which endures a long hot summer, facilities for swimming are surprisingly limited. The Olympic pool at the Piscine delle Rose (Viale America 20, in the E.U.R. district) is open from mid June until mid September daily 9am–6 or 7pm. Those preferring a swim in the sea can take the Metropolitana Line B to Lido di Ostia. Water quality here, however, is not the best.
Tennis	The main event is the "Italian Open", Rome's international tennis tournament in which the world's top players compete, takes place in May. Ticket sales: Viale dei Gladiatori 31, tel. 3 21 90 64. Tennis is played mainly in private clubs. There are however a few public courts – at the Foro Italico for example (see below). For a fee non-members can also play at the Oasi della Pace (Via degli Eugenii 2(off Via Appia Antica), tel. 7 18 45 50).

Sports facilities

Foro Italico	The large sports complex below Monte Mario, close to the Tiber, was begun for the Fascist Academy of the Farnesina in 1938 and finished after the Second World War. Major improvements were carried out for the world football championship in Italy in the summer of 1990.
Stadio Olimpico	This football and athletics stadium with seating for 100,000 spectators was the venue for the Final of the 1990 world football championship. The complex also has tennis courts.
Stadio dei Marmi	The first sports ground at the Foro Italico was this marble stadium. Holding more than 20,000 spectators, it hosts the annual athletics meeting normally held in September.
Stadio del Nuoto	This large swimming arena with indoor and outdoor pools accommodates 16,000 spectators. The pools are not however open to the general public.

244

The vast domed EUR sports centre in the Piazzale dello Sport provides a venue for basketball, boxing and tennis tournaments as well as rock and pop concerts.

Palasport

This sports centre, also located in the EUR district, has hockey, football and rugby pitches, athletics and roller-skating tracks, and a number of sports halls.

Tra Fontane

Situated near the Piazza Apollodoro, the small Palazzetto dello Sport is used for boxing, roller-skating, wrestling and tennis and fencing tournaments.

Palazzetto dello Sport

In addition to a football stadium holding 45,000 spectators, this complex in the Viale Tiziano has an indoor pool, a gymnasium and fencing hall.

Stadio Flaminio

Taxis

Taxis in Rome are either white or yellow. Always make sure the taximeter is properly set at the start of the journey. A surcharge is applied on night-time journeys between 10pm and 7am, and on Sundays and public holidays; also for luggage, waiting- and call-out time and journeys from and to Fiumicino airport. To avoid any nasty surprises it is best to establish the likely fare before you hire.

Tel. 38 75, 49 94, 8 81 77, 35 70

Radio taxis

Telephone

In Italy the telephone and postal services (see entry) are completely independent. Telephone services are provided by Telecom Italia.

Telephone offices

International direct dialling is only possible from public telephones displaying the orange-red receiver symbol. Public pay phones take both tokens (gettoni, value 200 lire) and 100, 200 and 500 lire coins. Most public pay phones also accept phonecards (carta telefonica), remember to tear off the corner strip before using. Costing either 5000, 10,000 or 15,000 lire, these are obtainable from tobacconists and Telecom Italia. There are also public pay phones in most bars (look for a circular yellow disc above the entrance). Cheap-rate applies between 10pm and 8am on weekdays and throughout the day as well at weekends.

Public telephones

To the United Kingdom: 00 44
To the United States or Canada: 001

International dialling codes from Rome

International directory enquiries: 176
Intercontinental directory enquiries: 1790

From the United Kingdom: 00 39 06
From the United States and Canada: 011 39 06

International dialling codes to Rome

N.B. When dialling an international call the initial zero is normally omitted from the local dialling code.

Theatres

Rome has numerous theatres; new ones open from time to time, and old ones sometimes close. The principal theatres are:

Teatro Argentina – Teatro di Roma
Largo di Torre Argentina 52, tel. 68 80 46 01/2.
Mainly productions of Italian classics

Teatro Belli
Piazza Sant'Apollonia 11a (Trastevere), tel. 5 89 48 75
Small theatre with modern and classical repertoires
Mainly light theatre

Teatro delle Arti
Via Sicilia 59, tel. 4 74 35 64

Teatro della Cometa
Via del Teatro Marcello 4, tel. 6 78 43 80

Teatro Eliseo
Via Nazionale 183, tel. 488 2114

Teatro Ghione
Via delle Fornaci 37, tel. 6 37 22 94

Teatro Manzoni
Via Montezebio 14/c, tel. 3 22 36 34

Teatro Nazionale
Via del Viminale 51, tel. 48 54 98 or 487 0614

Teatro Quirino
Via Marco. Minghetti 1, tel. 6 79 45 85

Teatro dei Satiri
Via di Grottapinta 19, tel. 6 87 70 68

Teatro Sistina
Via Sistina 129, tel. 4 82 68 41

Teatro Valle
Via del Teatro Valle 23/a, tel. 6880 3794
Light theatre and touring opera

Teatro Vascello
Via Giacinto Carini 72 (Monteverde), tel. 5 88 10 21

Advanced booking
Since the various box offices have different opening times it is always best to check beforehand. The most usual hours are 10am–1pm and 4–6.30pm.

Tickets may be purchased in advance at:
Agenzia Orbis, Piazza dell'Esquilino 37, tel. 4 82 74 03
'Box office' Via del Corso 506, tel. 361 2682

Time

Italy observes Central European Time (GMT +1; US and Canada Eastern Time +6). Summer Time (GMT +2; US and Canada Eastern Time +7) is in force between March and October.

Tipping (Mancia)

Despite the fact that in hotels and restaurants service is included, a tip of 5 to 10% of the bill is still expected. In "bars" (Italian cafés) service is not included and a tip of 12 to 15% is the norm. For taxis the usual practice is to round up the fare. Porters expect about 3000 lire per case.

Transport

Several tram routes and about 300 bus routes ensure an excellent public transport system in Rome; the heavy inner city traffic means however that progress is often very slow.

Buses and trams

Multiple tickets and season tickets can be bought at the municipal transport authority (A.T.A.C.)'s information office on the Piazza dei Cinquecento, opposite the Stazione Termini; there are also ticket machines.

Information

Tickets are not obtainable on buses (except at night) or trams, so must be purchased before boarding, either singly or in packs of 10. They are available from tobacconists ("tabacchi") and newspaper kiosks. Once cancelled a ticket remains valid for 75 minutes. There are no conductors on buses; passengers board at the rear of the vehicle where there is an orange-coloured machine for cancelling tickets.

Tickets

The day ticket "BIG" is valid for 24 hours on all routes. For tourists special weekly tickets are available, valid from the day of purchase on all routes at any time of the day or night. For a longer stay in Rome a monthly ticket ("tessera intera rete") is recommended. All these tickets can be obtained at the A.T.A.C. information desk (see above). Monthly tickets can also be bought in tabacchi.

Metropolitana stations are signposted by a large M on a red background. There are only two lines (A and B).

Metropolitana (Underground)

Line A: Ottaviano (near St Peter's), Lepanto, Flaminia (Piazza del Popolo), Spagna, Barberini, Repubblica, Termini, Vittorio Emanuele, Manzoni, San Giovanni and as far as Anagnina.

Line B: Stazione Termini, Via Cavour, Colosseo, Circo Massimo, Piramide and as far as Laurentina.

Tickets for the Metropolitana, valid for a single journey only, can be purchased in tobacconists and from ticket machines in Metropolitana stations. There are also day and monthly tickets.

Roma – Lido (a branch of Metropolitana Line B, Piramide Station, to Lido di Ostia).

Ferrovia (local railway)

Roma – Nord (from Metropolitana Line A, Flaminia Station, to Prima Porta).

Travel documents

Passport

Citizens of the United Kingdom, Republic of Ireland, the United States of America, Canada, Australia, New Zealand and many other countries require only a valid passport.

It is always a good idea to make photocopies of travel documents. This makes it easier to obtain replacements in the event of loss (keep the copies separate from the originals).

Vehicle documents

Motorists should carry their driving licence and car registration documents. An international insurance certificate ("green card") is not obligatory but is strongly recommended. Foreign cars must display an oval nationality plate.

When to Go

The best times to visit Rome are the months from April to June, when the average temperature hovers around 15°C/59°F, or September/October when the average is 20°C/69°F. For these months early booking is essential.

In July and August Rome is populated almost entirely by tourists; the Romans themselves flee to the coast or into the country to escape the often unbearable heat (up to 40°C/105°F, average temperature 25°C/77°F).

In winter, with an average temperature of 8°C/46°F, even Rome can be unpleasantly cold and heating is often less than adequate. Still, the winter months offer an opportunity to enjoy the sights of the Eternal City in relative peace. During Christmas, Easter and Whitsun on the other hand, Rome is inundated with pilgrims; hotels and pensions are certain to be fully booked.

Youth Hostel (Albergho per la Gioventó)

Foro Italico – A. F. Pessina
Viale delle Olimpiadi 61
1–00194 Roma
Tel. 3 23 62 67 or 324 2571, fax 3 24 26 13
334 B; open: 7–9am, noon–midnight

Index

Index

The Principal Sights at a Glance

Imprint

107 illustrations, 17 maps and plans, 1 large map at end of book

German text: Dr Madeleine Reincke, Evamarie Blattner, Helga Cabos, Peter M. Nahm, Michael Machatschek, Andreas März, Dr Reinhard Paesler and Reinhard Strüber

Editorial work: Baedeker-Redaktion (Dr Madeleine Reincke)

Cartography: Franz Huber, Munich; Franz Kaiser, Mairs Geographischer Verlag GmbH, Ostfildern (regional map)

General direction: Rainer Eisenschmid, Baedeker Ostfildern

English translation: James Hogarth, David Cocking, Wendy Bell

Source of illustrations: Alitalia (1), Anthony (1), Archiv für Kunst und Geschichte (1), Baedeker Archive (12), Borowski (4), Cabos/Reincke (132), Eid (3), Eisenschmid (3), Frei (1), HB-Verlag Hamburg (1), Hotel Albani (1), Hotel Plaza de Russie (1), IFA (4), Mader (5), Mauritius (1), Schuster, (1), Strüber (1), ZEFA (5)

Front cover: Powerstock/Zefa. Back cover: AA Photo Library (P. Wilson)

6th English edition 1999
Reprinted 2000

© Baedeker Ostfildern
Original German edition 1997

© 1999 The Automobile Association
English language edition worldwide

Published by AA Publishing (a trading name of Automobile Association Developments Limited, whose registered office is Norfolk House, Priestley Road, Basingstoke, Hampshire RG24 9NY. Registered number 1878835).

Distributed in the United States and Canada by:
Fodor's Travel Publications, Inc.
201 East 50th Street
New York, NY 10022

A CIP catalogue record for this book is available from the British Library.

Licensed user:
Mairs Geographischer Verlag GmbH & Co.
Ostfildern

Printed in Italy by G. Canale & C. S.p.A., Turin

ISBN 0 7495 1993 2